Information Management

Information Management
The evaluation of information systems investments

Leslie Willcocks

*Oxford Institute of Information Management,
Templeton College, University of Oxford, UK*

CHAPMAN & HALL
University and Professional Division
London · Glasgow · Weinheim · New York · Tokyo · Melbourne · Madras

Published by Chapman & Hall, 2-6 Boundary Row, London SE1 8HN

Chapman & Hall, 2-6 Boundary Row, London SE1 8HN, UK

Blackie Academic & Professional, Wester Cleddens Road, Bishopbriggs, Glasgow G64 2NZ, UK

Chapman & Hall GmbH, Pappelallee 3, 69469 Weinheim, Germany

Chapman & Hall USA, One Penn Plaza, 41st Floor, New York, NY10119, USA

Chapman & Hall Japan, ITP - Japan, Kyowa Building, 3F, 2-2-1 Hirakawacho, Chiyoda-ku, Tokyo 102, Japan

Chapman & Hall Australia, Thomas Nelson Australia, 102 Dodds Street, South Melbourne, Victoria 3205, Australia

Chapman & Hall India, R. Seshadri, 32 Second Main Road, CIT East, Madras 600 035, India

First edition 1994
Reprinted 1995

© 1994 Leslie Willcocks

Typeset in 9.5/11.5pt Meridien by Excel Typesetter Co. Ltd., Hong Kong
Printed in England by Clays Ltd, St Ives plc

ISBN 0 412 41540 2

A Catalogue record for this book is available from the British Library

Library of Congress Cataloging-in-Publication Data available

∞ Printed on acid-free text paper, manufactured in accordance with
   ANSI/NISO Z39.48-1992 and ANSI/NISO Z39.48-1984
   (Permanence of Paper).

Contents

Contributors

James Bacon is senior lecturer in information systems at the University of Canterbury in Christchurch, New Zealand. He was previously for many years a systems consultant in London and New York. Recent publications cover decision criteria in project selection, data privacy and data freedom, principles of systems decentralization, and business benefits of the object-oriented paradigm. His current research is aimed at developing a valid and useful paradigm for the management of information systems/technology.

Tom Coleman is a senior consultant with Ochre Management Services. Previously he worked for the BT and Prudential where he focused on advanced technologies and latterly on investment appraisal systems. His primary interests are in achieving maximum total value from IT expenditure, and in reducing the implementation and benefit delivery risks of IT projects and programmes. He has also published a book *Expert Systems for the DP Manager*.

Catherine Griffiths is Research Fellow at the Kobler Unit, Imperial College, and a director of Canmore Consultants Ltd. She has over ten years' experience working with industry and government on such areas as investigating the strengths and weaknesses of current IT/S practices; evolving relevant and coherent strategies; identification of hidden costs in management approaches to IT investments. She is a regular speaker at conferences and seminars and author of a number of reports and articles, including co-author of *Controlling IT Investments – Strategy and Management* (Chapman & Hall), and is featured in The Sunday Times Video Series (1991).

Beat Hochstrasser is consultant for the Management of Information Technology at the Kobler Unit, and also a Research Fellow of Imperial College, London. He is also a member of the steering group comprising the Foundation of IT in Local Government and the Society of IT Managers. Previously he held management positions for ten years in Switzerland, Germany and France, in manufacturing, retail and financial service sectors. His present research and consultancy work focuses on designing evaluation methodologies and metrics to control IT investments for various companies. With Catherine Griffiths he has published two Kobler Unit reports on the management of IT.

Malcolm Iliff is a chartered accountant and director of Canmore Consultants Ltd, a company that specializes in information management. His work with Canmore concentrates on increasing the effectiveness of investment in IT. During a career in the financial services sector, he has held senior line management roles in Coutts and Co., and in Amsterdam Bank NV. He had overall responsibility for operations and administration in the London branch. He is on the editorial board of the *Journal of Information Technology* and is treasurer of the Association for Information Technology.

Mark Jamieson is a computer systems manager for Allen Overy – a leading London law firm. Previously he worked in the IT industry for 11 years for IBM in New Zealand, Wang in the United Kingdom and as a consultant for Ernst Young in their London information systems group. He has collaborated with Tom Coleman on several projects, including a 1991 UK study on the evaluation of intangible benefits of information technology.

Stephanie Lester is a computer services consultant with Hoskyns plc, where for three years she has worked on and managed facilities management contracts. She also specializes in business applications of PC-based networks. Previously she worked in audit for six years in a major government department. She holds an MSc in management from City University Business School and has, with Leslie Willcocks, published several papers on IS evaluation.

Helen Margetts is a research officer in the Department of Government at the London School of Economics. She is currently working on the US budget with Professor Patrick Dunleavy. She has co-authored publications on electoral systems and their reform and recently won the Haldane essay competition run by the Royal Institute for Public Administration for her work on the computerization of the Department of Social Security. She worked for several years as systems analyst in the private sector and is completing a PhD on comparative institutions for IT management in the UK and US public sectors.

Glen Peters holds a PhD from Henley Management College. He is a partner at Price Waterhouse responsible for consultancy activities in the energy and petrochemicals sector. He is a chartered engineer specializing in developing IT investment strategies for companies in the petrochemical, engineering and defence industries. IT investment mapping was the subject of this PhD thesis.

Brian L. Dos Santos is Frazier Family Professor of Computer Information Systems at the College of Business and Public Administration, University of Louisville, Kentucky. He received a PhD in Management from Case Western Reserve University. His research interests are in the design and development of decision support and expert systems and in the management of information systems. He has published numerous articles in journals such as *Management Science, Omega, Information and Management, Journal of Management Information Systems*, and has presented papers at many national and international conferences.

Veronica Symons has a BSc in Mathematics and a PhD in Management Studies from the University of Cambridge. Having worked as a business consultant for Shell International Petroleum Company, she is currently employed by Leicester City Council as a senior management services officer. Her primary responsibility is the development of computing and statistics applications within the Personnel and Management Services department. Her research, which focuses on the analysis of multiple perspectives in information systems evaluation, has been published in a number of research journals and conference proceedings.

John Ward is Professor of Strategic Information Systems at Cranfield School of Management. He acts as consultant to a number of major organizations and has recently co-authored *Strategic Planning for Information Systems* (John Wiley & Sons). Prior to joining Cranfield he was systems development manager at Kodak. He has a degree in natural sciences from Cambridge University and is a Fellow of the Chartered Institute of Management Accountants.

Devra Wiseman is the managing director of Devra Wiseman Associates, an information service consultancy. She has over 20 years' experience working as a manager, educator and consultant with leading systems and technology vendors. Her major concerns are with the strategic use of information systems and technology to improve organizational performance, and in enabling users to understand and manage information systems. She has pioneered in the United Kingdom the use of the information economics approach to valuing information systems. She is currently engaged in evaluation issues where Civil Service activities are exposed to competition through the market testing process.

Leslie Willcocks is a Fellow in Information Management at Templeton College Oxford, and co-editor of the *Journal of Information Technology*. Previously he worked in accountancy and management consultancy for seven years, for Touche Ross and several smaller firms, and as a director of a research centre in information management at City University Business School. Co-authored publications include *Computerising Work* (Blackwell Scientific), two books on systems analysis and design, and *Rediscovering Public Service Management* (McGraw-Hill). Research interests are in information systems – human, organizational and evaluation issues.

Introduction: of capital importance

Leslie Willcocks

Introduction

Information Technology (IT) – here used as a generic term for the convergence of computers, telecommunications, and electronics and the resulting technologies – is now, in many senses, of capital importance. There is the sheer size of the IT industry, and of expenditure on IT, in the developed and developing economies. Comparing figures from studies by Electronic Industries Association of Japan, IDATE and Texas Instruments, the worldwide revenues from telecommunications services and equipment, electronics, IT products and semiconductors exceeded $840 billion in 1985, $1490 billion in 1990, and are predicted to exceed $2100 billion in 1995. In North America in 1991 the revenues of the largest IT companies exceeded those of the oil business and oil refining and processing sectors; by 1993 the computer and electronics sector may well constitute the largest single US industry. On some predictions, by the year 2000 the whole IT industry will account for some 10% of world economic activity – a doubling of the 1990 figure (Cane, 1992; Heath and Swinden, 1992).

There is also the rising trend in IT expenditure over the last two decades. In the 1980s IT investment by user organizations had an annual growth rate of nearly 15%. Different sources for the USA, Europe and Japan show this as slowing, and sometimes negative, at different times and for different countries, in the 1989–92 period. Apart from economic recession, one reason may be the size and maturity of

Information Management: The evaluation of information systems investments.
Edited by Leslie Willcocks.
Published in 1994 by Chapman & Hall. ISBN 0 412 41540 2.

the IT industry. Despite this, most sources suggest, however, that the higher growth trend in IT expenditure will return from 1993 as economic recession recedes (Bryan, 1990; Guterl, 1992; Johnston, 1992; Marion, 1992; Price Waterhouse, 1992; KEW Associates, 1993). Clearly the high availability of goods and services on the IT market needs to be addressed as a more central issue in management thinking in work organizations than ever before. Together with the rising expenditure trend it also raises ever more urgent questions, including: what are competitors doing with IT; how are we disadvantaged without IT; how can performance and/or competitiveness be improved with these technologies?

There is every indication that the inclination to increase IT spend has been widespread – at individual organizational level the above figures often translate into large IT investments indeed. At the general level the figures can only be indicative. However, in the USA IT investment may approach 4% of revenues or more in some companies (McKeen and Smith, 1992). According to Price Waterhouse (1991, 1992) in the United Kingdom the national average for organizations with a data processing department of five or more staff has varied between 0.9 and 1.3% of turnover, but by 1992 was 1.5%, representing £3.9 million (Price Waterhouse, 1992). In the more information intensive industries, for example finance, IT investment in individual companies may exceed 10% of turnover. By 1992 public and private sector IT expenditure in the UK exceeded £15 billion per annum (KEW Associates, 1992). It is probable that, globally, computer and telecommunications investments now amount to nearly half of most large firms' annual capital expenditures (Earl, 1989; Franke, 1987; Keen, 1991; Loveman, 1988). On size of organizational expenditure and on rising trends in this expenditure alone, clearly the financial aspects of IT have become a critical management responsibility and focus for attention in work organizations.

IT is of capital importance in a deeper sense. This is its large potential impact on organizations and their stakeholders. How IT is applied can have massive implications including for how an organization functions, can be structured, what it can achieve and how, changed ways of working, winners and losers, positioning in the marketplace, and the possibility of switching into new sectors of operation (Dunlop and Kling, 1991; Forester, 1989; Keen 1986; Scott-Morton, 1991; Willcocks and Mason, 1987). Many organizations are also already highly dependent on information technology. For example studies suggest that if a bank loses the use of its main computer centre for more than 48 hours its very existence is threatened (Morris, 1992). All this also demands priority attention from those responsible for managing organizations. Furthermore there is a burgeoning literature pointing out the centrality of information assets, underpinned by information technologies, for many existing and most future organizations (see for example Drucker, 1991; Quinn, 1992; Zuboff, 1988). Information-based assets and the capabilities they offer, embodied in people, technology and/or their combination may well form a core competence in many industries, producing ways of differentiating the organization in terms of both offering and performance (Itami, 1987; Prahalad and Hamel, 1990; Quinn *et al.* 1990).

A further meaning contained in the phrase 'of capital importance' presents itself. Given the large and rising expenditure on IT and its potential critical importance, clearly, the evaluation and control of IT investments becomes a vital management task. There is a more fundamental issue that arises at this point. IT is used here to refer to the supply of information-based technologies. What matters, however, is how the IT becomes translated into information systems (IS), that is organizational applications, more, or less, IT-based, delivering on the information needs of the organization and its stakeholders. It is the evaluation of IS investments that becomes of capital importance. This is reinforced still further when the evidence on three issues is taken into account. Firstly there is very wide questioning and uncertainty about whether IT/IS investments are actually paying off (see for example Hackett, 1990; Roach, 1991; Sequent, 1991; Weill, 1991). The 1993 abandonment of a 5 year project like Taurus in the UK London financial markets, in this case at a cost of £80 million to the Stock Exchange, and possibly £400 million to City institutions, provides only high profile endorsement of underlying disquiet on the issue (Waters and Cane, 1993). Secondly, there is emerging from a range of studies accumulating evidence of difficulties in, and also of indifferent, IT/IS evaluation practice (for example Farbey et al., 1992; McKeen and Smith, 1992; Weill and Olson, 1989). Thirdly, as shown in Chapter 3, much management attention does focus on the critical prioritization and feasibility stages of IT/IS projects, even if less attention is paid to subsequent possible evaluation stages and evidence. Much weight therefore falls upon getting the evaluation at these early stages right. Yet there is much evidence showing inappropriate techniques and poor processes being used (see below and Chapters 2 and 3). The book therefore focuses predominantly on these early stages, with a companion volume dealing with evaluation and management across systems lifetime (Willcocks, 1994).

There is a lack of understanding of IT as a major capital asset in organizations. While the annual expenditure on IT may receive detailed attention amongst senior managers as well as IT directors, there is little awareness of the size of the capital asset that has been bought over the years. IT, and the information asset it underpins, is rarely seen as a balance sheet item, a fixed asset. Too often, like people, IT is seen as an expense, and treated as one. If the cost of accumulating such a potential asset were more often understood, information assets may well be less under-managed than they are at the moment. Clearly, improved evaluation and control again have roles to play here in bringing the critical issue of the cost of this IT/information asset, as well as its potential value, to detailed management attention.

The above points offer the rationale for the book. Its theme is evaluation practice at strategic levels and during the pre-purchase phases of IS assessment. These are taken as composed of investment appraisal, prioritization and evaluation at the feasibility stage. The focus is on both describing and also improving evaluation practice in these areas. We begin the process by firstly providing an outline of the findings from the more recent research studies. We then provide a detailed review of the major weaknesses in evaluation practice as identified in those studies. The major points are summarized in Figure 1.1. The issue of terminology then receives detailed attention. Finally there is an overview of the structure of the book, and of the contents and individual relevance of each of its chapters.

Overview of research studies

Some key general points emerge from reviewing the major research studies in the area. Firstly, **the record on controlling and measuring IS investments has not been impressive. This is shared across private and public sector organizations**. Managers have found it increasingly difficult to justify the costs surrounding the purchase, development and use of IT (Aggarwal et al., 1991;

Hochstrasser and Griffiths, 1991; PA Consulting Group, 1990; Price Waterhouse, 1989; Weill, 1989). The value of IT/IS investments are more often justified by faith alone, or perhaps what adds up to the same thing, by understating costs and using mainly notional figures for benefit realization (Peat Marwick, 1989; Strassmann, 1990). A whole string of second-order costs is often missed out of the evaluation (Hochstrasser, 1990; Keen, 1991; National Audit Office, 1987, 1989; Strassmann, 1992). Hochstrasser and Griffiths found only 16% of their sample relying on rigorous methods to calculate the benefits of investment in IT. Over a quarter of managers did not know (presumably because it was not measured) whether or not IT was producing better or worse returns than other investments. In a survey of 90 UK managers Vowler (1990) found 66% admitted their organizations were poor at measuring the IT contribution to the business. Grindley (1991) found 83% of IT directors admitting that the cost/benefit analyses supporting proposals to invest in IT are a fiction.

Secondly, **the difficulties in measuring benefits and costs are felt, in both private and public sectors, to be the major constraints to IS investment**. A.T. Kearney (1990) found that credibility in identifying benefits from a system is the top constraint closely followed by cost justification. This is explained as companies being aware of benefits but being unable to quantify them and therefore being sceptical of their scale. This scepticism may be reinforced by a degree of disenchantment engendered by past experiences with IS projects. One can add from 1990–92 research that the large and increasing size of IS spend increasingly brings IS to the attention of senior managers, particularly in a period of recession when expenditure is more closely scrutinized (Willcocks, 1992). Wilson (1991), in researching 550 companies, also found measuring benefits as the major barrier to the setting up of an IS strategy, and the third most critical in implementing strategy (after difficulties in recruiting IS staff and 'nature of business'). Grindley (1991), researching over 5000 IT directors found the intangible nature of benefits as amongst the top five problems facing them, and held to be the main problem by 27%. Kobler Unit (1987) found the difficulties of cost justifying new IS proposals as the second major constraint on future investment. In surveying over 450 organizations Touche Ross (1991) found that in 35% of cases potential users of office automation were held back by lack of clarity (or intangibility) of IS benefits.

In the UK public sector a 1992 survey of 210 managers found some 16% as 'successful users' of IS as measured on objective criteria, and 24% 'very unsuccessful users' (Willcocks, 1993). The detailed results show respondents rating themselves generally lower on control than on planning, organization and management issues in Generating the Context for IS, Design and Development and Implementation and Operations phases of IS projects. These results reinforce those of Bacon (1991). In looking at 23 government organizations he found most 'clearly unhappy . . . with regard to the value of benefits set out in the business cases for their strategies.' Futhermore 'few departments . . . had performance indicators or intended to place the mechanisms by which appropriate information could be collected. There is recognition that the measurement of the success of the strategies will be very difficult because of the lack of performance indicators for large areas of business where the benefits are intangible'. In looking at public and private sector experience with office automation, Touche Ross (1991) found fewer than half of users set criteria for assessing benefits. Most criteria were qualitative; only 27% set quantitative criteria.

A third key point, however, is that **there is a strong correlation between control and measurement of IS and higher effectiveness with IS, however**

measured (Shank and Govindarajan, 1992; Smith and McKeen, 1992; Strassmann, 1990; Weill and Olson, 1989). For example, in the UK AT Kearney (1990) found that successful users are twice as likely to set formal targets for return on investment and to measure the performance of new IS systems against them as are unsuccessful users. Kobler Unit (1987) found that the top management of market leader companies tended to be better informed about the performance of IS installations than the top management of less successful counterparts. Peters (1990) found that IS projects which had clearly defined responsibilities, a project board, and regular monitoring of key metrics over-performed on the original appraisal of anticipated net benefits. Given the strong correlation between IS control and measurement and IS success, and the large deficiencies identified in private and public sector practice, a much higher profile for this relationship, and appropriate measures and processes for tracking IS effectiveness would seem to be needed.

Given these findings, we will now review the main limitations, constraints and problems experienced in IS evaluation practice as they emerge from the research studies, including the author's own. These are summarized in Figure 1.1. The review will be used as a basis for suggesting ways forward on how evaluation of IS investments may be conducted.

Investment climate, strategy and alignment

The organizational investment climate has a key bearing on how investment is organized and conducted, and what priorities are assigned to different IT investment proposals. According to Butler Cox (1990) the investment climate is affected by:

● the finanical health and market position of the organization;
● industry sector pressures;

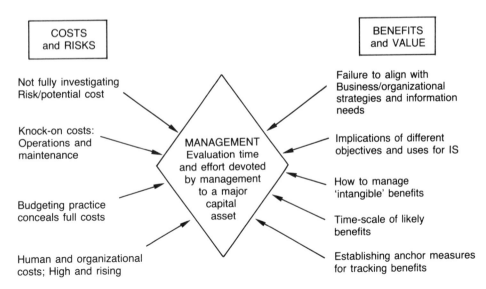

Figure 1.1 Evaluating the IS contribution: emerging problems.

- the management and decision-making culture; and
- the business strategy and direction.

On the first, the 1990–93 period of UK recession has seen a marked concern for cost containment and for improved justification of IS investment in both private and public sectors. As an example of the second, 1989–90 research by Datasolve shows IS investment priorities in the retail sector focusing mainly on achieving more timely information; in financial services around better quality service to customers; and in manufacturing on more complete information for decision-making. In government the focus has tended to be on cost reduction and containment, doing more or the same with less. As to decision-making culture, senior management attitude to risk can range from conservative to innovative, their decision-making styles from directive to consensus-driven. As one example conservative consensus-driven management would tend to take a relatively slow, incremental approach, with large scale IT investments being unlikely. As an example of how tensions can develop, in the UK public sector 1980s moves to an innovative-directive management approach to risk and decision-making on both IS and non-IS issues would seem to require a move toward IS investment being assessed on judgement, based on business strategies and objectives, and resulting in top-down introduction. However there is conflict between this and the Treasury regulatory procedures and other guidelines and their emphasis on financial justification and monitoring.

On the fourth issue, shaping the context in which IS evaluation is conducted is a necessary prelude to then applying appropriate evaluation techniques and approaches. A fundamental starting point emerging from the research studies is the need for alignment of business/organizational needs, what is done with IS, and plans for the human resources, organizational structures and processes. The highly publicized Landmark Study tends to conflate these into alignment of business, organization and IT strategies (Scott-Morton, 1991). A simpler approach is to suggest that the word 'strategy' should be used only when these different plans are aligned. There is much evidence to suggest that such alignment rarely exists. Thus in a study of 86 companies Ernst and Young (1990) found only two aligned. In detailed research Willcocks (1991) has shown the lack of alignment to be a common problem in public sector informatization.

The case of an advertising agency is instructive. In the mid-1980s the agency installed accounting and market forecasting systems at a cost of nearly £100 000. There was no real evaluation of the worth of the IT to the business. It was installed largely because one director had seen similar systems running at a competitor. Its existing systems were adequate, and the market forecasting system ended up being used just to impress clients. At the same time as the systems were being installed, the agency was sacking over 35 staff. The company was taken over in 1986. Clearly there had been no integrated plan on the business, human resource, organizational and IT fronts. In the end the IT amplifier effect may have operated. IT was not used to address the core, or indeed any, of the needs of the business. A bad situation was made correspondingly worse by the application of IT (Willcocks and Margetts, 1992). Thus one result of such lack of alignment is that IS evaluation practice tends to become separated from business needs and plans on the one hand, and from organizational realities that can influence IS implementation and subsequent effectiveness on the other. Both need to be included in IS evaluation, and indeed are in the more comprehensive evaluation methods, notably the Information Economics approach (see Chapter 9).

Another critical alignment is that between what is done with IS and how that fits with the information needs of the organization. Most management attention has tended to fall on the 'technology' rather than the 'information' element in what is called IS. Hochstrasser and Griffiths (1991) found in their sample no single company with a fully developed and comprehensive strategy on information. Yet it would seem to be difficult to perform a meaningful evaluation of IS investment without some corporate control framework establishing information requirements in relationship to business/organizational goals and purpose, prioritization of information needs, and, for example, how cross-corporate information flows need to be managed. An information strategy directs IS investment, and establishes policies and priorities against which investment can be assessed. It may also help to establish that some information needs can be met without the IS vehicle.

In fact there are many methods available for focusing management attention on the IS evaluation question: where does and will IS give us added value? Two are detailed in early chapters of this book. Thus the use of McFarlan and Mckenny's IT strategic grid is discussed in Chapter 4. An investment mapping approach to relating IS investments to organizational/business needs has been developed by Peters (see Chapter 5). Of other methods available, Porter and Millar (1985) have been useful in establishing the need for value chain analysis. This looks at where value is generated inside the organization, but also in its external relationships, for example with suppliers and customers. Thus the primary activities of a typical manufacturing company may be: inbound logistics; operations; outbound logistics; marketing and sales; and service. Support activities will be: firm infrastructure; human resource management; technology development and procurement. The question here is what can be done to add value within and across these activities? As every value activity has both a physical and information processing component, it is clear that the opportunities for value-added IS investment may well be considerable. Value chain analysis helps to focus attention on what these will be.

Earl (1989) has also proposed a particularly useful multiple methodology for IS strategy formulation. This again helps in the aim of relating IS investment more closely with the strategic aims direction of the organization and its key needs. One element here is a **top-down approach**. Thus a Critical Success Factors (CSF) analysis might be used to establish key business objectives, decompose these into critical success factors, then establish the IS needs that will drive these CSFs. A **bottom-up evaluation** would start with an evaluation of current systems. This may reveal gaps in the coverage by systems, for example in the marketing function, or in terms of degree of integration of systems across functions. Evaluation may also find gaps in the technical quality of systems and in their business value. This permits decisions on renewing, removing, maintaining or enhancing current systems. The final plank of Earl's multiple methodology is **inside-out innovation**. The purpose here is to 'identify opportunities afforded by IT which may yield competitive advantage or create new strategic options'. The purpose of the whole multiple methodology is, through an internal and external analysis of needs and opportunities, to relate the development of IS applications to business/organizational need and strategy. All such methods help to establish the right strategic climate and context for evaluating the feasibility of individual IS projects.

Identification of full costs

Costs can be understated where size of IS budget, present and predicted, is used to evaluate an IS investment proposal. Recent studies in both the USA and UK show that up to 40% of relevant costs incurred on IS can be outside the traditional IS budget (Hodges, 1987; Keen, 1991; Moad, 1991; Price Waterhouse, 1990; Strassmann, 1990). In one large manufacturing company studied by Willcocks and Lester (1991), user department IS and training costs were in fact 29% of total costs but hidden in departmental, often non-IS related budgets. It should be noted that this trend toward IS costs being incurred in user department IS and non-IS budgets looks set to increase. Clearly, the IS budget as a control mechanism may need to be reformulated to reflect full costs. IS costs are no longer anything near equatable with the budget of the IT/IS department.

As hardware and equipment costs get driven down, IS-related human and organizational costs are rising. Strassman (1990, 1992) estimated these to be as much again over the lifetime of a system. At the US Department of Defense he found for every $1 spent on IT equipment, a further $7 needed to be spent on people and training. Hochstrasser (1990) suggests that human and organizational costs can be as much as three to four times as high as hardware/equipment costs. Invariably, however, these costs are rarely fully budgeted for in IS investment proposals, and may partially explain the phenomenon of cost-creep that occurs over the course of most IS projects. In a retrospective analysis of an insurance company database application, the author and project manager analysed human and organizational costs three years after development began. These included such items as training, management and staff time, extra staff, staff turnover, losses in productivity and organizational restructuring during changeover. These were over two times equipment costs, and only 20% were included in the original feasibility assessment (Willcocks, 1992).

There may be political reasons for understating costs, the main one being to gain support for, and acceptance of the project from senior managers. Furthermore, in a recessionary climate, a concern for cost-justification, quick returns and, indeed applying IS for cost reduction purposes would seem to be paramount (Price Waterhouse 1991). This again can pressure proponents of IS into understating costs. A major problem area is where knock-on costs are understated. Thus maintenance costs may well be one to four times as much again as systems development costs, and are not avoidable over the lifetime of a system (Laudon and Laudon, 1991; Swanson and Beath, 1989). According to research on IS projects by Keen (1991), operational and maintenance costs were 2.4 times systems development costs over the four year life of the system. An additional problem is incurred here. Development costs incur maintenance costs that then feed into the future IS budget. If IS is being measured by size of spend, the picture will be one of rising investment. However this will conceal the fact that most of the expenditure will be on existing systems; it will not be focused on future systems possibly critical to the organization's competitiveness or health.

Research shows less than impressive figures for IS projects coming in within time and under budget (see for example Chew *et al.*, 1991; Grindley, 1991; AT Kearney, 1990; KPMG Peat Marwick, 1990). Estimates do tend to improve with greater IS experience, that is more experienced staff being used and/or organizational experience with previous IS projects (AT Kearney, 1990; Sequent, 1991; see also Chapter 11). However, overstatement of time and cost may actually become a politically astute move by those responsible for IS delivery. In two projects researched by the author it was clear that the project managers overstated costs at the feasibility stage with the express purpose of making sure they could deliver systems within time and budget. In one case a £500 000 home help organizer system was delivered to a social services department within 3 years. In another, a CAD/CAM system was brought into a small manufacturing company within the £2.1 million budget, though 2 months outside deadline. In each case the project manager revealed political astuteness and gained a reputation for effectiveness. Clearly the political issues inherent in IS evaluation and measurement need to be borne in mind when metrics, control parameters and what amounts to success/effectiveness are being defined.

From this brief review it would seem advisable for organizations to identify how budgetary procedures can disguise full IS costs; may inhibit proper funding or appropriate allocation of financial resources between human, organizational and technical requirements; and can lead to IS metrics being set up that monitor only partial costs. Organizations could usefully detail all likely costs in an IS project, categorized by type (for an example see Chapter 8).

The issue of intangible benefits

There is a whole raft of such benefits, some quite critical to operation and future competitiveness and direction, that are regularly omitted from feasibility proposals and subsequent monitoring, often on the grounds that they cannot be financially quantified, are not cost justifiable, are not certain and/or cannot produce obvious short-term paybacks.

To some extent this caution is understandable. Thus at Trustee Savings Bank the Banking Division in 1990 contained some 1600 branches. A very large 6 year strategic Network Redesign project was undertaken to automate branch administration and sales support systems. According to its director, a rigorous business case had to demonstrate early payback; therefore the first two years focused on automation of administrative tasks. In fact subsequent phases produced major intangible benefits excluded from the original business case, notably increased office space worth £15 million, reduction in headcount, and redesigned branch layout to give 75% of the space to customers and new revenue generating opportunities (Willcocks, 1992).

Nevertheless, failure to assess, and take into account, intangible benefits may well check potentially profitable proposals. Some, possibly the major, potential benefits from IS are not measurable using traditional financially-based evaluation techniques. These include: improved customer service, development of systems architecture, higher job satisfaction, higher product quality, improved internal/external communications and management information, gaining competitive advantage, cost avoidance, avoiding competitive disadvantage, improved supplier relationships. Thus at National Westminster Bank the card service department introduced document image processing technology with a resulting cost-justified 40% productivity increase. However the project manager rated the less tangible benefits much higher: 'Quality of service is becoming increasingly important as a competitive edge. We know card holders are impressed if the clerk can instantly say, "yes, I have your letter in front of me"' (Ring, 1991). Strassmann (1990) suggests that direct benefits such as cost reduction, cost displacement and revenue growth appear quickly and are relatively easy to track. Indirect benefits such as cost avoidance and risk reduction, and inferred benefits such as from relationship redesign, competitive gain and competitive survival occur over longer time periods and are more difficult to relate as due to IT investments. Techniques for identifying such benefits are discussed throughout this book.

Another problem on assessing intangible benefits is where evaluation procedures lead to understating costs, as discussed above. A corollary is to be lazy on searching for benefits to match against those costs. Thus bad practice reinforces itself, and can lead to pursuing very limited objectives relative to what IT could do for the organization.

Finance-based cost benefit analysis

It is useful at this stage to consider the more traditional and widely used techniques for feasibility evaluation. Willcocks and Lester encountered many of these in their 50 respondent organizations drawn from private and public sectors (see Chapter 3). Here, a variety of methodologies were used. A common element, however, could be characterized as cost benefit assessment described in monetary terms, allied with managerial judgement. The more traditional techniques of relating benefits to the costs of obtaining them are discussed by Coleman and Jamieson (1991); Earl, (1989); Farbey et al. (1992); and Parker et al. (1988). The main methods include: return on investment (ROI); discounted cash flow/internal rate of return (DCF/IRR); net present value (NPV) and profitability index (PI); payback period, and present worth. Some limitations of these specific methods can be noted.

ROI is the ratio of the average annual net income of the project divided by internal investment in the project. It is widely used as a 'hurdle rate' against which the merits of different projects are assessed. Dangers occur where the method is not allied to discounting cash flow, for example failure to account for variations in timing and risk. DCF/IRR are the most widely used, according to the studies described in Chapters 2 and 3. This establishes the discount rate at which the present value of cash receipts equals the present value of cash expenditures. Drury (1988) notes that it finds favour because of its relative simplicity but fails to take account of the relative scale of projects and the time loading mentioned in the Net Present Value method. NPV/PI are discounting techniques taking cash flows back to their value at the commencement of the project. Much depends on the discount rate adopted. If used alone, normally the project with the highest NP will adopted. PI is used less for IT projects. PI involves dividing estimated cash flows by the initial capital investment, but, as discussed above, IT projects rarely incur most costs at their beginning. The payback method is frequently used because it determines the amount of time required for the cumulative cash inflow to equal the initial investment. Managers find attractive the question: how long will the project take to pay for itself? However, Parker et al. (1988) noted technical deficiencies with this method. Present Worth assumes that the funding acquired to support a cost justified project is borrowed or acquired through the sale of stock. Simple ROI calculations are extended by discounting future cash flow on the basis of the cost of acquiring funds.

There are more sophisticated methods for developing a cost-benefit analysis. These include probability of attainment, decision models, break-even analysis, structural models and the hedonic wage model (Sassone, 1988). A number of composite methods have also been developed. However all methods reviewed in this section need to be used with some care:

• In themselves they largely exclude the significant problem of risk. Coleman and Jamieson (1991) convincingly make the case for more widespread use of risk analysis, based round formal techniques like measures of variance, sensitivity analysis and simulation/modelling techniques.

● Based on monetary value they can exclude costs and benefits that may be difficult to quantify but could be critical to the evaluation. For example, some of the best returns may well be from IS projects that deliver competitive advantage, improved customer service, higher product quality, innovation, more timely information. One manufacturing company installed a flexible manufacturing system costing $18 million. The project's return would only be 10% per annum, even taking into account significant labour savings over a 20 year period. The project would be appraised as unprofitable against typical hurdle rates of 15% expectations of payback within 5 years. However it offered significant productivity and performance benefits, as well as flexibility (Earl, 1989). Kaplan (1986) makes the point that the major benefits from computer integrated manufacturing − such as quality, flexibility, responsiveness, functional integration − fall very much in the intangible class.

● Arising from the above it is clear that discount rates may be difficult to arrive at for IS projects. Also hurdle rates set for non-IS capital investment may need to be lowered for IS with the capability of impacting on competitive advantage, creating new businesses or that represents significant innovation with unclear payoffs. This applies especially to application projects like CIM, electronic mail networks, and to infrastructure investment. These will tend to have a longer useful life than non-IS projects and deserve different treatment in feasibility evaluation (Kaplan, 1986). Unfortunately ROI type measures can create minimum hurdle rates that shield managers from understanding the differences between IS projects, and between IS- and non-IS projects.

● In his case study work Norton (1986) usefully concludes that, in respect of IS, CBA and ROI approaches are microeconomic, encouraging low risk investments with small returns; are the result of a manufacturing economy that treats labour as an expense; and the analysis tends to be static and short-term.

Some further work has been done by Kaplan (1986) in providing a refined NPV model. However this does not give explicit attention to strategic issues and concerns. Conversely, approaches like that of Porter (1985) (see above) do link technology decisions to strategic analysis, but do not give explicit attention to financial analysis. Several useful attempts have been made to address these limitations. Thus Noble (1989) suggests a threefold methodology. Firstly a strategic justification needs to be carried out, evaluating IS capability to meet corporate goals and objectives; assessing customer needs and industry trends and where IS would affect market position and share for each product line; assessing, through top-down functional analysis where IS can add value in functions and processes. Secondly, a modified cost justification is needed. This means using ROI and expected value analysis, but also assessing costs and benefits against the competitive consequences of implementing, or not implementing IS; analysing likely costs on an organization-wide basis; assessing cost savings; and taking an 8−10 year time horizon. Thirdly, a benefits analysis is needed to assess intangible benefits that arise for each strategic alternative. This can be accomplished by listing each potential benefit, assigning a weight, then scoring the benefit on its value in current operations, as against if the IS is implemented.

Shank and Govindarajan (1992) have also proposed a threefold approach, called a strategic cost management framework. Their intention is to shift attention away from conventional management accounting approaches to how IS investments are evaluated. This involves, first, replacing conventional, project-level, value-added calculations with a quantified benefit analysis derived from applying Porter's value chain analysis. Secondly, a cost driver analysis is performed. Costs are seen as a function of 'structural' drivers (e.g. scale, product line complexity, scope of operations, experience, and technology) and 'executional' drivers (such as Total Quality Management, capacity utilization, and workforce participation). There are multiple drivers of cost. Technology must be an important driver of cost at critical steps in the value chain. Thirdly, a competitive advantage analysis establishes whether technological change will enhance the way a firm has chosen to compete, either on the basis of cost or on the basis of differentiation. The authors claim that each analysis is necessary, but only all three in combination form a sufficient basis for assessing IS investments.

These more modern approaches usefully expand the traditional management accounting base of investment appraisal. They recognize that for the assessment of IS investments there is a need to integrate strategic analysis with modified financial and non-financial appraisal techniques. Thus while finance-based cost–benefit analysis and measures continue to serve important purposes for organizations, it is also important to realize, in detail, their limitations, and the need to supplement them with other quantitative non-financial and qualitative/subjective approaches and measures.

Risk analysis for information systems

There emerge from the research studies three major areas of risk that are frequently downplayed in evaluating IS proposals. Firstly the failure to build in adequate risk assessment of different IS options at the prioritization and feasibility stage of projects. This in itself constitutes a risk. Yet Coleman and Jamieson (1991) and Willcocks and Lester (1991), for example, found little concern for such assessment amongst respondent organizations. The second is the cost to the organization where implementation may be less than smooth, and where additional implementation time begins to add very large cost burdens. As one example in the £2 billion Department of Social Security Operational Strategy in the United Kingdom much of the speed in implementation from 1987 to 1992 can be explained in terms of the otherwise inhibiting costs of delay (see Chapter 11). The risk of disruption to the organization and to customers, indeed loss of customers, may also not be fully assessed (Tate, 1988). The enhanced cost–benefit analysis technique suggested by Parker et al., (1988) goes some way toward addressing these omissions. However their listing of possible risks to be assessed is not exhaustive and would need to be tailored to the specific sector and circumstances in which an organization finds itself. Additionally risk analysis is recommended which takes into account sufficient optimistic and pessimistic parameters, investigation of optimistic bias, and assessment of variability and uncertainties. Techniques such as sensitivity analysis and structured scenarios to take account of multiple factors and their interrelationships can also be useful, as can pay back period and premium on the discount rate to qualify financial estimates arrived at through cost–benefit analysis (see also Chapter 10). However, the research shows that, unfortunately, these techniques are rarely acted upon in practice.

The third area involves the risk exposure of the organization in terms of security and what happens when, for example, a complex network management system is no longer functioning. A networked organization like a bank or an airline and its booking system need very high reliability and back-up systems. When systems are not working, neither is the business. Managing such risk can incur substantial costs, and only some of the risk can be offset through insurance. Keen (1991), in a review of studies in this area, suggests that security to minimize different forms of risk exposure is expensive, and much of the risk is hidden. The research suggests that firms spend too little time analysing IS risk exposure, and are reluctant to make 'just-in-case' investments in IS security. The major problem here, is lack of measurement and assessment of risk. In the public sector it also may be the case that scarce financial resources in IS projects are prioritized elsewhere, especially where IS risk is not assessed in detail.

In looking at risk analysis in capital budgeting in 146 companies Pike and Ho (1991) found the most common barriers in order of significance as:

- Managerial understanding of techniques;
- Obtaining input estimates;
- Time involvement;
- Cost justification of techniques;
- Human/organizational resistance;
- Trade-off between risk and return;
- Understanding of output of analysis.

Clearly, means for reducing these barriers need to be adopted if risk analysis techniques are to be utilized as properly as they should be in IT projects. Organizations do not focus enough on the risks inherent in implementing and using information systems. There is a widespread need to promote education on, and use of, risk analysis techniques for use in IS investment proposals, but also in the development, implementation and routine operations of information systems.

The selection of IS performance measures

It is now widely accepted that certain measures in themselves do not assist the process of establishing how IS adds net value to an organization. As McKeen and Smith (1992) pointed out, it is not enough to simply identify the financial outlay on IS. One must also investigate how well, or poorly, the money is spent, that is the effectiveness of the investment. Strassman (1990) argues convincingly that size of IS spend bears no relationship to subsequent IS effectiveness. It is how the IS is used and managed, not the size of expenditure, that determines IS effectiveness. This is important to bear in mind because IS suppliers and management consultants frequently make comparisons on IS spend between companies, and between private and public sector organizations, to encourage further expenditure (Bacon, 1991; Grindley, 1991). Relatedly, IS expenditure as a percentage of turnover, then compared to an industry average, or what a competitor is spending, will do little to focus investment on where IS adds value to the organization (Kobler Unit, 1987; Hochstrasser and Griffiths, 1991). Internal systems efficiency measures do not relate performance to added value for the organization (Butler Cox, 1990). A common practice is to take the previous year's IS budget as a guideline, then add or deduct a percentage to arrive at the current year's planned expenditure. This in itself is not an effective substitute for identifying where IS will add value, and planning expenditure around what is required.

The more appropriate measures relate IS investment not to revenue but to profitability. However, even here the more traditional measures of profit, for example return on assets, return on sales, tend to penalize IS investments, particularly where the payoffs are likely to be long-term. Several commentators suggest that tracking IS progress over time is most meaningful in relation to organizational revenue or profit per employee (Chakravarthy, 1986; Keen, 1991; Smith and McKeen, 1992). This is because IS rarely reduces cost; rather its main value more often is changing the cost structure of the organization so that it can increase sales or output without increasing personnel.

The IS impact may also be traced by establishing non-financial measures around key business processes where IS is now being heavily used, for example ratio of seats occupied to seats available in an airline. Given the unreliability of single measures it may be wise to use several. Butler Cox (1990) suggest that IS expenditure can be usefully controlled and evaluated if measured against revenue, IS spend per employee, business volume (measured non-financially), and key business process measures. An example of their approach is shown in Figure 1.2.

Another area that can be usefully evaluated is levels of customer/user satisfaction with what is delivered (Miller, 1989; Remenyi *et al.*, 1991). A certain amount of work has also been done to establish that IT utilization can be a useful measure of systems effectiveness over the long term; the argument here is that if a system is effective, then people will use it; otherwise it will fall out of use (Smith and McKeen, 1992; Trice and Treacy, 1986).

One way forward here is to establish appropriate measures in financial or quantified terms wherever possible, but recognize their limitations and place alongside these where appropriate, measures that are subjective and qualitative in nature. Another

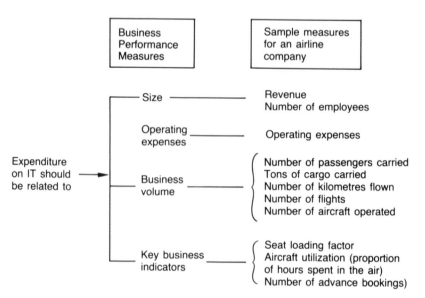

Figure 1.2 Possible performance measures – AIRLINE.

complementary approach is to develop a battery of measures to cover a range of stakeholder concerns (Gold, 1992; Kaplan and Norton, 1992). Thus Carlson and McNurlin (1992) suggest measures to cover five areas – IT resources used, IS efficiency (such as cost per thousand lines of code), IS effectiveness (for example levels of user satisfaction), business efficiency (for example labour productivity), and quality management (such as delays in problem correction, and levels of customer service). This theme is developed in Chapter 3 with the balanced scorecard approach.

Matching measurement techniques to types of IS investment

Much of the research shows strongly that there is a preference for more traditional, financially-based cost benefit approaches to IS assessment. It also shows that these approaches are not appropriate for all types of IS investment (Hochstrasser and Griffiths, 1991; Scott-Morton, 1991; Ward, 1990). A major way forward on IS evaluation is to match techniques to objectives and types of projects.

A starting point is to allow business strategy and purpose to define the category of IS investment. From their research Weill and Olson (1989) suggest, first, the need to identify a Strategic Business Unit (SBU). An SBU will be a separate business unit with a distinct set of products or services, group of customers and a defined set of competitors. They indicate the importance of choosing measures that can be logically linked to the performance objectives of each type of IS investment. Four types of IS investment are identified. They offer the following as a general guideline, with the measures needing to be tailored to the industry and a specific organization's needs:

Strategic investments. Made with long term goals relating to competitive advantage. The recommended performance measure is the revenue growth rate of the SBU.

Informational investments. Made with medium-term goals of improving management decision-making. The suggested performance measure is Return on Assets (ROA). This is justified by reference to a study of 16 financial measures by Grinyer and Norburn (1975). The study showed that in the assessment of firm size, profitability, performance and growth, statistically the measure of ROA could substitute for all the others.

Transactional investments. Generally made with goals of reducing the costs of doing business by substituting capital for labour. The suggested performance measure is changes in the cost of indirect labour (adjusted for sales).

Threshold investments. Such IS investments may be required in order to compete in an industry. Weill and Olson point out that such investments may have negative ROI but be essential to the firm's survival. They do not make a suggestion for a performance measure for this type of investment.

This type of approach is supported by Quinn (1992). In looking at the more advanced users of IT in service industries, he and his co-researchers found most tending to separate out different types of investments and systems problems, and, with clear reasons, carrying out detailed cost–benefit analyses on some items, but not on others. Most used a classification system which included at least the following:

1. **Cost-reducing and new product investments.** Respondents claimed they could carry out all the standard cost−benefit calculations when for example eliminating routine accounting tasks or using IT to support a specific new product entry. The problem was that most of such investments had already been made and their payoffs achieved. Also, even in these areas where results were more quantifiable, they found difficulty in separating out IT from non-IT contribution to performance.

2. **Infrastructure investments.** These were considered necessary for competitive service levels and even survival. Standard financial evaluations (ROI or PV) were often inappropriate or useless. This classification of investment is similar to the threshold investment identified above. Also falling into this classification are attempts to automate and integrate office activities across organizations, and interconnect knowledge workers through data networks so they can be better informed.

3. **Strategic technology investments.** These are defined as investments that either change the firm's basic position in the marketplace or ensure its very viability. Quinn found that if the investment created a totally new business, benefits could usually be quantitatively measured and justified. Where they merely improved the quality of outcomes few metrics, other than managerial judgement, seemed appropriate. As one example a company installed Electronic Data Interchange to get closer to a particularly large customer. It was not known whether they would have lost the account without EDI, whether the customer would have cut back purchases without it, or whether the competition would have installed EDI in a pre-emptive move. Evaluation could not really be made in financial or probability terms. The issue was the $20 million size of the account and the fact that the customer wanted better service.

There are several variations on these types of approach and these receive further attention in Chapter 3. It is useful however to point to one development away from large-scale projects noted by several commentators. This is the breaking down of very large IS projects into smaller, discrete investments and projects which can be justified individually, but which can also be linked into a larger scale system. To a certain extent this can avoid some of the problems of evaluation prevalent with the infrastructure and strategic technology type investments discussed above. It can also have more usable learning for future projects – one of the desired outcomes from carrying out any evaluation. Quinn (1992) points out the advantages: 'By breaking down programs into definable, smaller projects, each with a finite timing and payoff, both risks and total investments can be decreased. Initial feedback from early projects can be used to guide those later in the sequence. Project management is simplified and more focused . . . . "mega projects", by contrast, generally turned out to be major sources of corporate inefficiency . . . . respondents said that even for strategic projects, they had moved to more discrete, incremental development patterns'.

Time and effort required for a major capital asset

Many of the studies discussed so far support the notion that most organizations have a range of deficiencies in their IS evaluation and measurement practice. As argued earlier, this remains surprising in the light of the substantial investment IS now represents in most organizations. The problem arises partly because managers fail to understand how substantial that investment really is. Keen (1991) is useful here in suggesting the need to create what he calls an 'IT balance sheet'. Senior management rarely know how much capital is tied up in IS resources. In one bank Keen investigated, management were aware of the $200 million annual IS expenditure, and the $120 million value of centrally managed computers. However when personal computers, departmental telecommunications, small items, and the cost of creating the software and data currently in use were added together, the bank possessed an IS asset worth $2 billion. Keen's point is a good one. Failure to appreciate the size of this investment leads to IS being undermanaged, a lack of serious attention given to IS investment evaluation and control, and also a lack of concern for discovering ways of utilizing this IS asset base to its full potential. Drawing up such a balance sheet, and auditing that balance sheet, may well be a significant stimulus to improved IS evaluation and measurement techniques and approaches. Organizations could usefully adopt the idea of drawing up IS balance sheets to establish were IS assets and costs are and the size of these assets and costs, and encourage their improved management.

Time-scale of likely benefits

The search for quick payoffs from IS is understandable. However even in fairly straightforward office systems, automation, for example bringing in word processors, can have delayed cost savings. As a matter of experience the full impact of process innovation – aimed at efficiency and cost savings, that is doing existing things better – can take over two years to materialize, and would still be difficult to isolate on traditional financial statements like cash flow and profit and loss statements.

As Keen (1991) suggests, we are still learning about the likely time-frame for assessing the impact of IS investments. In fact he suggests that infrastructure investments – for example those in telecommunications networks, shared database management resources, network management utilities – may be long-term, critical but difficult to evaluate. They need to be evaluated separately and funded by top or corporate divisional management as a long-range capital investment justified by corporate policy requirements.

The issue of time-scale of benefits is illustrated by the case of a US manufacturing company (Willcocks, 1989). Here, one casualty of erosion of market share was the IS budget. The plan to migrate existing applications to a common manufacturing, engineering and purchasing database was deferred. However, sales people were to get laptop computers because competitor salesforces were seen to make good use of these for rapid order entry. The problem rested in the evaluation approach adopted. Traditional cost–benefit analysis proved the need for a freeze on IS spending. Only when the long-term 1987–92 implications of IS spending on core activities were taken into account, did it emerge that without such expenditure the very survival of the firm was jeopardized. As Strassmann (1990) establishes, there is no real way of knowing what IS can do for the business, and the risks of not using, as compared with using IS, always have to be significant factors in the subsequent investment appraisal. In the case in question the real way to evaluate IS plans was to establish the value added by comparing the business plan with changes to IS costs over five years against the business plan without changes to IS costs. This would seem to be a fundamental method for adoption in appraising and tracking IS investments in organizations.

On terminology and definitions

A final problem area needs to be addressed. It is endemic to discussions on IT/IS, strategy and evaluation for the relevant terms to be used in loose and unclear ways. Not only do different commentators use the same words but impute different meanings to them. Often the use of a term is not defined in the first place. Moreover the meaning of a term can often change in the course of the same article or book, without the author noting the different usage. The problem is compounded when an author refers to other sources and imports the language and arguments of those sources without fully noting differences in meanings assigned to terms. This set of problems stems from the relative immaturity of IS/IT and information management as subject disciplines. It also relates to the practical, inter-disciplinary nature of those subjects. A very wide range of interested parties across the academic–practitioner spectrum is involved in constructing the discourse.

It is difficult to avoid completely these problems of language and meaning in a book by many authors from different backgrounds. However, the major terms used throughout the book are defined and discussed in this section, with a view to offering some clarity for the reader. If a contributor uses terms in different ways from those now cited, the different uses will be made explicit at relevant points in the text. The definition of terms leads into a more extended consideration of several root concepts in the IS evaluation debate, namely economy, efficiency, effectiveness and value for money.

There are three clusters of concepts that commonly run through discussions on evaluation of information systems investments and that therefore need working definitions. These clusters are:

1. Information Technology, Information Systems, Information Management, IS Strategy and Strategic Information Systems;
2. Evaluation, cost, benefit, risk and value;
3. Efficiency, economy, effectiveness and value for money.

IT/IS/IM strategy

Information Technology (IT) is taken to refer to the hardware, software and communications technologies – essentially equipment – and attendant techniques. **Information systems (IS)** is a wider concept referring to how designed information flows attempt to meet the information needs of the organization. IS may be more, or less, IT-based. The process of managing the information needs of the organization is often referred to as **information management (IM)**. **IS strategy** slightly amends the Earl (1989) definition: it is a long-term directional plan which decides what to do with IT and information. It is business/organizational led, demand-oriented and mainly concerned with exploiting IT either to support business strategies or create new strategic options. **A strategic information system** is taken to be one on which the organization's survival, growth and future direction is critically dependent.

Evaluation

From a management perspective **evaluation** is most commonly taken to be about establishing, by quantitative and/or qualitative means, the worth of IS to the organization. Evaluation brings into play notions of cost, benefit, risk and value. It also implies organizational processes by which these are assessed, whether formally or informally. A method of evaluation needs to be reliable, that is consistent in its measurement over time, able to discriminate between good and indifferent investments, able to measure what it purports to measure, and be administratively/organizationally feasible in its application.

Hard costs associated with an investment are those agreed by everyone to be directly attributable to the investment, and which can be easily captured by accounting procedures. There may however be **hidden costs** that are more difficult to identify and quantify, but still need to be attributed to the investment for measurement purposes. An **IS benefit** can be seen as an advantage or good, something produced with the assistance of computers and communications for which an organization is prepared to pay, or has experienced as supporting the business and technical goals and priorities of defined stakeholders. **IS risk** relates to the degree to which the organization, through IS, is vulnerable to threats, which can disadvantage the goals and priorities of the organization. HM Treasury (1991) usefully defines **cost–benefit analysis** as 'the most comprehensive form of economic appraisal which seeks to quantify in money terms as many of the costs and benefits of a proposal as possible, including items for which the market does not provide a satisfactory measure of economic value'. Cost–benefit analysis will also seek to take into account **opportunity cost** – 'value in most valuable alternative use of resources; this may or may not be measured in monetary terms' (HM Treasury, 1991). The emphasis on costs and benefits in money terms is important to developing IS metrics. However not all costs and benefits relevant to IS can be tracked adequately using money-based measures. Quantitative, non-money based, and qualitative measures also need to be employed to capture fully the costs and benefits often referred to as 'less tangible'. One way forward, based loosely on Parker *et al.* (1988), is to expand the measurement of **cost** to cover financial, quantifiable and qualitative costs and risks (potential costs). Relatedly the measurement of **benefits** can be extended to cover financial, quantifiable and qualitative desired/preferred outputs and outcomes. What then becomes important is the establishment of the **net value** or worth of the potential or actual IS performance to the organization. This is done through netting off the results from taking an enhanced view of costs and benefits.

Net value as such expresses the degree to which business/organizational performance is enhanced through IS. At the feasibility stage of an IS project, net value is a calculation of potential. One should note that post-implementation evaluation often highlights **unanticipated, desired benefits of IS**. Thus AT Kearney (1990), surveying over 400 companies, found 22% experiencing greater benefits than expected with IS. To some extent this reflects limitations in evaluation techniques at the feasibility stage of projects. Additionally, however it is important for the evaluation process to be flexible enough to include such benefits in the assessment of net value at the post-implementation stage, and for the discovery of unanticipated, less 'tangible' benefits to guide evaluation processes and measures in future computerization. However, discussion of net value cannot be isolated from that of effectiveness, as emerges below.

Economy, efficiency and effectiveness

The interrelationships between the concepts of economy, efficiency and effectiveness are presented in Figure 1.3, which is based on the work of Metcalfe and Richards (1990).

Economy can be defined as the purchase and provision of a service at lowest possible cost consistent with a specified quality and quantity. Some writers have seen economy in terms of how actual input costs compare with planned or expected costs, or, simpler still, just minimizing resource consumption. It practice economy is often defined exclusively in terms of costs, in particular as the ratio of the resources consumed relative to planned consumption, that is the difference between planned and actual inputs. By focusing solely on inputs this approach ignores the quality of the output, that is whether it is of an acceptable standard. **Efficiency** is often used as both a measure and an objective of computerization. Efficiency seeks to ensure that maximum output is obtained from resources devoted to a computerization programme, or that only the minimum level of resources is devoted to a specified level of output. As a measure it can be seen as a ratio of actual input to actual output, or rate at which inputs are converted into outputs. Put more simply it is the ratio of resource consumption to benefits produced. **Effectiveness** relates to comparing actual performance against planned, whether original or subsequently chosen,

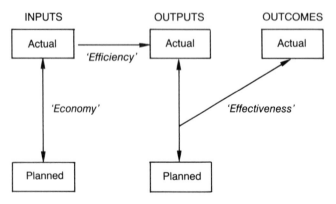

Figure 1.3 Economy, efficiency and effectiveness.

targets/outputs, outcomes and policy objectives. In other words effectiveness is a measure of actual performance against planned, subsequently chosen and/or preferred performance. Here 'performance' is used in a wide sense of the word. **Value for Money (VFM)** can be seen to come from the economic, efficient and effective use of resources. It is a balance of quality, time, cost and risk. Value here is an expression of relevance to requirement in the light of alternatives for spending the money.

Economy, efficiency and effectiveness: further considerations

A detailed discussion of this third cluster of concepts appears in Willcocks and Harrow (1992). Some further comment on some difficulties in applying the concepts in IS projects and programmes is appropriate here.

The quantification problem

There is an inclination to resort to quantification in IS evaluation, following the much quoted prescription: 'what gets measured, gets done'. However a concentration on measurable efficiency of IS can have several undesirable consequences. First, because costs are more easily measured than benefits, efficiency often reduces to economy. This can lead to savings in money and human resources becoming the prime measure of improvement. Secondly, because human social and organizational costs are more difficult to measure than technical and economic costs, e.g. of hardware and software, the latter often receive most attention. Thirdly, economic benefits are more easily identified than human, organizational and social benefits and efforts to increase efficiency often lead to redefining performance criteria in ways that lend themselves to easier measurement. The pursuit of efficiency can be demoted into a numbers game (Metcalfe and Richards, 1990). This may lead to minimizing inputs regardless of outputs. Where the essential input–output relationship is of less significance than the reduction of inputs as such, this can no longer be described as a concern with efficiency.

Interlinks

It is clear that the concepts of efficiency, economy and effectiveness are interlinked, and that changes in one need to be traded off against the others. For example a badly maintained printer may consume more paper or toner (an economy issue), or it may not have the performance anticipated (an effectiveness issue), or both may occur. But such a situation with extra raw material costs or unsatisfactory output can be due to inefficiency. This interlinking needs to be taken into account when devising and interpreting metrics for IS performance.

Outputs and outcomes

It is by no means easy to arrive at definable, non-conflicting intentions, objectives and planned targets. Furthermore, placing priority on any one goal in isolation may have a detrimental effect on the pursuit of other, conflicting goals. Additionally, if effectiveness is seen, as it frequently is, as 'the ratio of output to planned output' this leads, in practice, to an over-emphasis on achieving economy and efficiency at the expense of a broader concept of effectiveness. Indeed, in practice effectiveness may come to be conflated to mean the achievement of economy and efficiency. Relatedly, in practice, effectiveness may mean no more than the achievement of targets, narrowly conceived. These definitions limit effectiveness to an evaluation of outputs of specific programmes or IS projects, that is the use of limited 'within time and budget, to required standard' type criteria. The result may be no attempt to link outputs with the broader concept of outcomes, and no assessment measures set up to link actual outputs and outcomes with the overall strategic aims of an organization. It is therefore important in measuring IS effectiveness to distinguish between **outputs/targets**, that is the service provided by the IS, and the wider concept of **outcomes**, that is the impact of that service on overall preferred policy objectives in the public sector or strategic objectives in private sector organizations.

Model of rational choice

A final difficulty relates to the model of rational choice based on given objectives that underlies much IS performance measurement found in both private and public sector organizations. Conventionally IS evaluation is dependent on a prior definition of outputs, outcomes and policy objectives. However, objectives, and related outcomes and outputs, are notoriously difficult to define, are frequently in conflict and are often subject to revision. Moreover IS evaluation is an inherently political process, with different stakeholders bringing a variety of perceptions and interests to bear on the selection and in the use of evaluation techniques and approaches (Willcocks and Mason, 1987).

Recent literature has tended to reformulate the problem of organizational and IS effectiveness. Instead of assuming given objectives and seeing organizations as goal-seeking systems, effectiveness is increasingly defined in terms of innovativeness, adaptability, organizational learning and capacity to manage change (see for example Kaplan and Norton, 1992). Against this backdrop, the way forward on IS evaluation practice is conceiving this as a learning process capable of adapting and revising measures where objectives change. It also needs to be a continuous, integrated process with wide stakeholder involvement in both setting goals and measures and in being accountable for the delivery of benefits and value (Eason, 1988; Gregory and Jackson, 1991; Hawgood and Land, 1988; Hoff, 1992). These issues receive some attention in Chapters 3, 12 and 13.

This book

These considerations underpin and inform the contributions that follow. The book is organized into four parts. The focus throughout is very much on the front end of IS evaluation, that is strategy, investment appraisal, prioritization and evaluation at the feasibility stage. Part One is an overview, designed to provide insight into, and commentary on, current IS evaluation practice in organizations. The first contribution here is by James Bacon. Taking an 80 company sample of American, British, Australian and New Zealand companies, he investigates the criteria these organizations used, how they arrived at decisions, and the type and quality of the decisions made. Bacon provides his own critique of current capital budgeting theory and also points out the importance of the process adopted when arriving at IS capital expenditure decisions. He poses three main types of criteria for investigation – financial, management and development. From the survey results, he is able to generate ten proposals that might be considered by organizations in making decisions on their information systems projects and investments. The second overview contribution is by Leslie Willcocks and Stephanie Lester. Their UK-based survey and interview programme seeks to investigate criteria and processes adopted by private and public sector organizations considering the feasibility of potential IS investments. Their findings largely complement those of Bacon, and pinpoint some common weaknesses and areas for improvement in IS evaluation practice. They also build on their recommendations by appraising less traditional approaches to IS feasibility evaluation including Return on Management, Information Economics, SESAME, Contingency approaches and the Balanced Score-Card approach.

Part Two of this book is devoted to four chapters on the strategic dimension in IS evaluation. The first, by John Ward, uses the work of Parker, Benson and Trainor, and of McFarlan, as a platform for the development of a portfolio approach to evaluation. He explores the nature of benefits that can accrue in relation to the business objectives of IS investments. He also has an extensive discussion on how risk assessment can be incorporated into the portfolio model. Ward has produced here a high level approach to evaluation that facilitates the maintenance of a coherent strategy for managing IS investments. In the next chapter Glen Peters also develops a method for evaluating IS investments against business strategy. He does this from research into over 50 IS projects in the UK. From the research base he builds an investment mapping procedure by which the benefits and investment orientation applied to IS can be compared to those inherent in the business strategy. Gaps between the IS and business investment criteria can then be identified and closed.

Malcolm Iliff's chapter is concerned also with the issue of aligning IS/IT strategies with those of the rest of the business. He introduces the concepts of Information Technology, Information Systems and Information Management strategies, based on Earl's work, and provides a planning model for aligning IS with business needs. He also introduces a 'Portakabin' approach to developing systems outside the strategic IS migration path, and gives rules for how this approach can be applied. Brian Dos Santos provides the last chapter in this part. His work counterbalances other contributions by showing how a financial assessment of strategic IT applications can be conducted. Financial analysis, based upon traditional NPV analysis and options pricing models is proposed, together with an appropriate development process. A case is described wherein an options model was used to estimate the value of a prototype project. The chapter also discusses the effects of project and firm characteristics on the value of an IS investment.

Part Three deals in detail with modern techniques for evaluation of IS investments. Beat Hochstrasser, in Chapter 8, puts forward a categorization of types of investment and IT/IS projects, and a framework for evaluating and prioritizing non-infrastructure investments. The approach consists of four modules, to be applied in a sequential fashion: corporate standards for new IT initiatives; developing awareness of potential wider effects; establishing business performance indicators; and how to assess the relative merits of individual projects against one another through a Project Priority Value calculation exercise. Devra Wiseman then deals in detail with the Information Economics (IE) approach. She shows the adaptability of the approach through her own case study work in both private and public sector organizations.

Tom Coleman and Mark Jamieson also demonstrate the applicability of the IE approach in Chapter 10. They move from a critique of existing methods to show how intangible benefits can be included in evaluation schemes. They illustrate how a business case can be built for IS investment, then detail a methodology and process called 'total benefit management' developed at The Prudential insurance company. The final chapter in this part is by Leslie Willcocks and Helen Margetts. They point to the frequent under-analysis of risk in evaluation practice. The chapter considers a variety of methods that can be adopted for risk analysis, and stresses the need to take a broader perspective on risk than is prevalent through using techniques from the project management, operational research and financial management fields. A case study approach is used to develop a new risk profiling framework.

The final part of the book has two chapters focusing on evaluation processes. Earlier chapters make clear a number of weaknesses in the IS evaluation processes adopted in organizations. As the final chapters establish, however, processes are not only vehicles for operationalizing techniques; they can be formative of the very nature of techniques, and are an important ingredient in establishing the acceptability and credibility of the resulting evaluation. In Chapter 11 Catherine Griffiths looks at who has, and who should have, responsibility for IS decisions. From her research she finds a common pattern of IS responsibility being slotted into traditional manage-ment structures without any recognition of the broader impact that IS management should have on existing processes, communication practices and organizational structures. She details what happens when IT directors, finance directors, business units or the Board are in charge of IT, and makes proposals for how evaluation processes can be better staffed, organized and managed. Veronica Symons, in the final chapter, uses a detailed case study to bring home the point that formal–rational, finance-based evaluation techniques and processes can be dysfunctional. She suggests the need for multiple perspectives to be incorporated into the evaluation process, and the usefulness of a wider stakeholder involvement in IS evaluation practice. This endorses many of the findings and prescriptions made in the first section of the book, and provides a fitting message with which to end it – techniques mean little if the right processes are not in place to operationalize them.

References

Aggarwal, R., Mellen, E. and Mellen, L. (1991) Justifying investments in flexible manufacturing technology: adding strategic analysis to capital budgeting under uncertainty. *Managerial Finance*, **17** (2/3), 77–88.

Bacon, N. (1991) Information systems strategies in government – recent survey evidence. *Journal of Information Technology*, **6** (2).

Bryan, E. (1990) Information systems investment strategies. *Journal of Information Systems Management*, Fall, 27–35.

Butler Cox Foundation (1990) *Getting Value from Information Technology*. Research Report 75, June. Butler Cox, London.

Cane, A. (1992) A hiatus for the high-tech dream. *Financial Times*, 21st. August.

Carlson, W. and McNurlin, B. (1992) *Basic Principles for Measuring IT Value*. I/S Analyser, October, pp. 1–15.

Chakravarthy, B. (1986) Measuring strategic performance. *Strategic Management Journal*, **7**, 437–58.

Chew, B., Leonard-Barton, D. and Bohn, R. (1991) Beating Murphy's Law. *Sloan Management Review*, **32** (1), 5–16.

Coleman, T. and Jamieson, M. (1991) *Information Systems: Evaluating Intangible Benefits at the Feasibility Stage of Project Appraisal*. Unpublished MBA thesis, City University Business School, London.

Drucker, P. (1991) The Coming of the New Organization. In *Revolution in Real Time* (ed. W. McGowan), HBS Press, Boston.

Drury, C. (1988) *Management and Cost Accounting*. Van Nostrand Reinhold, London.

Dunlop, C. and Kling, R. (1991) *Computerization and Controversy: Value Conflicts and Social Choices*, Academic Press, Boston.

Earl, M. (1989). *Management Strategies for Information Technology*, Prentice-Hall, London.

Eason, K. (1988) *Information Technology and Organisational Change*, Taylor & Francis, London.

Ernst and Young (1990) *Strategic Alignment Report, UK Survey*. Ernst and Young, London.

Farbey, B., Land, F. and Targett, D. (1992) Evaluating investments in IT. *Journal of Information Technology*, **7** (2), 100–12.

Forester, T. (1989) *Computers in the Human Context*. Basil Blackwell, Oxford.

Franke, R. (1987) Technology revolution and productivity decline: The case of US banks. *Technology Forecasting and Social Change*, **31**, 143–54.

Gold, C. (1992) *Total Quality Management in Information Services – a balancing act*. Ernst and Young Center for Information Technology and Strategy, Boston.

Gregory, A. and Jackson, M. (1991) Evaluating organizations: a systems and contingency approach. *Systems Practice*, **5** (1), 37–60.

Grindley, K. (1991) *Managing IT at Board Level*, Pitman, London.

Grinyer, P. and Norburn, D. (1975) Planning for existing markets: perceptions of executives and financial performance. *Journal of the Royal Statistical Society*, Series A (138, part A), 70–97.

Guterl, F. (1992) The Datamation 100 – European 25. *Datamation*, July, 60–6.

Hackett, G. (1990) Investment in technology – the service sector sinkhole? *Sloan Management Review*, Winter, 97–103.

Hawgood, J. and Land, F. (1988) A Multivalent Approach to Information Systems Assessment. In *Information Systems Assessment: Issues and Challenges*, (eds N. Bjorn-Andersen and G. Davis), Elsevier North-Holland, Amsterdam.

Heath, W. and Swinden, K. (1992) The chips are down for Europe. *Management Today*, October, 92–110.

HM Treasury (1991) *Economic Appraisal in Central Government. A Technical Guide for Government departments*. HMSO, London.

Hochstrasser, B. (1990) Evaluating IT investments – matching techniques to projects. *Journal of Information Technology*, **5** (4), 215–21.

Hochstrasser, B. and Griffiths, C. (1990) *Regaining control of IT investments – A Handbook for Senior UK Managers*, Kobler Unit, London.

Hochstrasser, B. and Griffiths, C. (1991) *Controlling IT Investments: Strategy and management*. Chapman & Hall, London.

Hodges, P. (1987) DP Budget Survey. *Datamation*, April 1st., 69–73.

Hoff, J. (1992) *Criteria for Evaluation of IT in the Private and Public Sector: Should They Be the Same?* Paper at the Conference of the European Group of Public Administration, Pisa, 2–5 September.

Itami, S. (1987) *Mobilising Invisible Assets*. Harvard University Press, Boston.

Johnston, M. (1992) Mixed year for Asia's IT industry. *Datamation*, 1 September, 62–84.

Kaplan, R. (1986) Must CIM be justified by faith alone? *Harvard Business Review*, March–April, 87–95.

Kaplan, R. and Norton, D. (1992) The balanced scorecard: measures that drive performance. *Harvard Business Review*, January–February, 71–9.

Kearney, A. T. (1990) *Breaking the Barriers: IT Effectiveness in Great Britain and Ireland*, AT Kearney/CIMA, London.

Keen, P. (1986) *Competing in Time*, Ballinger, Cambridge, USA.

Keen, P. (1991) *Shaping The Future: Business Design through Information Technology*, Harvard Business School Press, Boston.

KEW Associates (1992) UK IT market analysis. *Computer weekly*, Autumn 1992 edition, London.

Kobler UNIT (1987) *Does Information Technology Slow You Down?* Kobler Unit, London.

KPMG Peat Marwick Mitchell (1990) Quoted in Datalink, 12 March, page 1.

Laudon, K. and Laudon, J. (1991) *Management Information Systems*, Macmillan, New York.

Loveman, G. (1988) An assessment of the productivity impact of Information Technologies. Working paper, *Management in the 1990s*. Sloan School of Management, MIT.

Marion, L. (1992) The Datamation 100 Overview. 15 June, pp. 12 *et seq.*

McKeen, J. and Smith, H. (1992) *Linking IT Investment with IT Usage*. Working paper 92–20, June, School of Business, Queen's University, Ontario.

Metcalfe, L. and Richards, S. (1990) *Improving Public Management*, Sage, London.

Miller, J. (1989) Information Systems effectiveness: the fit between business needs and systems capabilities. *Proceedings of the 10th International Conference on Information Systems*, Boston, Mass.

Moad, J. (1991) DP budget survey. *Datamation*, April 15, 44–7.

Morris, B. (1992) *Improving Returns on Investment on IT at National Westminster Bank*. Conference Presentation, Cafe Royale, London, 2 December.

National Audit Office (1987) *Inland Revenue: Control of Major Developments in use of IT*, HMSO, London.

National Audit Office (1989) *Department of Social Security: Operational Strategy*. January Session 1988–89, HC–111, HMSO, London.

Noble, J. (1989) Techniques for cost justifying CIM. *Journal of Business Strategy*, January/February, 44–9.

Norton, D. (1986) A case study: Hercules incorporated. *Stage By Stage*, **6** (5), 11–17.

PA Consulting Group (1990) *The Impact of the Current Climate on IT – The Survey Report*. PA Consulting Group, London.

Parker, M. M., Benson, R. J. and Trainor, H. E. (1988) *Information Economics*, Prentice-Hall, London.

Peat Marwick (1989) *IT survey among CEOs*, Peat Marwick, London.

Peters, G. (1990) Beyond strategy – benefits identification and the management of specific IT investments. *Journal of Information Technology*, **5** (4), 205–14.

Pike, R. and Ho, S. (1991) Risk analysis in capital budgeting: barriers and benefits. *Omega*, **19** (4), 235–45.

Porter, M. (1985) Technology and competitive advantage. *Journal of Business Strategy*, Winter, 60–78.

Porter, M. E. and Millar, V. E. (1985) How information gives you competitive advantage. *Harvard Business Review*, **63** (4) July–August, 149–60.

Prahalad, C. and Hamel, G. (1990) The core competence of the corporation. *Harvard Business Review*, **68** (3), May–June, 79–91.

Price Waterhouse (1989) *Information Technology Review 1989/90*, Price Waterhouse, London.

Price Waterhouse (1990) *Information Technology Review 1990/1*, Price Waterhouse, London.

Price Waterhouse (1991) *Information Technology Review 1992/3*, Price Waterhouse, London.

Price Waterhouse (1992) *Information Technology Review 1992/3*, Price Waterhouse, London.

Quinn, J. (1992) *Intelligent Enterprise: A Knowledge and Service Based Paradigm for Industry*, Free Press, New York.

Quinn, J., Doorley, T. and Paquette, P. (1990) Technology in services: rethinking strategic focus. *Sloan Management Review*, **31** (2), 79–87.

Ring, T. (1991) Counting the cost. *Computing*, 24 October, 20–2.

Roach, S. (1991) Services under siege: the restructuring imperative. *Harvard Business Review*, September–October, 82–91.

Remenyi, D. and Money, A. (1991) A user satisfaction approach to IS effectiveness measurement. *Journal of Information Technology*, **6** (3/4), 162–75.

Sassone, (1988) A survey of cost benefit methodologies for Information Systems. *Project Appraisal*, **3** (2), 73–84.

Scott-Morton, M. (1991) *The Corporation of the 1990s*. Oxford University Press, New York.

Sequent Computer Systems (1991) *The Boardroom Guide to Effective Computing*, Sequent, Weybridge.

Shank, J. and Govindarajan, V. (1992) Strategic cost analysis of technological investments. *Sloan Management Review*, **34** (1), 39–51.

Smith, H. and McKeen, J. (1992) *The Relationship Between Information Technology Use and Organizational Performance*. Working Paper 92–11, April, School of Business, Queen's University, Ontario.

Strassmann, P. (1990) *The Business Value of Computers*, The Information Economics Press, New Canaan.

Strassmann, P. (1992) The politics of downsizing. *Datamation*, 15 October, 106–10.

Swanson, E. and Beath, C. (1989) *Maintaining Information Systems in Organizations*, Wiley, Chichester.

Tate, P. (1988) Risk: the third factor. *Datamation*, 15 April, 58–64.

Touche Ross/IAM (1991) *Office Automation, The Barriers and Opportunities*, Touche Ross, London.

Trice, A. and Treacy, M. (1986) Utilization as a dependent variable in MIS research. *Proceedings of the 7th International Conference on Information Systems*, December.

Vowler, J. (1990) The theory – and the reality. *Computer Weekly*, 15 November, p. 18.

Ward, J., Griffiths, P. and Whitmore, P. (1990) *Strategic Planning for Information Systems*, Wiley, Chichester.

Waters, R. and Cane, A. (1993) Sudden death of a runaway bull. *Financial Times*, 19 March, p. 11.

Weill, P. (1989) *The Relationship Between Investment in Information Technology and Firm Performance in the Manufacturing Sector*. Working Paper No. 18, August, Graduate School of Management, University of Melbourne, Melbourne.

Weill, P. (1991) *Do Computers Pay Off?* ICIT Press, Washington D.C.

Weill, P. and Olson, M. (1989) Managing investment in Information Technology: mini case examples and implications. *MIS Quarterly*, March, 2–17.

Willcocks, L. (1989) Measuring the value of IT investments. *Journal of Information Technology*, **4** (4), 239–42.

Willcocks, L. (1991) Informatization in public administration and services in the United Kingdom: toward a management era? *Informatization and the Public Sector*, **1** (3), 1–23.

Willcocks, L. (1992) Evaluating information technology investments: research findings and reappraisal. *Journal of Information Systems*, **2** (3), 243–68.

Willcocks, L. and Lester, S. (1991) Information Systems investments: evaluation at the feasibility stage of projects. *Technovation*, **11** (5), 283–302.

Willcocks, L. and Harrow, J. (eds) (1992) *Rediscovering Public Services Management*. McGraw Hill, London.

Willcocks, L. and Margetts, H. (1992) *Information Systems as risk: private and public sector comparisons*. Paper at the Conference of the European Group of Public Administration, Pisa, 2–5 September.

Willcocks, L. (1993) Managing Information Systems in UK public administration: issues and prospects. Public Administration, Winter (in press).

Willcocks, L. and Mason, D. (1987) *Computerising Work: People, Systems Design and Workplace Relations*. Blackwell Scientific, Oxford.

Wilson, T. (1991) Overcoming the barriers to the implementation of Information System strategies. *Journal of Information Technology*, **6** (1), 39–44.

Zuboff, S. (1988) *In the Age of the Smart Machine*. Basic Books, New York.

Part One

Overviews

2

Why companies invest in information technology

C. James Bacon

Introduction

Why do companies invest in information technology? What criteria do they use and how are such decisions made? Are they 'quality' decisions – that is, do they support strategic business goals and effectively target the use of **information technology** (IT), as well as maximizing short- and long-term returns? Finally, what proposals might be developed for the purpose of optimizing the way in which such decisions are made?

In 1990, the author undertook a survey of American, British, Australian and New Zealand companies to try to find some answers to these questions. The survey was based on the premise that the quality with which investment decisions are made on IT projects has become critical to the organization. To begin with, the amount of money being spent on IT now makes it 'stand out on the balance sheet' (Sullivan-Trainor, 1989). At the same time, increasing economic and competitive pressures are compelling companies to cut costs further, and forcing them to scrutinize their IT operating and capital budgets more carefully, so as to allocate limited resources among competing projects in the best way possible (Carlyle, 1990). Thus, careful and correct IT investment (or project selection) decisions are becoming more of an economic and competitive necessity.

Information Management: The evaluation of information systems investments.
Edited by Leslie Willcocks.
Published in 1994 by Chapman & Hall. ISBN 0 412 41540 2.

There is no uniform definition of what constitutes an IT investment, and not all investment in **information systems and/or technology** (IST), is of a **capital** nature. The current cost of processing and operations is clearly not; neither is 'routine' systems maintenance. But outlays for hardware, network facilities and externally developed software products are clearly capital expenditures. In addition, in-house development projects involving new systems and significant enhancements would also seem to represent capital expenditures.

Capital expenditures in general have been defined as:

> investments to acquire fixed or long-lived assets from which a stream of benefits is expected.... Capital expenditure decisions, therefore, form a foundation for the future profitability of a company. (International Federation of Accountants, 1989).

An investment in the form of salaries to pay for 'in-house systems development may not appear to fit the capital definition, in that it may not involve the implicit external expenditure. However, the decision to go ahead with such a project generally commits the organization to significant internal expense, and the decision is based on a stream of expected benefits. Consequently, giving the go-ahead on an in-house systems development project, notwithstanding the absence of external expenditure, would seem to have the economic nature of a capital investment decision.

An IST capital investment is therefore defined as follows:

> A capital investment in information systems and/or technology (IST) is any acquisition of hardware or software, or any 'in-house' development project, that is expected to add to or enhance an organization's information systems capabilities and produce benefits beyond the short term.

Capital investment and budgeting are concerned with the process of planning for and deciding upon capital investments. This is therefore the general area of theory and practice within which investments in IST might be considered.

Much of the theory of capital investment/budgeting focuses on the evaluation of cash flows, based on the time value of money, and using **discounted cash flow** (DCF) techniques. DCF techniques reduce all projected cash outflows and inflows associated with a given investment or project back to point zero, the present, so as to express everything in present money values. This way, cash flows in different periods and in different projects have a common basis of comparison. There are also non-DCF techniques that ignore the time value of money. These are the **payback** (PBK) and the **accounting rate of return** (ARR) methods. PBK evaluates a project on the basis of how quickly it takes to pay for itself, whereas ARR divides the average annual income from a project by its initial capital investment. These non-DCF techniques are frequently used as 'yardsticks' or benchmarks, in conjunction with DCF techniques.

There are two basic DCF techniques:

1. **Net present value** (NPV), which discounts all estimated cash flows for a project to present value, using a required rate of return or 'hurdle-rate'. It may also be referred to as **expected present value** (EPV), to reflect the incorporation of probability and expected value estimates. If the present value of the cash inflows exceeds the present value of the cash outflows, including the initial capital investment, this will give a positive net present value, and possibly project acceptance.

2. **Internal rate of return** (IRR), which aims to find the discount rate that would equate the present value of estimated cash outflows with the present value of inflows. If this rate is greater than the required rate of return, the project may be accepted.

A third technique, the **profitability index method** (PIM), is an extension of the two basic DCF techniques.

However, a limitation with current capital budgeting theory, insofar as it relates to investments in information systems and technology, is that its starting point is the cash flows as given; it essentially assumes that those cash flows are known. Even risk analysis only provides for the estimation of cash flows after the underlying flows have been determined. Therefore, capital budgeting provides little insight into the quantification of benefits and estimation of cash flows.

A further limitation is that capital budgeting theory concentrates almost exclusively on the financial criteria. While it might be said that every business decision finally comes down to financial criteria, there are other criteria that should, and in practice are, considered by the managerial decision maker. This applies particularly to investments in information systems and technology.

A third limitation is that current capital budgeting theory does little to address the organizational and behavioural factors that make the **practice** of capital budgeting so different from its theory (Hellings, 1985; Kennedy, 1986; Weaver *et al.*, 1989). These issues receive further discussion in Chapter 3.

Background to the investment criteria

There appears to be an increasing need to subject investments in IST to more rigorous analysis and justification, comparable to that undertaken for other investments (Silk, 1990). This is especially so when studies suggest that investments in IST do not necessarily provide a high return but may, in fact, result in costs that contribute to a **loss** in competitive capability (Strassmann, 1985). Given this need, a two-fold question presents itself: how do organizations **decide** on their information systems (IS) investments, and how **should** they decide?

The complementary question is then: what is the **process** in arriving at the IS capital expenditure decision, and what are the **criteria** or methods used?

The **process** is concerned with the formal and informal organizational dynamics involved, starting with the initiation of an IS project or investment, and culminating in review and approval. It answers the question: **how** was the investment decision made? The **criteria** are concerned with the financial and non-financial justification used in proposing and then deciding upon the project or investment. They answer the question: **why** was the investment decision made?

There has been some research on the first part of the question, concerning the process and its organizational dynamics (McKeen and Guimaraes, 1985; Doll and Torkzadeh, 1987; Davenport *et al.*, 1989). Some work has also been done on the ranking process (Buss, 1983).

Regarding the second part of the question, concerning criteria, there has been discussion on whether financial criteria alone should be applied to IST investments, given the intangible and strategic nature of some of the benefits (Davenport, 1989; Badiru, 1990; Polakoff, 1990). And even since the early days of information systems there has been work done on the value of information (Boyd and Krasnow, 1963).

Lastly, the book of Parker *et al.* on *Information Economics* provides a major contribution in considering IST investment benefits based on six classes of value: return on investment, strategic match, competitive advantage, management information support, competitive response and strategic IS architecture (Parker *et al.*, 1988). Their approach receives more detailed attention in the chapters that follow, by Willcocks and Lester, and by Wiseman.

The criteria used in making the decision on IST investments are at the heart of that decision, and they have significance for a number of reasons. First, the criteria used or not used, and the way in which they are applied or not applied, significantly impacts the effectiveness with which IST investment decisions are made. They determine whether the optimal projects are selected and the suboptimal rejected.

Secondly, the criteria used by an organization in deciding upon IST investments tend to reflect the effectiveness with which IST resources are being used, the degree to which senior management are involved, and the level of integration between corporate/business-unit strategy and systems strategy.

Thirdly, the criteria are significant for the organization's finance and management accounting function, in terms of its role in optimizing return on investment, and its involvement in the cost–benefit analysis that may precede an IST capital investment decision. This factor is emphasized when the IST function comes under the responsibility of the chief financial officer.

There is one other reason why the criteria used in IST investments have significance, and it is concerned with achieving the right 'balance' in the use of criteria. There are essentially two opposing views in considering cost–benefit analysis for the purpose of evaluating and selecting information systems projects/investments. One is that a cost–benefit analysis, beyond an intuitive assessment, is neither feasible nor useful, especially when the numbers seem to be stretched to fit the need. This is reinforced by the belief that, even if the projected benefits are realized, it is difficult to prove that they are attributable to the IST investment. Neither is it always easy to quantify the 'soft' or indirect organizational costs involved, which may be greater than the hard/direct costs (Hochstrasser, 1990). Similarly, it has been suggested that ROI analysis is applicable to transaction-oriented systems, but not information support, or those undertaken for strategic, market-oriented purposes (Weill and Olsen, 1989).

All of this has some truth, and the quantification implicit in cost–benefit analysis may not always be feasible. In fact it may even turn into a 'numbers game' that displaces real analysis. Nonetheless, quantification should always be optimized, and procedures put in place to ensure evaluation, screening and benefit tracking (International Federation of Accountants, 1989). Otherwise, there may be an absence of disciplined analysis, no real basis of objective measurement, and limited awareness of the true costs and benefits of IST investments. Furthermore, the feedback and learning process is likely to be a 'hit or miss' affair.

The other view is that which imposes a **universal** requirement for a clear, measurable, and reliable return on investment, and that over two years or less. It is oriented to traditional, cost-saving, productivity-oriented projects, and it tends to screen out those providing better customer service, improved decision support, enhanced communication, and similar strategic payoffs. It denies the reality of intangible benefits, ignores any beneficial 'ripple' effects and dismisses any associated cash inflows, due to the difficulty of measuring such inflows (Downing, 1989; Parker *et al.*, 1988). The problem with this view is that the traditional project often fails to produce the expected cost savings and productivity improvements.

Survey and study background

In an effort to gain some answers on the IST capital investment (project selection) decision criteria used in practice, a survey was undertaken in 1990 of 80 American, British, Australian and New Zealand companies. A one-page survey form was used that provided 15 possible IST investment criteria, a means of indicating whether they are used or not, the percentage of projects to which each criterion is applied, and an overall ranking in terms of total project value for each criterion. The criteria are shown in Table 2.1.

The criteria are categorized into financial, management, and development criteria. They were developed, first, through interviews with some 20 chief information officers (CIOs) in Britain and the United States. These CIOs were questioned on what criteria their organizations use in selecting IST investment projects, with the aim of developing a full list of the criteria used in practice. Secondly, the criteria and the form were tested and refined in a pilot study with some 12 companies.

The criteria used in the survey and listed in Table 2.1 are **primary** level criteria. That is, they are oriented to the **basic** IST project selection and investment decision; the basic reason for the investment. This distinguishes them from **secondary** level criteria, such as functionality or viability of hardware or software, that might be used in selecting a particular IST **vendor**. For example, the criterion technical/system requirements is not a secondary level, vendor-oriented criterion. It applies where hardware or software requirements are a major factor or need behind the investment decision (irrespective of vendor).

An important finding in developing the criteria was the need to distinguish between those information systems projects undertaken in support of **implicit** business objectives, as opposed to those in support of **explicit** business objectives. For example, a significant machine upgrade might be undertaken due to volume

Table 2.1 Criteria used in the survey of information systems and technology (IST) project selection decisions

---

Financial criteria
Discounted cash flow (DCF)
 1. Net present value
 2. Internal rate of return
 3. Profitability index method

Other financial
 4. Average/accounting rate of return
 5. Payback method
 6. Budgetary constraint

Management criteria
 7. Support of explicit business objectives
 8. Support of implicit business objectives
 9. Response to Competitive systems
10. Support of management decision making
11. Probability of achieving benefits
12. Legal/government requirements

Development criteria
13. Technical/system requirements
14. Introduce/learn new technology
15. Probability of project completion

---

constraints with existing hardware, and there may or may not be specific objectives attached to the upgrade. Essentially, it is a response to a problem. Presumably however, the project also provides support for basic business objectives such as profitability, increase in sales, etc. On the other hand, there may be investment in new or additional hardware as part of a specific plan and *explicit* business objectives. Thus, there is a basic difference between those IST projects or investments undertaken in support of implicit business objectives, as opposed to those undertaken in support of explicit business objectives.

Another important finding was the need to separate the probability (and risk) of success (or non-success) relating to an information systems project into two parts. Some organizations engaging in R&D recognize **technical** success, i.e. meeting all specifications and tests, as distinct from **marketing** success, i.e. the finished product selling well (Gaynor, 1990). In the field of information systems, this is equivalent to probability of project completion and probability of achieving benefits. Probability of project completion concerns the probability of the project being completed according to time, cost and quality requirements. Probability of achieving benefits relates to the probability and risk attached to the desired revenue flows and business effects.

Table 2.2 Number of survey responses by company size (annual sales) for 80 sample companies

Annual sales (in millions of US dollars)	No. of companies
0–99	11
100–499	11
500–2499	17
2500–9999	30
10 000 plus	11

Table 2.3 Survey responses by industry for 80 sample companies

Industry or type of company	No. of companies
Food and beverage	11
Industrial and automotive	10
Banking and finance	8
Electronics	6
Insurance	5
Retail	5
Petroleum	4
Metal and metal products	3
Transportation	2
Telecommunications	2
Process industries:	
Chemicals and pharmaceuticals	7
Building and construction	4
Paper manufacturing	3
Utilities	3
Media	2
Forestry and mining	2
Cement products	2
Photographic products	1

Lastly, it became evident that the competitive environment is having a real and increasing impact on the selection of IST projects/investments, so that response to competitive systems became a further, important criterion. This bears out the literature on such use of IST (Ives and Learmonth, 1984; Porter and Millar, 1985; Tavakolian, 1989). Thus, an information systems project may be undertaken to achieve a competitive advantage for the organization, or it may be undertaken in response to other organizations trying to do the same thing.

A letter inviting participation in the survey, with the survey form enclosed, was sent to 203 companies. A follow-up letter was also sent. Of the 80 companies providing a *usable* reply, 25 were American, 23 British, 11 Australian, and 21 were New Zealand companies. In terms of size, they are mostly 'Fortune 500' types of company. As a consequence, the survey and sample was biased away from small companies. The breakdown of the sample by company size, in terms of annual sales, is shown in Table 2.2.

The industries in the sample represent a broad mix of different types of businesses. These are shown in Table 2.3.

Survey results

The first question asked of companies in the survey was:

1. Excluding routine maintenance work, which of the following criteria do you use in making the basic go-ahead decision on system development projects and computer hardware or software facilities?

Table 2.4 Companies using a given IST investment (project selection) criterion

Criteria	% of companies using
Financial criteria	
Discounted cash flow (DCF)	
1. Net present value	49
2. Internal rate of return	54
3. Profitability index method	8
Other financial	
4. Average/accounting rate of return	16
5. Payback method	61
6. Budgetary constraint	68
Management criteria	
7. Support of explicit business objectives	88
8. Support of implicit business objectives	69
9. Response to competitive systems	61
10. Support of management decision making	88
11. Probability of achieving benefits	46
12. Legal/government requirements	71
Development criteria	
13. Technical/system requirements	79
14. Introduce/learn new technology	60
15. Probability of project completion	31

The survey results in answer to this first question provided the percentage of companies that use a given IST project selection (investment) criterion. This is shown in Table 2.4.

For example, 68% of the companies indicated that they use budgetary constraint (implying that there is probably a capital budget for IST), as one of their criteria in deciding on IST projects/investments. As a further example, 16% of the companies said that they use average/accounting rate of return as a criterion in selecting their IST projects.

The second question asked of companies in the survey was:

2. What is your estimate of the number of projects to which a given criterion applies, as a percentage of the total number of projects?

The survey results in answer to the second question provided the average number of projects, as a percentage of the total number of projects, to which a given criterion is actually applied, for those companies in the sample using the criterion. These application percentages are shown in Table 2.5.

For example, the results indicated that those companies using net present value as a decision criterion apply it, on average, to 58% of their projects.

The percentage application of a given criterion for **all** projects in **all** companies in the sample, including those companies **not** using the criterion, can be determined by multiplying the criterion usage per cent in Table 2.4 by the application per cent in Table 2.5. For example, the net present value method is applied to only 28% (0.49×0.58) of **all** projects across **all** companies in the sample. Also, only 40% of all projects in all the companies are subjected to some type of DCF method.

Table 2.5 Percentage of IS projects to which a given investment/selection criterion is actually applied by companies using the criterion

Criteria	% of projects to which applied
Financial criteria	
Discounted cash flow (DCF)	
1. Net present value	58
2. Internal rate of return	54
3. Profitability index method	47
Other financial	
4. Average/accounting rate of return	47
5. Payback method	51
6. Budgetary constraint	64
Management criteria	
7. Support of explicit business objectives	57
8. Support of implicit business objectives	44
9. Response to competitive systems	28
10. Support of management decision making	29
11. Probability of achieving benefits	63
12. Legal/government requirements	13
Development criteria	
13. Technical/system requirements	25
14. Introduce/learn new technology	13
15. Probability of project completion	62

Table 2.6 Ranking of IST investment/selection criteria in terms of total project value by companies using the criterion

Criteria	Ranking by total project value
Financial criteria	
Discounted cash flow (DCF)	
1. Net present value	4
2. Internal rate of return	2
3. Profitability index method	14
Other financial	
4. Average/accounting rate of return	10
5. Payback method	5
6. Budgetary constraint	8
Management criteria	
7. Support of explicit business objectives	1
8. Support of implicit business objectives	3
9. Response to competitive systems	6
10. Support of management decision making	7
11. Probability of achieving benefits	9
12. Legal/government requirements	13
Development criteria	
13. Technical/system requirements	12
14. Introduce/learn new technology	15
15. Probability of project completion	11

The third question asked of companies in the survey was:

3. What ranking would you give to each criterion in terms of the overall value of projects to which it applies?

The survey results in answer to the third question enabled a determination of the average ranking of each criterion, based on the total **value** of projects to which the criterion is applied (for those companies using the criterion). This ranking is shown in Table 2.6.

For example, the results indicated that those companies using net present value as a decision criterion ranked it fourth in importance (on average), in terms of the total value of projects to which it is applied.

Thus, the survey results show: (1) the percentage of companies **using** a given criterion, (2) the percentage of projects to which it is actually **applied** by those companies using it, and (3) the ranking of each criterion in terms of total project **value** to which it is applied.

Discussion of financial criteria and survey results

An initial question in scrutinizing the survey results was: how many organizations use **some** form of DCF? The results showed that 75% use some form of DCF in selecting their IST projects, with some companies using more than one criterion/ technique.

Net present value and internal rate of return were ranked quite high, in terms of project **value**, by the companies that use these DCF criteria. However, the rate of **application** to their IS projects was moderate, being 58 and 54% respectively. This may indicate that NPV and IRR are only important in evaluating large projects.

The survey indicates that the internal rate of return (IRR) method may be more widely used in evaluating IST investments than net present value (NPV), with 54% of the sample companies using IRR versus 49% for NPV. This is consistent with previous surveys of capital budgeting practice (Farragher, 1986; Cook and Rizzuto, 1989; Pike, 1988). This finding may seem surprising, given the theoretical superiority of NPV over IRR. IRR may, in fact, give misleading information in comparing projects of different size or timing in cash flows, since the highest rate (IRR), may not indicate the highest available return in actual/current dollars. There may also be more than one rate for a project whose whose net cash flows change from positive to negative and back again in different periods. Lastly, the IRR method implicitly assumes that net cash inflows can be reinvested at the same rate in succeeding periods, which is unlikely (Brigham and Gapenski, 1991).

However, the difference between theory and practice in using IRR and NPV may be understandable in that: (a) managers may be better able to identify with a rate of return for a project as opposed to a net present value, and (b) the NPV method predicates a discount rate that may be difficult to determine.

The profitability index method (PIM), sometimes known as the project selection index, is the least used of all criteria, being used by only 8% (i.e. 6 out of 80), of the companies surveyed. However, these few companies apply the criterion to nearly half (47%), of their projects. In most cases, PIM is used in conjunction with NPV.

Overall, the moderate use of DCF techniques raises questions as to the extent of quantification in support of selection decisions on IST projects (even though quantification cannot/need not always be in financial terms). Quantification of estimated revenue flows or cash savings will not always be feasible. For example, it may be difficult to give reliable estimates of the added revenue that would accrue from improved customer service through a new on-line system. And quantified DCF benefits may be transcended by other criteria, such as the need to make quicker

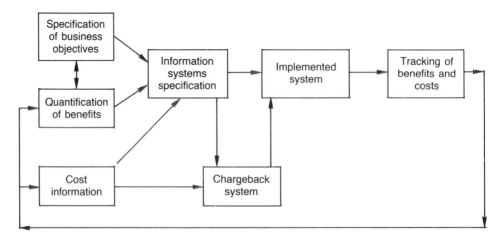

Figure 2.1 The feedback of quantified cost and benefit information from prior to prospective systems projects/investments.

decisions or meet the level of service provided by competitors. However, the moderate use of DCF methods suggests that there may be some question as to whether quantification of cost vs benefit, which is a basic aim of DCF, is being optimized in IST investment decisions.

Quantification becomes more feasible when there is an effective chargeback system in operation for the use of IST resources. It becomes even more feasible when there is a benefit-tracking programme in operation for IST projects, since there can then be feedback of cost and benefit information from prior to prospective systems investments. This process is shown in Figure 2.1.

For example, if a new system or technology improvement were thought to have a positive effect upon such an intangible as employee morale, this benefit might be broken down into quantified estimates of lower employee turnover, reduced absenteeism, reduced accidents, reduced wastage, higher quality, and repeat sales through improved customer service. In the case of improved customer service, variables such as waiting time, in-stock response, and frequency of sales/service calls might be quantified. The revenue estimates and associated costs might then be monitored, and future estimates could benefit through the data captured and learning gained from such prior projects.

But even if quantification is considered feasible, management might not consider the effort worth the time and cost involved. This could be the case where a systems project is virtually mandated, owing to technical, legal, or competitive requirements. Or where the project may not be considered large enough. Even in these cases, however, it would seem that a clear evaluation and tracking of cost vs benefit would assist the formulation of current and future IST investment (project selection) policy, through a better understanding and identification of IST-related benefits and costs.

The payback (PBK) method, a non-DCF method, is used by 61% of the companies in the sample (which is more than NPV or IRR). PBK ignores the time value of money, as well as any cash flow following the payback period. Also, there is no minimum rate nor any factoring for risk. However, two companies participating in the survey indicated that they use the **discounted** payback method, which at least factors in a time value for money.

The continued use of the payback method and its implicit short-term orientation, notwithstanding its theoretical shortcomings, may have some justification. To begin with, it is easy to understand and use. Secondly, the complexity and consequential difficulty in making predictions within today's economic, political and technological environment may lead some managers not to trust in long- or even medium-term DCF projections, since change in any one of these areas could have a material effect on estimated cash flows. Thirdly, in today's business environment, change occurs so rapidly that time is 'compressed'. Fourthly, in an environment of international corporate raiding and unfriendly takeover, management may feel that the company's stock market value needs to be kept high through a quick and reliable return on investment aimed at maximizing current profits, the objective being to keep raiders and takeover merchants at bay.

With respect to IST investments in particular, there is a rapid rate of enhancement in the field of information technology, so that today's technology may be obsolete in two or three years' time. In addition, the general cost of computing power continues to decline significantly year by year. Consequently, tomorrow's technology may be cheaper than today's. In such an environment the use of the payback method, oriented to the short term as it is, may reflect nothing less than the 'real world'.

The financial criterion that figures mostly in IST project selection is that of budgetary constraint (i.e. 'did we budget for it?'). Of the companies surveyed, 68% use budgetary constraint as a project/investment approval criterion. It is applied, by those companies that **use** it as a criterion, to 64% of their projects. Thus, it is not applied to all projects, and this represents nothing less than the 'real world', where it is not always possible to plan and budget for every IST capital expenditure.

Of 15 critera, budgetary constraint is ranked eighth in importance/value by those companies **using** the criterion. This may support a general principle of capital budgeting theory that provided the weighted average cost of capital remains the same, wealth maximization of the firm requires the avoidance of **strict** capital rationing. That is, all projects that contribute to profitability should be accepted, whether budgeted or not, unless there is some strategic reason or impending change that rules out (current) acceptance. Thus, where a capital budget has been established for information systems projects, that budget may be waived if a given project offers a positive and reliable net present value, or if it is imperative in supporting some strategic corporate objective.

Discussion of management criteria and survey results

Overall, the support of explicit business objectives is the most important criterion used by companies in selecting IST investments/projects. This criterion refers to a given IST project or investment that supports business objectives specifically indicated in some sort of **plan**. In comparison, support of **implicit** business objectives is a decision criterion justifying a project that fulfils or is in accordance with business objectives/aims that are 'understood', though not necessarily formalized in any plan.

Support of explicit business objectives is used as an IST investment criterion by 88% (i.e. nine out of ten) of those companies that participated in the survey. These companies **apply** it, on average, to 58% of their projects. It is also the top-ranking criterion, in terms of project value, in deciding on IST projects. Thus, support of explicit business objectives is clearly considered important by those companies in the sample that have the experience of using it as an IST investment criterion.

Where support of explicit business objectives is **not** used as a criterion in deciding upon IST investments, there is reduced likelihood of performance meeting expectation in the use of IST resources. A 1986 UK survey showed that 61% of chief executives expected to obtain improved information and communication from IST, but only 31% explicitly targeted this objective. Similarly, 32% expected more support for sales strategy, but this was explicitly targeted by only 13% (Galliers, 1986). The implication is that, where senior management expectations of IST are clearly specified in explicit corporate/business-unit objectives, and these are integrated with IST objectives, the greater is the likelihood of those objectives being fulfilled.

In a business environment characterized by change and uncertainty it may not be possible to anticipate and plan every IST project. It may not be possible for every one to be initiated in fulfilment of one or more explicitly stated business objectives. There will always be a proportion of projects that are virtually mandated at short notice; that have not been planned. This applies especially to 'Must-Do' projects (Silk, 1990). However, in an increasingly competitive environment, there is a need to knit together the objectives of the IST function with corporate and business-unit strategy, so as to effectively utilize IST resources in sustaining competitive goals.

While it may not always be feasible to **quantify** the benefits of a prospective IST investment, such benefits can usually be represented in explicit corporate goals and objectives. If an IST investment is then directed towards the fulfilment of such goals and objectives, the *raison d'être* of the IST function has been satisfied, and quantified cost–benefit justification no longer dominates.

Response to competitive systems is used as a criterion by 61% of companies, and is considered their sixth most important criterion. This is a criterion that may not have been relevant in past years. The fact that it is now indicates the significance of IST in today's competitive business environment. In some cases, response to competitive systems may be the underlying criterion where an organization concludes that: *'we cannot afford not to invest'*. Without new information technologies there may be a serious loss in effectiveness and competitive standing, compared to competitors that *do* invest in them.

It is not surprising that support of management decision making is used as a criterion by 88% of the companies that participated in the survey. This reflects the importance of systems in supporting management with requisite information. What may be surprising is that these companies apply the criterion to only 29% of their projects and, in terms of project value, it is ranked seventh in importance out of 15 criteria. However, this ranking may be due to this 'almost-traditional' criterion being transcended by other criteria, as organizations mature to other emphases (such as competitive response), in the use of IST.

The probability of achieving benefits is a risk/probability criterion that is used by less than half (46%) of the companies who participated in the survey. These companies apply it to an average 63% of their projects, which makes the probability of achieving benefits the highest proportion of any management criteria, second only to budgetary constraint in its percentage application to IST projects/investments.

Although the probability of achieving benefits might be implicitly included with other criteria, it may be a criterion that is best applied separately and distinctly, because (a) it represents a fundamental risk that is inherent in most projects in today's turbulent business environment, (b) it could provide for a more conscious management focus on and analysis of such risk, and (c) it would facilitate the learning process relative to this probability/risk. There are some projects that might never be undertaken if the criterion were so applied.

Discussion of development criteria and survey results

Technical/system requirements is a **primary** level, not a secondary level, vendor-oriented criterion. The results show that it is used as an IST investment or project selection criterion by 79% of the companies that participated in the survey. This is not surprising, since such requirements are a necessity in most IST projects. For example, an organization may invest in an upgraded computer or network because it has outgrown the present configuration. Or a major rewrite of a system may be required because it is no longer maintainable in its present form. The issue with the technical/system requirements criterion is the **degree** to which it is used. In the survey and sample it is shown to apply, on average, to 25% of an organization's IST projects/investments. Where the proportion is **significantly** more than this average, it may indicate that the IST function and the organization itself is being driven by technical/system requirements, rather than strategic objectives. That is, 'the tail is wagging the dog'.

'Introduce or learn new technology' is a criterion that, like response to competitive systems, may not have been as relevant in past years. However, it is becoming more of a justification as information technology continues to grow in its impact upon business organizations. Most organizations in the survey (60%) use it as a criterion, even though it applies to only a small proportion of their projects (13%).

Probability of project completion is a risk/probability assessment criterion that is used as an investment criterion by one-third of the organizations that participated in the survey. This might be considered a low proportion of companies, given the high rate of failure of IS projects (McComb and Smith, 1991). If this risk/probability criterion were used more often, and a formal assessment of its factors undertaken, effective steps might be taken to reduce or avoid the risk. However, those companies in the sample that **do** use probability of project completion as a criterion apply it to 63% of their projects, which is the third highest application of any criteria to IST projects. Thus, probability of project completion is considered quite important by those companies that have the experience of **using** it in IST investment decisions.

The probability of a project being completed or not depends upon such factors as project size, technical innovation, definitional uncertainty, complex organizational integration requirements, life or death deadline, experience and ability of personnel, availability and dependence upon personnel, senior management support, and user participation. These risk factors seem to increasingly characterize today's business and systems environments. Therefore, probability of project completion is a risk/probability criterion that would seem to be valuable in the assessment of most IST projects/investments.

Summary and conclusions

Business competition is global, intense and dynamic, and information systems and technology (IST) is a key resource in responding to and proacting with this environment. Consequently, capital investment decisions in selecting systems projects and hardware/software acquisitions are of a critical nature within the organization's overall strategy. The basic question is, therefore, how do organizations make these investment decisions, and how should they? In responding to that question this study concentrates on the decision **criteria**, as opposed to the decision **process**.

Fifteen criteria – six financial, six management and three development – were used in a survey undertaken in 1990 of 80 major companies in four countries – the United States, Britain, Australia and New Zealand. The companies were asked to indicate which criteria they use, the percentage of projects to which each criterion is applied, and the overall ranking in terms of total project value for each criterion.

The criteria and the way in which they are used has significance in that they determine whether the optimal systems projects/acquisitions are selected and the suboptimal rejected. They also reflect the level of integration and consistency between corporate/business-unit strategy and systems strategy. Also, the criteria have significance in the balance that an organization achieves in their use, particularly between financial and management criteria.

Some of the general conclusions developed in the analysis and discussion of the survey results are prescriptive in nature. That is, based on the practice and experience of the 80 companies who participated in the survey, there appear to be a number of proposals that might be considered by organizations in making decisions on their information systems projects and investments. These are as follows:

Although discounted cash flow (DCF) criteria may not be feasibly applicable to all prospective systems investments in a firm, they should be applicable to at least some of them. (Proposal A)

More accurate quantification of cost vs benefit and more informed IST investment decisions are facilitated where there is effective benefit-tracking and chargeback in place. (Proposal B)

Although there will always be some projects that cannot be foreseen, it should generally be possible to plan and budget for the majority of IST projects. (Proposal C)

The system investment may be made, or the project go-ahead given, even if it has not been budgeted, as long as the investment/project provides (a) a positive net present value, or (b) is required in support of overriding strategic business objectives. (Proposal D)

If IST is to be harnessed in support of the organization's planned direction, then the support of explicit business objectives needs to be optimized in prospective IST projects/ investments. (Proposal E)

The Optimum is for an IST project or investment to be undertaken in pursuit of both (a) quantifiable net benefits and (b) explicitly planned business objectives. Apart from mandatory (must-do) projects, the aim should be for at least one of these basic criteria to be involved in an IST investment decision. (Proposal F)

The high application rate of probability of achieving benefits, as an IST investment criterion by some companies, indicates that it may be sufficiently important to be formally considered as a distinct criterion, in evaluating and deciding upon prospective IST capital investments. (Proposal G)

If information systems and technology (IST) resources are to be optimized and strategically directed, technical/system requirements should not generally be dominant as a decision criterion in an organization's IST projects and investments. (Proposal H)

If an organization wishes to gain access to the pertinent learning curve of new information technology likely to be of benefit, it may be necessary to regularly undertake some R&D funding by way of 'seed money' for such projects and investments. (Proposal I)

Probability of project completion is a risk/probability criterion that might be considered formally as a decision criterion in evaluating IST projects/investments in that it is, in any case, an element present in most of them. (Proposal J)

The underlying thrust of the study was and is towards application. The goal is to bridge the gap between practice and academia. However, these results, together with the analysis and proposals accompanying them, are only a beginning, or perhaps just a step along the way, in this key area of IST management decision making. The following chapter complements this study by looking in greater detail at investment appraisal criteria and practice.

Lastly, the sample of 80 organizations is only sufficient to provide some indication of actual practice, and only tentative conclusions. Further surveys will be needed, with comparable results, for these conclusions to become more firm.

References

Badiru, A. B. (1990) A management guide to automation cost justification. *Industrial Engineer*, February, 27–30.

Boyd, D. F. and Krasnow, H. J. (1963) Economic evaluation of management information systems. *IBM Systems Journal*, **2**, 2–23.

Brigham, E. F. and Gapenski, L. C. (1991) *Financial Management: Theory and Practice*, 6th edn, The Dryden Press, New York.

Buss, M. D. J. (1983) How to rank computer projects. *Harvard Business Review*, **83** (1), 118–25.

Carlyle, R. (1990) Getting a grip on costs. *Datamation*, 15 July, 20–3.

Cook, T. J. and Rizzuto, R. J. (1989) Capital budgeting practices for R&D: a survey and analysis for *Business Week*'s R&D scoreboard. *The Engineering Economist*, **34** (4), 291–303. (Survey done in 1985).

Davenport, T. H., Hammer, M. and Metsisto, T. J. (1989) How executives can shape their company's information systems. *Harvard Business Review*, **89** (2), 130–42.

Davenport, T. H. (1989) The case of the soft software proposal. *Harvard Business Review*, **89** (3), 12–24.

Doll, W. J. and Torkzadeh, G. (1987) The relationship of MIS steering committees to size of firm and formalisation of MIS planning. *Communications of the ACM*, **30** (11), 972–8.

Downing, T. (1989) Eight new ways to evaluate automation. *Mechanical Engineering*, **111** (7), 82–6.

Farragher, E. J. (1986) Capital budgeting practices of non-industrial firms. *The Engineering Economist*, **31** (4), 293–302. (Survey done in 1984.)

Galliers, R. (1986) A failure of direction. *Business Computing and Communications (U.K.)*, July/August, 32–8.

Gaynor, G. H. (1990) Selecting projects. *Research & Technology Management*, **33** (4), 43–5.

Hellings, J. Capital budgeting in the real world. *Management Accounting (UK)*, **63**, 38–41.

Hochstrasser, B. (1990) Evaluation of IT investments – matching techniques to projects. *Journal of Information Technology*, **5** (4), 215–21.

International Federation of Accountants, Financial and Management Accounting Committee (1989) *The Capital Expenditure Decision*. Statement on International Management Accounting Practice 2. September/October, 540 Madison Avenue, New York, NY 10022, USA.

Ives, B. and Learmonth, G. (1984) The information system as a competitive weapon. *Communications of the ACM*, **27** (12), 1193–1201.

Kennedy, J. A. (1986) Ritual and reality in capital budgeting. *Management Accounting* (UK), **64**, 34–7.

McComb, D. and Smith, J. Y. (1991) System project failure: the heuristics of risk. *Journal of Information Systems Management*, Winter, 25–35.

McKeen, D. J. and Guimaraes, T. (1985) Selecting MIS projects by steering committee. *Communications of the ACM*, **28** (12), 1344–52.

Parker, M. M., Benson, R. J. and Trainor, H. E. (1988) *Information Economics*, Prentice-Hall, New Jersey.

Pike, R. H. (1988) An empirical study of the adoption of sophisticated capital budgeting practices and decision-making effectiveness. *Accounting and Business Research*, **18** (72), 341–51. (Survey done in 1986.)

Polakoff, J. C. (1990) Computer integrated manufacturing, a new look at cost justification. *Journal of Accountancy (U.S.)*, March, 24–9.

Porter, M. E. and Millar, V. E. (1985) How information gives you competitive advantage. *Harvard Business Review*, **85** (4), 149–60.

Silk, D. J. (1990) Managing IS benefits for the 1990s. *Journal of Information Technology*, **5** (4), 185–93.

Strassmann, P. A. (1985) *Information Payoff: The Transformation of Work in the Electronic Age*, Free Press, New York.

Sullivan-Trainor, M. L. (1989) The push for proof of information systems payoff. *Computerworld (U.S.)*, **XXIII** (14), 55–61.

Tavakolian, H. (1989) Linking the information technology structure with organisational competitive strategy: a survey. MIS Quarterly, **13** (3), 308–17.

Weaver, S. C., Peters, D., Cason, R. and Daleiden, J. (1989) Panel discussions on corporate investment: capital budgeting. *Financial Management*, **18** (1), 10–17.

Weill, P. and Olsen, M. H. (1989) Managing investment in information technology: mini case examples and implications. *MIS Quarterly*, **13** (1), 2–16.

3

Evaluating the feasibility of information systems investments: recent UK evidence and new approaches

Leslie Willcocks and Stephanie Lester

Introduction

This size and continuing growth in IT investments in the United Kingdom, coupled with a recessionary climate and concerns over cost containment in the period from early 1990, have served to place IT issues above the parapet in most organizations, perhaps irretrievably. IT expenditure across private and public sectors in the United Kingdom exceeded £15 billion in 1992. In companies this represented a national average of 1.5% of turnover; in the public sector IT spend exceeded 1% of total public expenditure. All commentators predict a general rising trend for the 1993–95

Information Management: The evaluation of information systems investments.
Edited by Leslie Willcocks.
Published in 1994 by Chapman & Hall. ISBN 0 412 41540 2.

period (KEW Associates, 1992; Price Waterhouse, 1992; Willcocks, 1992). Further-more, it is likely that these figures only partially take into account rising costs on IT contained in non-IT budgets. This may represent anything between 20 and 40% in additional expenditure, depending on the organization (see Introduction, page 8).

Understandably, senior managers need to question the returns from such invest-ments, and whether the IT route has been, and can be, a wise decision. This is reinforced in those organizations where IT investment has been a high risk, hidden cost process, often producing disappointing expectations. This is a difficult area about which to generalize, but research studies suggest that at least 20% of expenditure is wasted and between 30 and 40% of IT projects realize no net benefits, however measured (see, for example, AT Kearney, 1987; Eason, 1988; KPMG Peat Marwick Mitchell, 1990; Willcocks, 1990). A more optimistic picture is suggested by a 1990 survey of over 400 UK companies (AT Kearney, 1990). However this contained mixed messages. On the one hand, some 17% of new systems did not bring the advantages expected of them, leaving 83% of projects producing benefits as expected or better. On the other, only 11% of respondent organizations were successful IT users according to the relatively modest objective criteria established by AT Kearney.

The reasons for failure to deliver on IT potential can be complex. Technical, human resource, environmental, organizational and management issues interrelate where explanations are sought. However, as the Introduction to this book makes clear, major barriers, identified by a range of studies, occur in how the IT investment is evaluated and controlled. This chapter focuses on identifying and improving information systems (IS) evaluation practice. Findings from research carried out in 1990–91 on evaluation practice at the critical feasibility stage will be reviewed. These results will then be used as a basis for assessing more recent approaches to evaluation, and for developing processes, methods and techniques for better practice. The importance of continuing the evaluation across the lifetime of IT-based systems will emerge as fundamental, but neglected. Above all, with IT development and usage, and evaluation practice itself, yet to be imbedded in the routine texture of how most organizations are managed, the chapter will stress the need for evaluation to be set up as a learning process – to build up experience and reduce risk on future IT investments. One conclusion is that, at the present stage of information manage-ment attained by many organizations, the process of evaluation may well be more important than the individual evaluation techniques adopted.

When discussing evaluation in the context of IT and organizations, it is useful to make explicit the meanings assigned to the terminology employed. For evaluation and its related terms, and for information technology (IT) and information systems (IS) we follow the definitions presented in the Introduction. It should be pointed out that the authors and others would see IS as essentially a human activity system and part of social community, incorporating formal and informal elements (Hawgood and Land, 1988; Hirschheim and Smithson, 1988; Stone, 1991; Willcocks and Mason, 1987). Taking a social action perspective on IS leads to increasing the categories of effectiveness and taking a multivalent approach to assessment. However the research reported below uncovered little inclination to adopt a wider social action perspective or move from a restricted assessment of what Lyttinen *et al.* (1991) have called 'the effectiveness of instrumental action' in its technology, language and organization contexts. As a related point, interviews conducted during the research reported here revealed a marked tendency among respondents to refer to IT rather than IS evalu-ation. As a result the term IT is used frequently, where felt appropriate, throughout this chapter.

Evaluating feasibility

How do organizations go about IT feasibility evaluation and what pointers for improved practice can be gained from the accumulated evidence? As detailed elsewhere in this book, the general picture has not been encouraging. The sources cited in the Introduction suggest that organizations have found it increasingly difficult to justify the costs and benefits surrounding the purchase, development and use of IT. This is reflected, for example, where justifications are based mainly on faith or on largely notional figures (Grindley, 1991; Peat Marwick, 1989). A particularly interesting question, however, is whether such studies are uncovering genuine difficulties, straightforward, poor and redeemable evaluation practice, or, as other evidence might suggest, more complex shades and relationships within these possibilities (Farbey *et al.*, 1992; Hochstrasser and Griffiths, 1991; National Audit Office, 1989; Willcocks and Margetts, 1993). Furthermore, a range of evaluation issues and practices have not yet been investigated in any detail in the United Kingdom context, or indeed elsewhere.

To gain insight into evaluation practice a survey was carried out in a 3-month period in late 1990. After a piloting of the draft questionnaire, 200 organizations were selected on a random basis from the Institute of Internal Auditors (IIA) membership mailing list. This source was used because its membership was identified as representing a reasonable cross-section of organizations in the UK private and public sectors. It may be that small organizations are under-represented and organizations carrying out evaluation over-represented in the sample because of its IIA origins. Fifty organizations responded, drawn from a cross-section of small, medium and large private and public sector manufacturers and services. There were 12 financial service companies, 8 companies in manufacturing, 6 in information technology, 4 in central government with the rest spread through retail and wholesale, education, broadcasting, oil, telecommunications, publishing, transport, accountancy and consultancy, computer manufacturing, betting and postal services.

The individuals who were selected for and completed the survey questionnaires were all of manager status or above. They were identified as organizationally responsible for and/or knowledgeable about IS evaluation methods and outcomes. There are well documented limitations to the type of evidence supplied by such questionnaires. In this respect elements of subjectivity and bias on the part of the respondents are difficult to identify, evaluate and counteract. We attempted to ask questions that would gain mainly factual replies rather than those calling exclusively for opinion. Additionally, in the case of 32 respondents, further in-depth information was gained from follow-up interviews from one to two hours in length. These were carried out from April to November 1991. Another reason for selection of these respondent types was the practical one of making the survey not only acceptable to the organizations but also usable. The results of evaluation tend to be mainly used and acted upon by management. They have a vested interest in reviewing the evaluation process. Furthermore, if management can identify where weaknesses exist and improvements can be made, it is primarily their dissatisfaction which will instigate the change.

There are various proposals in the literature as to the stages into which to divide an information systems project for the purposes of analysis. The present study used a five-stage cycle to guide research and organize its results. The stages were: proposal/feasibility; development; implementation; post-implementation; and routine operations. This paper only reports the findings on feasibility evaluation practice. The proposal/feasibility evaluation stage of a project, as communicated to respondents, involves:

> evaluating the financial and non-financial acceptability of a project against defined organizational requirements, and assessing the priorities between proposed projects. 'Acceptability' may be in terms of cost, benefit, value, socio-technical considerations.

A further paper, in Willcocks (1993), provides the detailed findings on evaluation practice at all five stages. It also reports on the findings of a second phase in the research carried out in the period April–November 1991. This involved further interviews and questionnaires. In phase two some triangulation of senior, IS and user department managers was achieved by extending the interview programme to half-hour structured discussions with two other managers in each of the 32 organizations.

Some general findings

This section looks at where in organizations IT issues are considered, at what stages evaluation of IS investments are carried out, and the degree of satisfaction/ dissatisfaction with evaluation procedures recorded by respondents.

Forty-six of the surveyed organizations have separate IT departments, 11 organizations give consideration to IT within individual departments (seven of these also have separate IT departments). In this context the consideration of IT involves all aspects of IT and not just evaluation. The fact that in some organizations IT is considered by both IT departments and individual departments should not be assumed to be over-kill. However the detailed results make it clear who is actually involved for the purposes of evaluation. One significant correlation was with organizational size, i.e. all organizations with separate IT departments have 500 staff or more. However, we found no strong correlation between the degree of satisfaction registered with evaluation procedures and whether evaluation was carried out in an IT department, user department or both.

All the organizations completed evaluation of IT at the feasibility stage. Between 82 and 88% of the organizations completed evaluation at the other stages. However, only 66% completed evaluation at all five of the stages. Thus considerable weight in the evaluation process seems to fall on getting an accurate evaluation at the feasibility stage.

The main measure for assessing the success or otherwise of evaluation procedures was respondent perceptions of 'levels of satisfaction'. There are considerable limitations with this measure, not least the subjectivity and personal bias that can creep into the assessment provided by respondents. A further measure sought to compare the effectiveness of IS investment in terms of return on investment (ROI). We asked questions designed to elicit the size of the ROI, whether it was higher, comparable to or lower than ROI on non-IS investments, and the type of evaluation procedures designed to measure financially the return on IS investments once a system is operating. Only 8% could answer these questions. In line with the findings of Hochstrasser and Griffiths (1990), the vast majority admit to making no such evaluation. This would suggest that respondents need to be less satisfied with their evaluation procedures than their opinions registered below merit. Additionally, as will emerge, there is internal evidence from the present survey to support the notion that, as far as IS investments are concerned, respondents tend to overestimate the efficacy of their evaluation procedures.

The organizations were asked to indicate the degree of satisfaction with their evaluation at each stage. The range, together with an 'Other' option, was as follows:

Very satisfied   Although perfection is impossible, the results from the evaluation reach a high standard.

Satisfied   The organization can use the results with a degree of satisfaction and reliability, but improvements would be welcomed.

Not satisfied   The evaluation process is not satisfactory and is therefore not reliable.

Obstructive   The evaluation is considered to have a negative effect and is therefore a hindrance rather than a help.

Pointless   The evaluation is of no benefit to the organization.

A high degree of satisfaction (as defined above) by the majority of organizations was registered for all stages at which evaluation takes place. However, of the 50 organizations who used evaluation at the feasibility stage only 14% are very satisfied with the results, 72% are satisfied and only 6% are not satisfied, although 8% stated that their results varied. It is interesting that no organization found this type of evaluation obstructive or pointless. The organizations who were very satisfied came from the IT, financial services, and consultancy functions. The organizations who were unsatisfied with their evaluation came from central government, telecommunications and pharmaceutical manufacturing.

These results show that, generally, there is no relationship between the type of organization and its likely success, or perceived success, at any stage of the evaluation. The exception here is that IT, financial and consultancy services tend to register higher satisfaction with their evaluation procedures than organizations from other sectors. One possibility is that, historically, they have more experience of introducing IS and have been able to develop more effective evaluation procedures over time. In this scenario, organizations in other sectors may still have some catching up to do. The size (number of staff) of an organization bore no relationship to the types of evaluation used or to the perceived success rate.

The feasibility stage: findings

There is a dearth of information on how the feasibility of IS projects is evaluated. In reviewing the empirically based literature, a number of major gaps presented themselves. The research focused on addressing this imbalance. The major areas investigated were: who completes the evaluation; when are projects proposed and by whom; the methodologies and criteria used; the priority assigned to different criteria; the extent of own methodology use; whose objectives project proposals were evaluated against; the extent of consultation of interested parties; and who makes the final 'go/no go' decision. Supporting data for what follows appear in Tables 3.1–3.11.

Who completes the evaluation?

The results in Table 3.1 detail the department or departments who complete the evaluation at this stage within the organizations surveyed. It is interesting to see that

Table 3.1 Who carries out evaluation?

Department	No. of organizations
One group:	
IT department	7
User department	3
Separate committee	7
Project office	1
Individuals	1
Several groups:	
IT department	30
User department	23
Separate committee	13
Management	1
Finance department	1

many organizations use several different groups and others use just one group or individuals, i.e. seven organizations use only the IT department, three use only the user department and one organization uses individuals. The organization that uses individuals to evaluate, stated that their satisfaction with the results varied.

This is not surprising considering that different people will be completing the exercise and there will be little in the way of comparisons.

Many of the organizations (32%) use the IT and user departments to complete the evaluation and 16% use the IT and user departments in conjunction with a separate committee. Although there is no direct relationship between the levels of satisfaction recorded and the means by which the evaluation is completed, it may be significant that two of the organizations who are unsatisfied with their evaluations use only the IT and user departments to perform evaluation. One limitation of the survey evidence, to be rectified in later follow-up interviews, is that it did not establish at what level within these groups the evaluation was completed. However, the Kobler Unit survey is at least suggestive on this issue, finding that the responsibility for the evaluation was at too low a level (Hochstrasser and Griffiths, 1990).

One organization that was very satisfied with the results uses only the IT and finance departments for feasibility evaluation. This would suggest a high degree of strict financial accounting with the IT department trying to interpret the costs and benefits into monetary terms. It would be interesting to ask this company how its IT investments fare against its other capital investments; it would also be interesting to

Table 3.2 When are projects considered?

When considered*	No.
As and when proposed	32
Management ask for projects periodically	3
Management advertise when necessary	2
As and when proposed, also management ask for projects periodically	6
As and when proposed, also management advertise when necessary	6
As and when proposed, also when strategy dictates	1

* One organization did not answer the question.

find out how many of its projects are abandoned at a later stage. The evidence from this survey is that when this company abandons projects at the later, development stage, it is because user requirements had changed. Clearly one can question here the extent to which user requirements receive much attention in evaluation at the feasibility stage. That said, it is important to point out that 56% of the organizations included the user department in the evaluation process. However, given the emphasis in the modern literature on the need to meet users' IS requirements (Eason, 1988; Friedman, 1990; Gunton, 1988), one must question why the other 44% in the sample excluded users from the evaluation process.

When are projects proposed and by whom?

Sixty-four per cent of the organizations only consider the projects as and when they are proposed by individuals or groups. An additional 24% consider the projects as and when proposed, and also when management ask for projects and/or advertise for them (see Table 3.2).

On investigating the proposer of projects the survey found that two organizations only allow projects proposed by the IT department and eight only have projects proposed by the user departments (see Table 3.3). One of these organizations receiving projects from the user department also allows the user department to evaluate the projects. This would appear to have weaknesses if a standard practice, although the organization concerned said it is satisfied with its evaluation process. Overall, 42% of the organizations allow and receive projects from the user and IT departments, 22% also receive projects from these two departments and additionally from individuals and 16% receive projects from only the user department (Table 3.3).

The number of organizations who allow individuals to suggest projects is relatively low. Logically it would seem best practice to accept proposals from as many sources as possible; certainly this seems a minority approach from the survey results. However, these considerations do not take into account the degree or lack of IS know-how within various groups in the organizations surveyed.

Table 3.3 Who proposes projects?

Department	No. of organizations
One department proposes:	
IT departments	2
User departments	8
Individuals	1
Several groups propose:	
IT department	36
User department	38
Individuals	14
Board members	3
Strategy panels	1

Table 3.4 Use of evaluation methods

Evaluation policy	No. of organizations
Same method for all projects	24
Methods change for each project	22
Same methods but they are reviewed regularly	4

Use of methodology

Fifty-six per cent of the organizations use the same method of evaluation for all projects, only 16% of these organizations also review the method regularly and 44% change the methods according to the project (Table 3.4). All three organizations who were unsatisfied with their evaluation process use different methods for each project.

Although many of the other organizations change their methods but also registered 'satisfaction' with their evaluation process, changing methods could be an influential factor for the three organizations concerned. Such organizations should perhaps find one evaluation process that they can adapt to their needs. Perhaps they are in the process of attempting to find one. However, none of these organizations reviews regularly the method used, suggesting a degree of 'adhocery' in approach. Following this it is also apparent that 84% of the organizations who are 'satisfied' have assumed that their process will be relevant indefinitely as they have made no arrangements to review its currency. One problem here is that learning from experience is being excluded from the evaluation process, at least at the formal level. This approach would seem to invite additional problems, given the increasingly sophisticated systems being made available, the great variety of uses to which IT can be put, the extent to which organizations may need to move to more strategic uses of IT, and the degree to which achievement of competitive edge may require new, destabilizing uses of IT. The issue of methods used is discussed further below.

Criteria

All except two of the organizations use cost–benefit analysis in their evaluation process and the next most popular considerations are competitive edge, service to the public and quality of the product. Table 3.5 shows these and the other criteria used in feasibility evaluation in the organizations surveyed. Overall the most popular combinations are as follows:

14%   Cost–benefit, competitive advantage and service to the public
12%   Cost–benefit, competitive advantage, service to the public and quality of product
10%   Cost–benefit, competitive advantage, service to the public, quality of product and job enhancement

Only 16% of the organizations base their evaluation on more than four criteria. Only one of the organizations who felt 'very satisfied' with the results actually uses over four criteria. Most recent work on evaluation at the feasibility stage (see KPMG

Table 3.5 Basis of evaluation

Basis	No. of organizations
Several methods:	
Cost−benefit plus	
competitive advantage	38
service to public	26
quality of product	26
job enhancement	10
improved management information	3
user requirements + timescale	2
legal requirements	3
strategic importance	2
Organization requirement and necessity	3
Other methods:	
Cost−benefit only	1
Legal requirements, strategic importance and service to users	1
Service to users and organizational requirements	1

Peat Marwick Mitchell, 1990; Parker *et al.*, 1988; Ward *et al.*, 1990 for examples) suggests the use of a wide range of criteria and points to the considerable limitations of cost−benefit dominated approaches. This would suggest, first, that most organizations assess IS projects on the basis of too few criteria, and that at least six of the organizations who are 'very satisfied' with their evaluation process may need to be less confident in that opinion.

The two organizations who do not use cost−benefit analysis used legal requirements, strategic importance, service to users and organization requirements. The two organizations concerned were from education and financial services. They would appear to be attempting to evaluate IS projects against less traditional criteria. However, these two organizations both use a maximum of three criteria in total.

Priority given to different criteria

The results in Table 3.6 show that 62% of organizations use cost−benefit as their first priority during evaluation at the feasibility stage; 46% use competitive advantage as their second priority; while the third priority was an even mixture. This is reflected in the fact that the most popular combinations are:

1. 38% of organizations using both cost−benefit and competitive advantage
2. 14% of organizations using cost−benefit, competitive advantage and quality of product
3. 12% using cost−benefit, competitive advantage and service to the public.

Looking at the preferences from the organizational split, the financial services and manufacturing and computer manufacturing sectors went along with the overall preferences. However, information technology, central government, publishing and education have their own mixture. It was noticeable from the survey data, and confirmed in follow-up interviews, that companies in financial services and manufacturing, frequently considered to be comparatively ahead in the game of introducing

Table 3.6 Order of importance of evaluation criteria

First	Cost−benefit	31	Competitive advantage	8
	Service to public	3	Quality of product	2
	User requirements/service to users	2	Legal requirements	1
	Management information	1	Varies	2
Second	Cost−benefit	8	Competitive advantage	23
	Service to public	5	Quality of product	7
	Job enhancement	1	Strategic importance	2
	Organization needs/necessity	1	Varies	2
	N/A	1		
Third	Cost−benefit	7	Competitive advantage	2
	Service to public	10	Quality of product	9
	Job enhancement	3	Improved management information	1
	Legal requirements	1	Organization needs/necessity	2
	Strategic importance	1	User requirements/service to users	2
	Varies	2		
	N/A	10		

IT into organizations, still prioritize as primary the use of cost−benefit and competitive advantage evaluation criteria. On the other hand, the IT sector, central government, publishing and education sectors use a variety of methods to assess their projects. Although the IT sector may not be considered a novice to the introduction of IT, the other sectors mentioned are relatively so. In some cases the reason for this outcome was that the more experienced sectors, excluding the IT industry, have not changed their evaluation criteria since they first introduced IT. Respondents explained this in several ways: for example, they do not have the necessary techniques for alternative evaluation; or they lack confidence in them and/or prefer to keep tried and tested formulae. However, further considerations present themselves. Traditional cost−benefit analysis is best used to evaluate internal effectiveness of IT investments and therefore this could signify that these industries mainly look towards internal benefits from IT. Less optimistically, the criteria used may have the effect of restricting and biasing the evaluation process, allowing through mostly projects where there are primarily or even exclusively internal net benefits from IS investments.

The other less experienced sectors, perhaps encouraged by the IT industry, are using more adventurous criteria as a priority over the traditional techniques. In this sense they may well be leapfrogging part of their learning curve on IS evaluation, while more experienced organizations are finding it difficult to shed their inherited legacy of techniques and criteria in this area. However, it could simply be that the financial services and manufacturing industries are satisfied with their evaluation methods and therefore do not need to look elsewhere, and the less experienced sectors have had to find new criteria because the established evaluation methods could not be adapted to their industries or specific needs.

Finally, given some of the contradictory evidence above, while competitive edge criteria is used widely, the survey did not seek to discover in detail at this stage how well this criterion, increasingly regarded in the literature as of primary importance, is served by a method. However, the evidence from the findings of the Kobler Unit (1990) would suggest that, though methods are available, the criterion is unlikely to be well served in practice.

Table 3.7 Evaluation methodologies

Return on investment (ROI)	CCTA guidelines
SSADM	Prince
PRISM	Common sense
Industry standards	Prompt
Arthur Andersen SD method	Risk assessment
Cost benefit	Finger in the air

Use of own methodology

Of the organizations in the survey, 46% used their own evaluation methodology at the feasibility stage but few were willing to give details. The methods used by the remaining 54% are detailed in Table 3.7.

Sixty per cent of the financial services and manufacturing organizations, and 30% of the computer manufacturing, consultancies, transport and IT industries, used their own methodology. However, it is interesting that two of the three organizations who were unsatisfied with their results used their own methodology. It would appear, therefore, that producing your own methodology does not guarantee better results. Most of the central government departments used CCTA guidelines. The two organizations who are unsatisfied are not using unusual criteria – in fact they use cost–benefit and competitive edge as their main criteria. It is also interesting that the majority (82%) of organizations who use their own methodology also use cost–benefit and competitive edge as their main criteria. The organizations who use different or more complicated criteria use a method prescribed by others.

It would appear that organizations who develop their own methodology use the tried and tested criteria on which to base their methods. In the case of the two unsatisfied organizations this was not successful and it may be that these two organizations need to be more adventurous or should have used a methodology designed for them by an outside body with experience in this area.

Objectives

Whose objectives are considered in the feasibility evaluation process? The results for the surveyed organizations are presented in Table 3.8, which shows the following spread of objectives that are considered:

Organization objectives	80%
Department objectives	68%
End-user objectives	52%
Individual management objectives	32%
Customer objectives	4%

(Note: for 6% of organizations this varied from project to project.)

Eighty per cent of organizations considered organizational objectives in their evaluation. This is in line with the recommendation of Porter and Millar (1985) that an organization's strategic goals should align the objectives of IS projects with the achievement of competitive edge. King and Raghunathan (1987) also show through

Table 3.8 Objectives considered in evaluation

Objectives considered	No. of organizations
One set only:	
Organization objectives	6
Department objectives	3
End users' objectives	1
A number of objectives:	
Organization objectives	34
Department objectives	31
End-users' objectives	25
Individual management objectives	16
Customer objectives	2

research that if the organization uses formal IS strategic planning, it has a positive effect on the success of the IS project. However, they also suggest, against the practice of some of our respondent organizations discussed above, that evaluation should be conducted by both management and user. We would argue that to be properly 'strategic', the assessment of project relevance should begin with the user and progress through all stages up to the executive board level. To this end, looking at Table 3.8, only 22% of the organizations in the survey are fulfilling this requirement by considering the objectives from the bottom to the top, i.e. considering all of organizational, departmental, individual and end-user objectives. The most popular combinations of objectives to be considered are as follows:

Organization, department, individual management and end-user	22%
Organization only	14%
Organization and department	14%
Organization, department and end-user	12%

To develop the argument further, only 4% consider customer objectives in the feasibility evaluation process, and yet a high percentage claimed to assess the competitive edge of the project. Porter and Millar (1985) suggest that competitive edge should link in with IS strategy, but if organizations are failing to consider customer objectives and requirements in the evaluation process, one can only posit competitive advantage being gained where the competition is so bad that customer focus is not a primary requirement. It appears then that, first, many organizations are not using a formal IS strategy against which to evaluate their projects, and therefore could improve their chances of success by doing so, and, secondly, many are not evaluating fully with their own suggested criteria.

Consultation

During the course of feasibility evaluation organizations consult a variety of groups. The nine major groups are shown in Table 3.9. One organization only consults the executive board. For the other organizations the number of people consulted varies, but 86% consult their IT department and the same percentage consult user department heads, while 76 and 74% consult project teams and executive boards respectively.

Table 3.9 Who is consulted about evaluation?

Who consulted*	No.
Various groups:	
Project team	38
IT department	43
User department heads	43
Audit	1
External consultants	1
Executive board	37
Unions	9
End-user	32
Financial department	1

* One organization did not answer the question; one consulted the executive board only.

Although fewer organizations consult end-users, 64% does indicate some recognition of the need to move to a more end-user-oriented approach in IS management. However, only 18% of organizations consult the unions. None of the unionized manufacturing firms do. Furthermore, 36% of organizations do not consult end-users. This is significant because it shows how infrequently many organizations are prepared to consult their workforces. There is a large literature establishing case histories where end-users not closely linked to an IS project develop limited perspectives on the change it represents, i.e. they may end up with a narrow definition of their own needs, and user resistance may build up against an unexplained imposed system (see, for example, Eason, 1988; Gunton, 1988; Willcocks and Mark, 1989). Union consultation is something on which UK managements often seem divided, and not just on the occasion of advanced technological change (Willcocks and Mason, 1988, 1990). However, one can put forward reasons why consultation should occur, not least to gain some idea of the degree of resistance and support to different types of system, and gain some feel of user opinion from what is often a major representative of user interests. As Gunton (1988) suggests, the lack of consultation of end-users and unions can result in problems for management at the later, more expensive stages.

There are many combinations of people who are consulted by the organizations. The most popular combinations were:

20% Project team, executive board, IT department, user department heads and end-users

10% Project team, executive board, IT department, unions, user department heads and end-users.

Nearly 80% of organizations consult project teams (see Table 3.10), which seems to be a popular method of organizing evaluation. However, the remaining 20% consulted three groups or less about evaluation, and this may represent less good practice. The survey did not investigate the degree of consultation, nor is it possible to assess at this stage of the research how far those consulted are influential in the evaluation process.

Table 3.10

Constitution	No.
Users	24
Internal audit	5
Project manager/leader	16
Analyst/programmers	10
CCTA representative	1
IT department	25
Planning department	2
Board	2
Managers	10
Finance	1

Table 3.11 Who makes the final decision?

Makes decision	No.
One group:	
Separate committee	7
Executive board	12
Board management	1
IT department	2
User department management	1
Executive committee	1
Several groups:	
Project team	3
IT department	2
User department management	1
Separate committee	17
Executive board	23
Finance department	2

Final decision

Who decides which projects should be accepted? The survey data are represented in Table 3.11.

The decision on whether to go ahead with a project rests with different sections within the different organizations. Seventy per cent of the organizations included the executive committee in the final decision. This gives the decision the high status that much of the literature suggests is needed as one of the precursors for IS project success (Earl, 1989; Keen, 1986; Hochstrasser and Griffiths, 1991; Willcocks, 1992). On the other hand, 30% did not pass up decisions to executive board level. This may well be explicable in a number of ways, including a degree of conscious decentralization of control, the fact that the financial investment is not large enough to merit executive board attention, or perhaps a failure of control at board level over significant investments in IT.

The most popular group or combinations of groups used by the organizations is/are as follows:

24%   Executive board and separate committee
22%   Executive board only
12%   Separate committee
 8%   IT department and executive board

This accounts for 66% of the organizations. The remaining 34% use another 13 combinations, indicating a considerable variety in practice on how final decisions are made on IS investments.

Discussion of findings

Organizations reveal a variety of practice on evaluation at the feasibility stage of projects, and their experience suggests the need for flexible, regularly reviewed approaches to IS evaluation of intended IS investments. This arises from each organization having its own IS objectives and strategies, which themselves may change over time. Most organizations surveyed used cost–benefit at the core of their evaluation process. However, it does not follow that this is the best way to evaluate IS projects. Indeed, as shown, some organizations are using different criteria and are equally satisfied with the results. Also, an organization that develops its own evaluation methodology is no more likely to produce better results than one utilizing more standardized approaches. The need for flexibility is widely recognized in practice, with 60% of respondents using different methods of evaluation for each project or reviewing their methods regularly in order to make necessary changes. Some 70% of organizations include the executive committee on the final 'go/no go' decision on IS investments. This gives the decision the high status suggested as necessary by much of the literature. However, the level of commitment subsequently given to the project by senior management is perhaps an even greater precursor of success (Earl, 1984; Keen, 1986). Follow-up interviews suggested that the level of senior management commitment required was forthcoming in a small minority of the cases investigated.

Respondent organizations expressed a high level of satisfaction with their evaluation procedures at all five stages of the IS project life-cycle. However, detailed investigation of evaluation practice revealed this satisfaction to be widely misplaced. Thus 34% of organizations do not evaluate IS payoffs at all five stages. This failure to promote continuous review breaks the learning cycle for each IS project. Review and learning also break down in most of the 56% of organizations that use the same evaluation method for all projects, with only 16% of these reviewing the method regularly.

All except two of the organizations surveyed used cost–benefit analysis in their criteria for evaluation. The literature shows that the cost–benefit analysis used by organizations is outdated and does not assess the true worth of IT. Cane (1987) found that organizations had not changed their analysis techniques even though their systems were becoming more sophisticated. Bailey (1987) showed the need for extra cost–benefit and risk assessment analysis for executive management information systems. Hochstrasser and Griffiths (1990) found that many organizations could not justify their future investments in IT because their calculations for investment in IT were not as rigorous as those for other capital investments. Goodwin (1984) shows that if quality is not assessed, projects which could give a better product or even significant competitive advantage are likely to be passed over. The case for enhanced cost–benefit analysis is regularly made in the literature. Malitoris (1990) is typical in suggesting that measurement techniques must match the task. Efficiency and effectiveness objectives are more easily measured using financial appraisal methods, but the rigour applied will vary with the likely size of perceived net benefit. Where benefits and inputs are increasingly intangible but sizeable, as is usual with innovation and competitiveness objectives, then the information economics approach of Parker *et al.* (1988) becomes more appropriate.

However, our sample evidence suggests that few organizations adopt these techniques, or such a planned, contingency approach to evaluation in practice. Senior managers increasingly talk of, and are urged towards, the strategic use of IT. This means doing new things, gaining a competitive edge and becoming more effective rather than using IT merely to automate routine operations, to do existing things better, and perhaps to reduce the headcount. However, only 16% of organizations use over four criteria on which to base their evaluation, and 62% use cost–benefit as their first criterion in the evaluation process. The survey evidence here suggests that organizations may not only be missing IS opportunities, but may also be taking on large risks, through utilizing narrow evaluation approaches that do not clarify and assess less tangible inputs and benefits. There is also little evidence of a concern for assessing risk in any formal manner. However, the need to see and evaluate risks and 'soft' hidden costs would seem to be essential, given the history of IS investment as a 'high-risk, hidden-cost' business. To help in this objective the case for using strategic IS planning, linked with the techniques detailed in the more modern literature (see below and later chapters) is strong, even if the payoff from such an approach is neither very immediate nor very measurable or discoverable, especially at the feasibility stage of an IS project.

A sizeable minority of organizations (44%) do not include the user department in the evaluation process at the feasibility stage, despite the frequent emphasis given in the literature, and by respondents, to the strong relationship between delivering on user requirements and developing effective systems. Only a small minority of organizations accept IS proposals from a wide variety of groups and individuals within the organization. Despite the large literature emphasizing consultation with the workforce as a source of ideas, know-how and as part of the process of reducing resistance to change, only 36% of organizations consult end-users about evaluation at the feasibility stage, while only 18% consult trade unions. While the majority of organizations (80%) evaluate IS investments against organizational objectives at the feasibility stage, only 22% of respondent organizations act strategically in considering objectives from the bottom to the top – that is, evaluating the value of IS projects against all of organizational, departmental, individual management and end-user objectives. This, again, could have consequences for the effectiveness and usability of the resulting systems and the levels of resistance experienced.

Finally, most organizations endorse the need to assess the competitive edge implied by an IS project. However, only 4% consider customer objectives in the evaluation process at the feasibility stage. This finding, together with many others discussed in this chapter, puts into a different context the high levels of satisfaction with evaluation procedures registered in most organizations. The fact that such satisfaction may well be misplaced in many cases is a matter for some concern, when it is clear that organizations tend to place much of their evaluation effort into the feasibility stage of IS projects. Furthermore, it is important to note that omissions and weaknesses in evaluation at the feasibility stage can ultimately be very costly to an organization.

This may be the case whether the outcome is continuance or cancellation of a particular IS investment.

Beyond cost–benefit: modern approaches appraised

How far are the prescriptions detailed in this chapter supported by the more recent advances to be found in the management-oriented literature? Much work has been done to break free from the limitations of applying to IT investments the more traditional forms of capital investment appraisal. The major concerns seem to be (a) to relate evaluation techniques to the type of IT project, and (b) to develop techniques that relate the IT investment to business/organization value. A further development is in more sophisticated ways of including risk assessment in the evaluation procedures for IT investment (see also Chapter 10). Again, it is noticeable how most work is being done in the area of feasibility evaluation techniques. There is growing concern for assessing the quality of service from the IT department, subcontractors or facilities management companies. However, as at 1993, beyond using user satisfaction surveys and similar techniques, there seems little inclination to conceptualize then assess information technologies in a systematic way as being components of information systems that comprise the outcomes of social and human activity. Some of the main developments will now be reviewed. The approaches detailed below are not exhaustive of those available, but they represent a selective list of approaches which, while not detailed in this book, are nevertheless considered by the present authors to be among the more useful for integrating into present evaluation practice.

Matching objectives, projects and techniques

One useful way forward on IT evaluation is to match techniques to objectives and types of projects. A starting point is to allow business strategy and purpose to define the category of IT investment. The Butler Cox Foundation (1990) have suggested five main purposes:

1. Surviving and functioning as a business
2. Improving business performance by cost reduction/increasing sales
3. Achieving a competitive leap
4. Enabling the benefits of other IT investments to be realized
5. Being prepared to compete effectively in the future.

The matching IT investments can then be categorized, respectively, as:

1. **Mandatory investments** – for example, accounting systems to permit reporting within the organization; regulatory requirements demanding VAT recording systems; competitive pressure making a system obligatory, e.g. EPOS among large retail outlets.
2. **Investments to improve performance** – for example, Allied Dunbar and several UK insurance companies have introduced laptop computers for salespeople, partly with the aim of increasing sales.
3. **Competitive edge investments** – for example, the SABRE airline reservation

system at American Airlines, and Merrill Lynch's cash management account system in the mid-1980s.

4. **Infrastructure investments**. These are important to make because they give organizations several more degrees of freedom to manoeuvre in the future.

5. **Research investments**. In our sample we found a bank and three companies in the computer industry waiving normal capital investment criteria on some IT projects, citing their research and learning value. The amounts were small and referred to CASE tools in one instance, and expert systems in the others.

Hochstrasser (1990) provides additional detail when suggesting that different business purposes will produce a classification of eight types of project. These are discussed in detail in Chapter 7. These seems to be no shortage of such classifications now available (for a review see Willcocks, 1990). One of the more simple but useful is the six-fold classification shown in Figure 3.1. Once assessed against, and accepted as aligned with required business purpose, a specific IT investment can be classified, then fitted on to the cost–benefit map (Figure 3.1 is meant to be suggestive only). This will assist in identifying where the evaluation emphasis should fall. For example an 'efficiency' project could be adequately assessed utilizing traditional financial investment appraisal approaches; a different emphasis will be required in the method chosen to assess a 'competitive edge' project. Figure 3.2 is one view (with no great claims of accuracy) of the possible spread of appropriateness of some of the evaluation methods now available.

Another, complementary, way of looking at evaluation methods is suggested by Silk (1990), for whom quantifying the benefits of IT/IS is the core problem in justifying IT investment. At the root of the evaluation methods available he finds

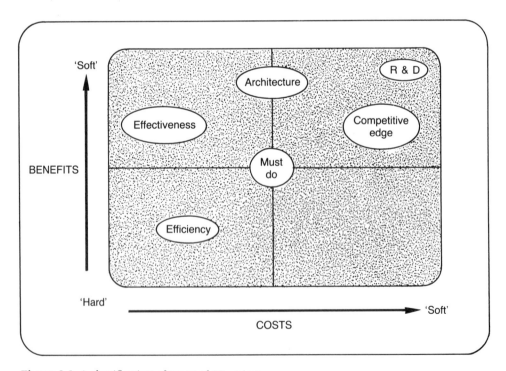

Figure 3.1 A classification of types of IT project.

seven types of benefit justification. In fact the first type involves little formal justification at all – that is, in the case of a 'must-do' project. An example is a clothing manufacturer required by British Home Stores to adopt Electronic Data Interchange as a condition of business. But should such investments be made at minimum cost with no benefit assessment? An assessment may be useful to see if additional benefits can be gained from higher investment.

Thereafter the modes of justification range from soft and subjective to hard and more objective, depending upon the generic benefit expected. Silk (1992) suggests there are three types of project and generic benefit, namely competitive edge, effectiveness and efficiency. (Note: his definitions of these types are his own and differ slightly from those of several other commentators.) As an 'act of faith' justification, Silk cites setting up a customer-operated information service in a food supermarket. Benefits might include better company image, higher turnover, need for new products identified, better understanding of customers. The decision might be based merely on senior management judgement or 'hunch'. A 'logic' justification would sharpen the business case by arguing how and why these benefits would materialize. A 'direction' justification would specify observable measures, e.g. more purchases, more shoppers. A 'size' justification would give a quantitative estimate of these changes. A 'value' justification would weigh the relative merits of different benefits – e.g. are more shoppers desirable even if each buys less? A 'money' justification would seek to express such benefits in terms of profit and/or revenue. Of course, in the case cited it might not be possible to apply all these justifications in an informed and useful manner. The point is to apply a mode of justification where it can contribute to sharpening the business case for a particular IT investment.

Developing the contingency approach

A further contingency perspective has been arrived at by Farbey *et al.* (1992). A description of their approach is particularly useful in bringing several strands together from the Introduction and this chapter. In the course of their research they found respondents mentioning five classes of factors influencing the way the investment decision was handled. These were:

1. **Role of evaluation.** The evaluation may occur early in the project, at requirements stage, or later, at the specification stage. Moreover, the level of the evaluation may vary between tactical and strategic.
2. **Decision environment.** This develops the description of the culture of organizational decision making, discussed in the Introduction to this book. Is the decision process standard for all projects or ad hoc? Are anticipated benefits hard and quantifiable or soft and qualitative? Are numbers attached to costs and benefits viewed as important, or not? Are cheap or expensive evaluation methods acceptable?
3. **The system.** The system may be a specific application or could be providing infrastructure. Secondly, the system may be in a supporting role, or core. (See Chapter 4 and the McFarlan matrix for the characteristics of such systems.)
4. **The organization.** Is the industry situation stable or turbulent? Does the organization intend to be leader or a follower in this industry?
5. **Cause and effect relationships.** Will the system have a direct or indirect impact upon the business? An example of the indirect benefits cited by Farbey *et*

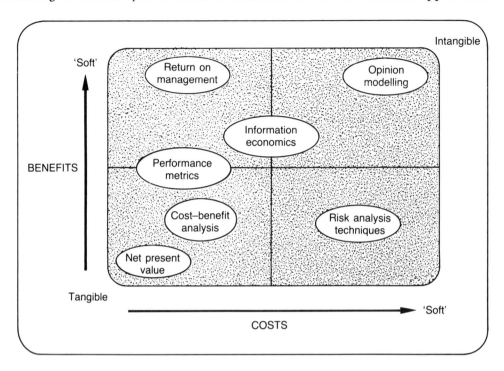

Figure 3.2 IT evaluation techniques: discovering appropriateness.

al. is where making an IT link between head office to branches depends on the ability of the staff to make use of the linkage. A second variable is the degree of predictability/unpredictability about the impact of the new system.

This adds up to a total of 12 variables. The authors allocate these to a 2 × 2 matrix, as shown in Figure 3.3. The characteristics of available evaluation techniques can be weighed against these variables, and each technique can then be allocated a position on the matrix. Some results of the process are shown in Figure 3.3. A few of the techniques mentioned in this figure are not described in detail elsewhere in this book. ROM, SESAME and IE receive attention below. Finance-based approaches are discussed in Chapters 1 and 2. The importance of multiple objective, multiple criteria approaches is discussed in Chapter 13. Here techniques are devised to reflect the perspectives and preferences of different stakeholders; the project will tend to be evaluated in utility terms other than just money (Hirschheim and Smithson, 1988; Walsham, 1992). Experimental methods refers to techniques associated with prototyping, simulation and gameplaying. These build in a more flexible, revisable approach to estimation. Boundary values are usually based on comparative ratios. Typical ratios may be IT cost as a percentage of revenue, IT as a percentage of total costs. These types of ratios, and their limitations in use, receive attention in the Introduction to this book. Value analysis tries to evaluate all benefits, including intangibles (see also Chapter 10). The focus is on value added, rather than on cost savings. Having identified and assigned utility values to the value added from applying IT to a work process, some techniques then convert these to money values, e.g. Meyer and Boone (1988).

	Direct Tactical Quantifiable Simple Support; Followers	Indirect Strategic Qualitative Sophisticated Core; Leader
Predictable specification: Numbers important Specific Stable	ROI P SES	CBA
Unpredictable requirements: Ad hoc Numbers unimportant Infrastructure changeable	MOMC EM	ROM VA IE BV

Key: ROI	– Return on investment	EM	– Experimental methods
P	– Payback	BV	– Boundary values
SES	– SESAME	IE	– Information economics
CBA	– Cost–benefit analysis	ROM	– Return on management
MOMC	– Multiple objective, multiple criteria	VA	– Value analysis

Figure 3.3 Techniques matrix (after Farbey *et al.*, 1992).

With minor variations in emphasis, the overall results in the matrix complement and add to our picture developed in Figure 3.2. Particularly noticeable is where the more traditional finance-based methods are located in terms of their suitability for use. It is important to emphasize that the matrices shown in Figures 3.2 and 3.3 should be used with care. They are useful for discovering appropriateness. In practice, objectives, type of project and situational factors may strongly indicate that techniques from just one quadrant will be most suitable. If this is the case, then more than one technique will probably be needed. More often, with IT in the 1990s, the analysis will suggest that a range of techniques from several quadrants will be most appropriate. In addition to techniques presented in later chapters, a number of additional recent methods fit within the context of the contingency approaches detailed above, and are now reviewed.

Return on management

Strassmann (1990) has done much iconoclastic work in the attempt to modernize IT investment evaluation. He has produced the very interesting concept of return on management (ROM). ROM is a measure of performance based on the added value to an organization provided by management. Strassmann's assumption here is that in the modern organization information costs **are** the costs of managing the enterprise. If ROM is calculated **before** and then **after** IT is applied to an organization, then the IT contribution to the business, so difficult to isolate using more traditional measures, can be assessed. ROM is calculated in several stages. First, using the organization's financial results, the total value added is established. This is the difference between net revenues and payments to external suppliers. The contribution of capital is then separated from that of labour. Operating costs are then deducted from labour value added, to leave management value added. ROM is management value added divided by the costs of management. There are some problems with the method of obtaining this figure, and whether it really represents what IT has contributed to business performance. For example, there are difficulties in distinguishing between operational and management information. Perhaps ROM is merely a measure in some cases, and a fairly indirect one, of how effectively management information is used. Farbey *et al.* (1992) also point out that, at the strategy formulation stage, any changes in ROM must rely on estimates of potential revenue, resource costs and contributions once the new system has been implemented. For them the difficulty of making such estimates suggests that the ROM method of evaluation is better suited to ex-post-evaluation of information systems projects. A further serious criticism lies with the usability of the approach and its attractiveness to practising managers. This may be reflected in its lack of use, at least in the UK, as identified in different surveys (Butler Cox Foundation 1990; Coleman and Jamieson, 1991; Farbey *et al.*, 1992; Willcocks and Lester, 1991).

SESAME

IBM have developed SESAME to provide a more flexible approach to cost–benefit analysis. Here the costs and benefits of an IT-based system are compared against an equivalent manual system. The Butler Cox Foundation (1990) note that it is essentially a method based on establishing the cost of clerical substitution, although it does incorporate the capacity for more sophisticated calculations. This method bases much of the assessment on user opinion, which may involve users more in the process of assessment; but user evaluation may not, in itself, be a sufficient benchmark of IT effectiveness. Lincoln and Shorrock (1990) also suggest that the flexibility of SESAME is highly dependent on the analyst who will need considerable experience of dealing with complex, unstructured issues. A limitation is that it seeks to compare the cost–benefits of an IT system with those of performing the tasks manually. This may be a cumbersome, and less than meaningful comparison to make in many already computerized operations. However, the IT projects to which it has been applied reveal generally good results, according to its proponents (Lincoln and Shorrock, 1990).

Information economics

A particularly ambitious attempt to deal with many of the problems in IT evaluation – both at the level of methodology and of process – is represented in the information economics (IE) approach (Parker *et al.*, 1988). They build on the critique of traditional approaches. Costs have been taken from the IT department who often use chargeback systems, or taken from departmental costings. Benefits are seen differently according to the department carrying out the calculation. Monetary gains may, or may not, be easy to evaluate, but matters like staff satisfaction and competitive advantage are not. One way to avoid this, of course, is to leave them out. At worst traditional modes of analysis ignore IT as an organizational asset, and all that it entails. Another problem occurs. Too frequently a Gresham law applies: technology management problems drive out business perspective and awareness. Furthermore, justification processes often fail to take account of, or are unable to quantify new risks associated with IT. IE emphasizes the necessity of dealing with these problems on the way to defining the value of information to an organization.

Parker *et al.* look beyond benefit to value. Benefit is a 'discrete economic effect'. Value is seen as a broader concept based on the effect IT investment has on the business performance of the enterprise. How value is arrived at, and full definitions of the terms used, are detailed by Wiseman in Chapter 9 and only an outline of the process is provided here. The first stage is building on traditional cost–benefit analysis with four additional techniques for establishing an enhanced ROI calculation: value linking, value restructuring, value acceleration, and innovation valuation. IE then enhances the cost–benefit analysis still further through business domain and technology domain assessments. Thus on the benefits/value side the valuable suggestions of Parker *et al.* may be summarized as expansion to include six classes:

- Enhanced view of ROI (established as above)
- Strategic match
- Competitive advantage
- Management information
- Competitive response
- Strategic IS architecture.

As an example of what happens when such factors and business domain assessment are neglected in the evaluation, Parker *et al.* point to the case of a large US truck-leasing company. Here they found that on a 'hard' ROI analysis IT projects on preventative maintenance, route scheduling and despatching went top of the list. When a business domain assessment was carried out by line managers a customer/sales profile system was evaluated as having the largest potential effect on business performance. An important infrastructure project – a Database 2 conversion/installation – also scored highly where previously it was placed bottom of eight project options. Clearly the evaluation technique and process can have a significant business impact where economic resources are finite and prioritization and drop decisions become inevitable.

Except for strategic IS architecture, all the above form part of the business domain assessment. When the cost–risk side of traditional analyses is expanded, the business and technology domains are also required to assess:

- Organizational risk (business domain)
- IS infrastructure risk

- Definitional uncertainty
- Technical uncertainty.

Parker *et al.* have provided an impressive array of concepts and techniques for assessing the business value of proposed IT investments. Their concern for fitting IT evaluation into a corporate-planning process, and for bringing both business managers and IS professionals into the assessment process is also very welcome. Some of the critics of IE suggest that it may be over-mechanistic if applied to all projects, it can be time-consuming, and may lack credibility with senior management, particularly given the subjective basis of much of the scoring. The latter problem is also inherent in the process of arriving at the weighting of the importance to assign to the different factors before scoring begins. Additionally there are statistical problems with the suggested scoring methods. For example, a scoring range of 1–5 may do little to differentiate between the ROI of two different projects. Moreover, even if a project scores nil on one risk, e.g. organizational risk, and in practice this risk may sink the project, the overall assessment by IE may cancel out the impact of this score and show the IT investment to be a reasonable one. Clearly, much depends on careful interpretation of the results, and much of the value for decision makers and stakeholders may well come from the raised awareness of issues from undergoing the process of evaluation rather than from its statistical outcome. Another problem area may lie in the truncated assessment of organizational risk. Here, for example, there is no explicit assessment of the likelihood of a project to engender resistance to change because of, say, its job reduction or work restructuring implications. This may be compounded by the focus on bringing user managers, but one suspects not lower level users, into the assessment process.

Much of the criticism, however, ignores how adaptable the basic IE framework can be to particular organizational circumstances and needs. Certainly this has been a finding in trials in organizations as varied as British Airports Authority, a central government department (see Chapter 9), and a major food retailer. In the latter case one of the authors and Ong (1991) investigated a three-phase branch stock management system. Some of the findings are instructive. Managers suggested including the measurement of risk associated with interfacing systems and the difficulties in gaining user acceptance of the project. In practice few of the managers could calculate the enhanced ROI because of the large amount of data required, and, in a large organization, its spread across different locations. Some felt the evaluation was time-dependent; different results could be expected at different times. The assessment of risk needed to be expanded to include not only technical and project risk but also the risk/impact of failure to an organization of its size. In its highly competitive industry any unfavourable venture can have serious knock-on impacts and most firms tend to be risk-conscious, even risk-averse. Such findings tend to reinforce the view that IE provides one of the more comprehensive approaches to assessing the potential value to the organization of its IT investments, but that it needs to be tailored, developed, and in some cases extended, to meet evaluation needs in different organizations. Even so, IE remains a major contribution to advancing modern evaluation practice.

The balanced score-card approach

Kaplan and Norton (1992) present this approach for top management use. Their version of the approach is applied to the business as a whole, but it is relatively easy

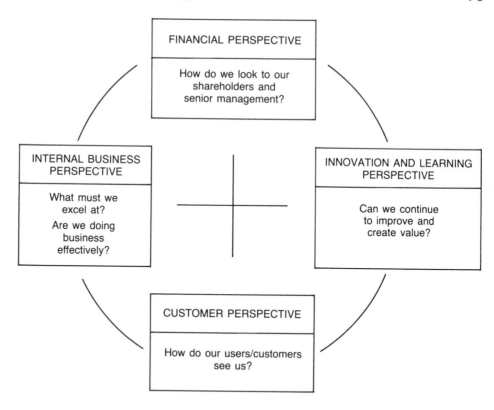

Figure 3.4 A balanced score-card approach (adapted from Kaplan and Norton, 1992).

to tailor the framework they use to the specific needs of IT investment evaluation. From research in 12 US companies, Kaplan and Norton identified four views to be represented in a balanced score-card. These, together with slightly revised questions, are shown in Figure 3.4.

Examples of typical measurable items are:

- **The financial perspective.** Market share, return on equity, cash flow, sales growth by business unit.
- **The internal business perspective.** Quality, cycle time, productivity, cost reduction, unit cost yield, actual new product introduction against plan.
- **The customer perspective**, e.g. on-time delivery (as defined by customer), quality, price performance relative to competitor, customer ranking of company, level of service experienced.
- **The innovation and learning perspective**, e.g. time to develop new applications, percent of sales from new applications, time to market.

As indicated, the framework is flexible enough to incorporate IT performance measurement, and several suggestions on this have already been put forward (Gold, 1992; Lockett, 1992). One danger those sources do not entirely avoid is being led into seeing the score-card approach from an IT department perspective. In this case the customer would be interpreted as referring, in practice, to the internal customer only, as is frequently found in the survey detailed earlier in this chapter. The

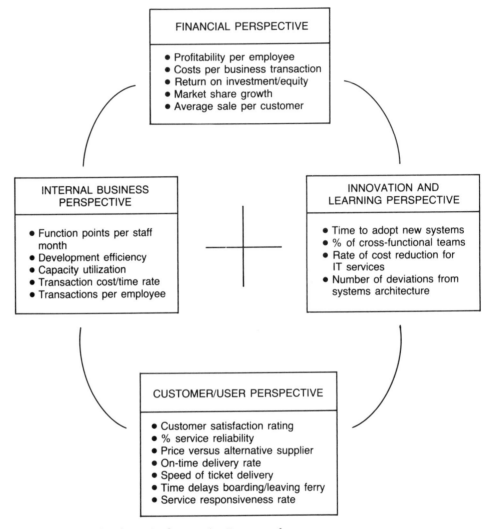

Figure 3.5 IT-related metrics for a major European ferry company.

financial perspective might come to be interpreted as: How do we in IT appear to senior management? A further note of caution is that there are probably no generic IT measures that fit all organizations. Metrics must fit a specific organization's goals, activities and customer base. Some examples developed for a major UK-based ferry company are shown, for illustrative purposes only, in Figure 3.5.

One should note that such high-level measures operate on the assumption that the IT investment is large enough to have a potential significant impact, or that the business processes are so dependent on IT as to make the measures meaningful in terms of expressing IT impacts. The measures probably can rarely isolate the impacts of IT from other factors influencing business performance. One way to handle the issue is to incorporate into the score-card portfolio a balance of both more business-related and more directly IT-related metrics. Figure 3.5 is merely indicative on this possibility. However, from a general management viewpoint, and as business processes in an organization come to be highly dependent on IT, this may cease to be recognized as a significant issue, as long as the critical business success factors are being delivered.

The strength of the balanced score-card approach is that it responds to the need, identified in the Introduction to this book, for a number of high-level measures to be developed, reflecting different viewpoints on the organization and performance. It can also be made to respond adequately to the frequently voiced need for quantified measures. Furthermore, it provides measures that can be usefully tracked beyond the investment appraisal stage and into the system's life-cycle. It also provides a framework of goals and high-level measures on which a hierarchy of more detailed measures can be erected, as recommended in Peters (1990) and Willcocks (1994).

Conclusions

The high expenditure on IT, its growing usage that goes to the core of organizational functioning, together with disappointed expectations about its impact, have all served to raise the profile of how IT investments can be evaluated. From the arguments and evidence in this chapter it is not only an underdeveloped, but also an undermanaged area which organizations can increasingly ill afford to neglect. Organizations need to shape the context in which effective evaluation practice can be conducted. Traditional techniques cannot be relied upon in themselves to assess the types of technologies and how they are increasingly being applied in organizational settings. A range of modern techniques can be tailored and applied. There is no single technique that can reliably report on the potential or actual value of IT to an organization. Broader thinking, in terms of IS investments, and a deeper understanding of IS as human activity systems, lead on to multiple effectiveness criteria and related measures. However, techniques can only complement, not substitute for developing evaluation as a social and organizational process, and the deeper organizational learning about IT that entails. Past evaluation practice has been geared to asking questions about the price of IT. Increasingly it produces less than useful answers. The future challenge is to move to the problem of value of IT to the organization, and build techniques and processes that can go some way towards answering the resulting questions.

References

AT Kearney (1987) *Corporate Organization and Overhead Effectiveness Survey*, IAM/CBI, London.
AT Kearney (1990) *Breaking the Barriers: IT Effectiveness in Great Britain and Ireland*, AT Kearney/CIMA, London.
Bailey, T. C. (1987) Some perspectives on the management of information technology. *Australian Journal of Management*, **12** (2), 159–83.
Butler Cox Foundation (1990) *Getting Value from Information Technology*. Research Report 75, June. Butler Cox, London.
Cane, A. (1987) Cost monitoring omitted in plans for technology. *Financial Times*, 30 November.
Coleman, T. and Jamieson, M. (1991) *Information Systems: Evaluating Intangible Benefits at the Feasibility Stage of Project Appraisal*. Unpublished MBA thesis, City University Business School, London.

Earl, M. (1984) Emerging trends in managing new information technologies, in *The Management Implications of New Information Technology* (ed. N. Piercy), UWIST/Croom Helm, Beckenham.

Earl, M. (1989) *Management Strategies for Information Technology*, Prentice-Hall, London.

Eason, K. (1988) *Information Technology and Organizational Change*, Taylor & Francis, London.

Farbey, B., Land, F. and Targett, D. (1992) Evaluating investments in IT. *Journal of Information Technology*, **7** (2), 100–12.

Friedman, A. (1990) *Computer Systems Development: History, Organization and Development*, Wiley, Chichester.

Gold, C. (1992) *Total Quality Management in Information Services – IS Measures: A Balancing Act.* Research Note, Ernst & Young Center for Information Technology and Strategy, Boston.

Goodwin, C. (1984) How OA can justify itself. *Computing*, 4 October, 6.

Gunton, T. (1988) *End User Focus*, Prentice-Hall, London.

Grindley, K. (1991) *Managing IT at Board Level*, Pitman, London.

Hawgood, J. and Land, F. (1988) A multivalent approach to information systems assessment, in *Information Systems Assessment: Issues and Challenges* (eds N. Bjorn-Andersen and G. Davis), Elsevier North-Holland, Amsterdam.

Hirschheim, R. and Smithson, S. (1988) A critical analysis of information systems evaluation, in *Information Systems Assessment: Issues and Challenges* (eds N. Bjorn-Andersen and G. Davis), Elsevier North-Holland, Amsterdam.

Hochstrasser, B. (1990) Evaluating IT investments – matching techniques to projects. *Journal of Information Technology*, **5** (4), 215–21.

Hochstrasser, B. and Griffiths, C. (eds) (1990) *Regaining Control of IT Investments – A Handbook for Senior UK Managers*, Kobler Unit, London.

Hochstrasser, B. and Griffiths, C. (1991) *Controlling IT Investments: Strategy and Management*, Chapman & Hall, London.

Kaplan, R. and Norton, D. (1992) The balanced scorecard – measures that drive performance. *Harvard Business Review*, January–February, 71–9.

Keen, P. (1986) *Competing in Time*, Ballinger, Cambridge, USA.

KEW Associates, (1992) *UK IT Market Analysis*, Computer Weekly Publications, London.

King, W. R. and Raghunathan, T. S. (1987) How strategic is information systems planning? *Datamation*, November, 133.

KPMG Peat Marwick Mitchell (1990) Quoted in Datalink, 12 March, page 1.

Lincoln, T. and Shorrock D. (1990) Cost justifying current use of information technology, in *Managing Information Systems for Profit* (ed. T. Lincoln), Wiley, Chichester.

Lockett, M. (1992) How IT could be measured. *Creating Business Value with IT Seminar, Templeton College, Oxford*, November.

Lyttinen, K., Klein, H. and Hirschheim, R. (1991) The effectiveness of office information systems: a social action perspective. *Journal of Information Systems*, **1** (1), 41–60.

Malitoris, J. (1990) IT measurement: delivering the goods. Paper at the Technology and People Conference, London, 15 June.

Meyer, D. and Boone, M. (1988) *The Information Edge*. Holt, Rinehart & Winston, Toronto.

National Audit Office (1989) *Department of Social Security: Operational Strategy*, January Session 1988–89, HC-111, HMSO, London.

Ong, D. (1991) *Evaluating IS Investments: A Case Study in Applying the Information Economics Approach.* Unpublished MBA thesis, City University Business School, London.

Parker, M. M., Benson, R. J. and Trainor, H. E. (1988) *Information Economics*, Prentice-Hall, London.

Peat Marwick (1989) *IT Survey among CEOs*, Peat Marwick, London.

Peters, G. (1990) Beyond strategy – benefits identification and the management of specific IT investments. *Journal of Information Technology*, **5** (4), 205–14.

Porter, M. E. and Millar, V. E. (1985) How information gives you competitive advantage. *Harvard Business Review*, **63** (4), 149–60.

Price Waterhouse (1992) *Information Technology Review 1992/3*, Price Waterhouse, London.

Silk, D. (1990) Managing IS benefits for the 1990s. *Journal of Information Technology*, **5** (4), 185–93.

Silk, D. (1992) *Planning IT*, Pitman, London.

Stone, D. (1991) Language, training and experience in information system assessment. *Accounting, Management and Information Technology*, **1** (1), 91–108.

Strassmann, P. (1990) *The Business Value of Computers*, The Information Economics Press, New Canaan.

Walsham, G. (1992) *Interpreting Information Systems in Organizations*, Wiley, Chichester.

Ward, J., Griffiths, P. and Whitmore, P. (1990) *Strategic Planning for Information Systems*, Wiley, Chichester.

Willcocks, L. (ed.) (1990) Theme issue: the evaluation of information systems investments. *Journal of Information Technology*, **5** (4).

Willcocks, L. (1992) Evaluating Information Technology Investments: Research Findings and Reappraisal. *Journal of Information Systems*, **2** (3), 243–68.

Willcocks, L. (ed.) (1994) *Evaluating and Managing Information Systems Investments*, Chapman & Hall, London.

Willcocks, L. and Lester, S. (1991) Information systems investments: evaluation at the feasibility stage of projects. *Technovation*, **11** (5), 283–302.

Willcocks, L. and Margetts, H. (1993) Risk assessment and information systems. *European Journal of Information Systems*, **3** (forthcoming).

Willcocks, L. and Mark, A. (1989) IT systems implementation: research findings from the public sector. *Journal of Information Technology*, **4** (2), 92–103.

Willcocks, L. and Mason, D. (1987) *Computerising Work: People, Systems Design and Workplace Relations*, Paradigm, London.

Willcocks, L. and Mason, D. (1988) New technology and human resources – the role of management. *Employee Relations*, **10** (4), 3–8.

Willcocks, L. and Mason, D. (1990) Managing new technology and workplace relations. *Employee Relations*, **12** (3), 3–11.

Part Two

The Strategic Dimension

4

A portfolio approach to evaluating information systems investments and setting priorities

John Ward

Introduction

Investments in systems and technology (IS/IT) compete with alternative investments, such as buildings, plant, equipment, R&D and advertising, for the organization's funds. While application software may for 'legal' reasons be written off as an expense item, it is in reality not a consumable item whose benefits accrue in the year it is purchased. It is an investment whose benefits accrue over time. Technology is normally treated as a capital item, to be offset over time against benefits which accrue from applications which use it. Projects involving IS/IT investments have traditionally been evaluated like 'capital projects', assuming a 'fixed cost' offset against net revenue over the 'life' of the application. This is not meant to be confusing, but is intended to show the rather odd status of IS/IT investments – the real 'asset' is the software, not the hardware. There is no simple answer to the question: 'On what basis should IS/IT investments be evaluated against other investments?' However, it is important that some general rules are established within

Information Management: The evaluation of information systems investments.
Edited by Leslie Willcocks.
Published in 1994 by Chapman & Hall. ISBN 0 412 41540 2.

which applications and supporting technology requirements are evaluated. Otherwise any strategy will be distorted over time by inconsistent, even arbitrary, decision making.

If the organization was able to develop at any one time all the applications demanded, inconsistent evaluation would not really matter. The overall return on IS/IT investment might be very poor but at least the worthwhile things would get done as well as the worthless! However, in most cases not all demand can be satisfied and priorities must be set.

If no consistent justification approach is followed, the more beneficial applications may well be deferred, allowing those that are worth less to proceed. Assuming that does not mean an opportunity completely foregone, which may occur with delay, the resources and funds invested have provided a poorer return than could have been achieved, to the overall detriment of the organization.

An obvious conclusion from the above is that the same principles and practice should govern the 'go/no go' decisions for individual applications *and* deciding priorities across applications competing for resources. The only additional factor, assuming that systems are not sequentially dependent, is the amount of resource consumed. The limiting factor is normally people in quantity or quality (particular skills) but the same logic applies whatever the limiting resource – priority setting should enable maximum return from the use of that resource.

The discussion below considers investment evaluation first and then priority setting, assuming not all applications can be achieved in parallel and skilled staff are the scarce resource.

Evaluating IS/IT investments

It is possible to argue that a 'technology' investment cannot strictly give a return on investment unless it replaces an older technology and carries out the same functions more efficiently. In practice, most 'technology' investments are justified on the back of applications. Even if capacity on computers and networks has to be purchased in advance of the need, the justification should be based on systems that will use that capacity and the benefits they will provide. However, as argued in the Introduction to this book, it is often difficult to associate all 'infrastructure' type investments with the subsequent benefits of using applications, even where sophisticated capital cost recovery accounting techniques are used. The arguments below will assume that reasonable cost allocations of shared resources can be arrived at – reasonable in the sense that

(a) unused capacity is not 'free' – there is at least an opportunity cost of using it for another application;
(b) each application need justify only the incremental capacity **it** requires, not the next capacity increment which has to be purchased;
(c) where the technology is dedicated to an application, the full cost is attributed to the application.

Another point of evaluation logic which is peculiar perhaps to IS/IT investments is the way particular costs and benefits should be treated. Most accounting evaluation practices are conservative, expecting the worst and mistrusting the best. Raw IT costs have been reducing at 25% per annum for some 25 years and this is difficult for accounting procedures to accept when evaluating systems with five-, eight- or ten-year lives. This changing reality of running costs of systems over time must be allowed for where shared resources are used. It is important to take a realistic (even marginal) view of the costs rather than a theoretical one. Some of the problems with applying traditional accounting practices to information systems evaluation are also discussed in the previous chapter.

On the other side of the coin, quantifying the benefits of any system can be a difficult, even impossible, task. In the book *Information Economics*, Parker *et al.* (1988) assess in detail the ways in which information and systems benefits accrue and how they can be quantified to help in justifying investments. They consider three main types of application:

1. **Substitutive** – machine power for people power; economics being the main driving force, to improve **efficiency**.
2. **Complementary** – improving productivity and employee **effectiveness** by enabling work to be performed in new ways.
3. **Innovative** – intended to obtain or sustain **competitive** edge by changing trading practice or creating new markets, etc.

They then identify the ways in which applications should be justified and define five basic techniques for evaluating benefits.

1. The traditional cost–benefit analysis, based on cost displacement by a more efficient way of carrying out a task. For example, preparing invoices by computer and transmitting them electronically via a data network is more efficient, both for the sender and the receiver, than printing and posting them.
2. 'Value linking', which estimates the improvement to business performance, not just savings made, by more precise coordination of tasks in different areas. Being able to bill customers more accurately, due to immediate delivery feedback, or satisfy a greater proportion of customer orders direct from stock due to the precision of the stock records, are examples of value linking.
3. 'Value acceleration', which considers the time dependency of benefits and costs in other departments, of system improvements, e.g. being able to prepare invoices one day earlier or giving sales data to buyers sooner, giving them more time to negotiate with suppliers. This implies that the benefit will occur in another area of the business.
4. 'Value restructuring', which considers the productivity resulting from organizational change and change of job roles, enabled by the new system. For instance, departments can be combined, even eliminated due to systems developed to carry out functions in an integrated fashion. Information intensive tasks such as forecasting, planning and scheduling can often be rationalized and improved.
5. 'Innovation evaluation' attempts to identify the value of new business or new business practices levered from IS/IT. The value may be in the application itself, e.g. the use of expert systems to diagnose machine faults, or in the image it creates for the company (e.g. Home Banking Services).

The above categories of benefit are suggested to be related to the application types, as shown in Table 4.1.

By assessing costs and benefits using these techniques the overall 'economics' of an application can be assessed. The ideas are certainly more creative in interpreting information's long-term value than traditional views of systems investments. A more detailed account of the information economics approach appears in Chapter 9.

While it is important to quantify and express in financial terms as many of the

Table 4.1 Relationship of benefits to application types* (after Parker *et al.*, 1988)

Type of application	Substitutive (efficiency)	Complementary (effectiveness)	Innovative (competitive)
1. Cost–benefit	***	**	*
2. Value linking	**	***	**
3. Value acceleration	*	***	***
4. Value restructuring		**	***
5. Innovation evaluation			***

*The number of stars indicates the relative importance of the type of benefit to the application type.

costs and benefits as possible, it is not essential to convert all 'intangibles' to financial figures. It is simply not possible to express all the benefits of 'systems' in quantitative terms and it serves no useful purpose to develop spurious calculations to quantify the unquantifiable. If a new system will improve staff morale because at last the company has seen fit to invest in improving office functions and modernize the environment, how can that increase be financially expressed even after the event, let alone before it has happened?

The application portfolio approach

What is more important is to use the appropriate basis for judgement of applications based on the role they are expected to fulfil in the business. A portfolio management approach can offer help in making such judgements. There are many ways of classifying information systems, but for investment appraisal purposes the role they play in the business and the contribution they are expected to make should be the key parameters for such a classification. This view can be achieved by adapting an idea originally devised by McFarlan (1984) for comparing the role of IS/IT across different organizations. It has been shown to be very helpful in gaining management understanding of the differing nature and importance of IS/IT investments and to demonstrate how, as with any investment portfolio, different management strategies are needed. The rationale for such an approach is explained in depth elsewhere (Ward, 1988).

The classification is based on a management judgement of the 'value' of the systems investments, in terms of one of four segments of a matrix – see Figure 4.1.

The objective of such a classification is to determine the criticality of the relationship between the investment and business success and hence determine how the application should be managed, including how the investments will be appraised. The business reasons for embarking on the applications, and hence the key issues to be managed, are different. Some critical aspects are described in Table 4.2.

The basic philosophy in the **high-potential** segment is R&D, whereas for **strategic** applications the drive is to achieve a business objective through an IS/IT investment – and managing the change in the business will be as critical as the effectiveness of the IS/IT application management.

Key operational applications are more familiar territory and involve improving the effectiveness and efficiency of how activities are carried out. Most 'systems development methodologies' were developed to deal with the challenges in creating

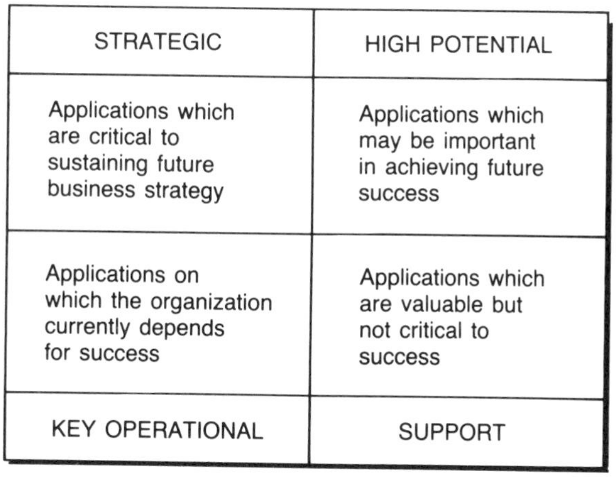

STRATEGIC	HIGH POTENTIAL
Applications which are critical to sustaining future business strategy	Applications which may be important in achieving future success
Applications on which the organization currently depends for success	Applications which are valuable but not critical to success
KEY OPERATIONAL	SUPPORT

Figure 4.1 Information systems application portfolio.

Table 4.2 Some key issues in the segments of the portfolio

Segment	Driving forces	Critical requirements
High potential	New business idea or technological opportunity	Rapid evaluation of prototype and avoid wasting effort/resources on failures
	Individual initiative – owned by a 'product champion'	Understand the potential (and the economics) in relation to business strategy
	Need to demonstrate the value or otherwise of the idea	Identify the best way to proceed – the next step
Strategic	Market requirement, competitive pressures or other external forces	Rapid development to meet the business objective, and realize benefits within the window of opportunity
	Business objectives, success factors and vision of how to achieve them	Flexible system that can be adapted in the future as the business evolves
	Obtaining an advantage and then sustaining it	Link to an associated business initiative to sustain commitment
Key operational	Improving the performance of existing activities (speed, accuracy, economics)	High-quality, long-life solutions and effective data management
	Integration of data and systems to avoid duplication, inconsistency and misinformation	Balancing costs with benefits and business risks – identify the best solution
	Avoiding a business disadvantage or allowing a business risk to become critical	Evaluation of options available by objective feasibility study
Support	Improved productivity/efficiency of specific (often localized) business tasks	Low-cost, long-term solutions – often packaged software to satisfy most needs
	Legal requirements	Compromise the needs to the solftware available
	Most cost-effective use of IS/IT funds and resources available	Objective cost–benefit analysis to reduce financial risk and then control costs carefully

long-term effective key operational systems. Their effectiveness is often dependent on the degree of integration with other systems in the business. Poor key operational systems can rapidly lead to business disadvantages. **Support** systems are again more familiar in type – producing improvements in efficiency throughout the business at a broad (e.g. maintaining personnel data) or local level (word processing, spreadsheets for planning, etc.). They need careful management to ensure that resources are not wasted since the overall business impact is less critical. An example portfolio for a manufacturing company is shown in Figure 4.2.

Clearly, over time, applications can migrate round the matrix, as the business and IS/IT use evolves. High-potential applications cannot be high potential forever. They either have significant potential and become strategic, have no potential and should be rejected, or have limited benefits of a support or key operational nature. As they move, further investment should be appraised based on their planned destination. Strategic systems will over time produce fewer advantages, as others catch up, or the industry or business objectives change. As they become the established way of doing business, they essentially become key operational systems and may have to be re-implemented to be more appropriate to that role – this implies further investment of resources and this should be argued from a key operational perspective. Equally,

STRATEGIC	HIGH POTENTIAL
Order management	EDI with wholesalers
Links to suppliers	Staff planning
MRP II	Decision support (capacity plans)
Sales forecasts and market analysis	Expert fault diagnosis
Product profitability analysis	etc.
etc.	
Bill of materials DB	Time recording
Inventory management	Budgetary control
Shop floor control	Expense reporting
Product costing	General accounting
Maintenance schedule	Maintenance costing
Employee DB	CAD for layout design
Receivables/Payables	etc.
CAD (product design)	
etc.	
KEY OPERATIONAL	SUPPORT

Figure 4.2 Example portfolio for a manufacturing company.

some key operational systems eventually only fulfil a support role, as the business changes and, hence, further investment should be severely curtailed, or again the system re-implemented to provide a better economic return over the long term by reducing support costs, etc.

Hence, over time an application will move at least partially round the matrix and as its contribution changes, so should the way further investments in the application are made be argued.

The rationale for developing applications or investing funds and resources in each segment of the matrix is different and therefore the evaluation process should be different. The arguments used to justify a prototype expert system to model customer buying behaviour are not the same as those used to justify a rewrite of the general accounting system. Equally, response to a competitor's action and a decision to integrate applications via a database require different approaches to evaluation. The risks of failure in the various segments are different. This can be allowed for by asking for a higher predicted rate of return where the risk is higher, although this may in turn merely lead to creative accounting for the benefits!

The application portfolio approach can be related to the types of benefits considered in the 'information economics' rationale. The mix of benefits expected from any application development in each segment will vary according to the contribution it is intended to make. Figure 4.3 attempts to show this.

In the high-potential segment the benefits are unknown and the purpose of the evaluation is, in part, to identify the types of benefits that might be achieved, and hence the nature of the system. Obviously if there are no benefits it should be rejected.

In the support segment the main likely benefits are of a substitution type —

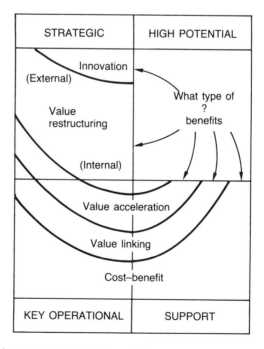

Figure 4.3 Information economics and the matrix.

replacing a less efficient means of carrying out a set of tasks – although some may accrue from linking tasks together or by enabling faster or earlier completion on non-critical tasks, releasing resources for other more critical activities. Most of the arguments should therefore be based on cost–benefit, value linking or value acceleration logic. A little value restructuring may be possible if the system enables tasks to be centralized or decentralized to be carried out more appropriately. This might be true in a general accounting system, for instance. Many of the arguments will be the same for key operational systems, although more emphasis will be placed on effectiveness through integrating activities, whereby the value-linking and acceleration benefits should increase in importance. Such benefits from systems integration may also force some internal restructuring of activities in the organization to ensure that the benefits are gained.

The strategic segment is about change – change of business relationships and practices to gain advantages and achieve objectives. Hence the types of benefits will accrue by innovation and by restructuring both internal organizational processes and the relationships with the outside world, especially customers and suppliers. Accelerating business activities and linking them more proficiently will contribute to this, but basic cost–benefit appraisals will be difficult due to the degree of change involved. It is similar to carrying out a new promotion campaign or reorganizing, where estimating payback is far from easy in advance.

The purpose of the above analysis is to enable management to consider the nature of the benefits they should be seeking for applications they deem to be in the various segments. As the nature of the benefits changes, the responsibility for overall success with the investment shifts. Identifying and then achieving the benefits becomes more critical as we move towards strategic systems, and the ability of the IS/IT department to achieve that success by improving delivery performance and controlling the cost side of the equation becomes less critical to overall success. This is depicted in Figure 4.4.

The portfolio approach and the information economics rationale suggest two further points.

1. Quantified justification of applications is easier in the key operational and support quadrants – where all aspects of the application will be better known or can be

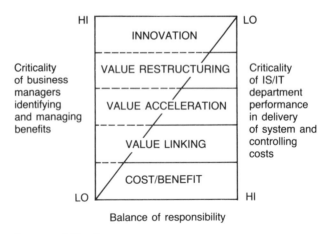

Figure 4.4 Overall responsibility for success.

determined and risks are lower and the rate of change is slower. High potential applications should be considered like other R&D investments rather than like key operational or support systems. Strategic applications may be difficult to argue quantitatively in advance, and timing may be critical to the achievement of benefits.

2. A singular approach to system justification will tend to produce one type of application to the exclusion of others. This argument is particularly strong where a deliberate scarce resource approach has been adopted and pure financial return on investment decides whether projects go ahead, and also the priorities. This will clearly favour the key operational and support quadrants.

The arguments surrounding the appraisal of applications in the different segments are now considered in more detail.

Support applications

The main argument for such systems is improving efficiency, which should be possible to quantify and convert into a financial argument for investment. Additional arguments may revolve around system and technology obsolescence and improving staff morale, and these may be difficult to quantify. If the application development requires the use of scarce (central) resources then, in this segment, it is reasonable to expect potential benefits to be estimated **before** resources and costs are incurred to identify the most economic solution within the benefits achievable. Again, if the application is contending with others for the limited resource, then a support application must show a good economic return for the allocation of a scarce resource.

If, however, the project can be carried out within the user department's control then it is reasonable that, since the budget or funding is under local control, the 'go/no go' decision is made by local user management. The IS/IT investment is an alternative use of funds to other investments locally and is not competing with alternative use of scarce IS/IT resources. Hopefully user management will expect the case to be argued in predominantly financial terms, but if not, that is their responsibility.

In summary, assuming a scarce resource strategy is being adopted 'centrally' for all support applications, then any allocation of that resource should be argued on economic, return on investment, grounds primarily. At the same time, some discretion can, without great risk, be left to local management via a 'free market' strategy. The balance of scarce resource/free market in this segment will depend on how centralized or decentralized the organization is overall.

Key operational applications

While as far as possible all costs and benefits of a new development/redevelopment/ enhancement to a key operational system should be converted to a financial evaluation, this may not allow for all the arguments involved.

For support systems it was suggested that benefits should be estimated before any resource is allocated or costs determined. This is inappropriate for key operational applications where financial benefits are not the only driving force, and also the most economic solution may not be the most effective. This is the area for strict 'feasibility study' to find the best solution from a range of alternatives, each with differing costs and benefits and risks.

The business success may be at risk if a system falls behind the business needs. It also might be worth spending more to achieve an integrated solution which meets a range of needs more effectively and upon which new strategic applications can be built. The relationship of the 'project' to other existing, proposed and potential systems must be included in the evaluation. Normally this will increase the cost and the 'intangible' benefits. Some of those benefits will be able to be related to critical success factors which by inference will, if achieved, lead to achievement of business objectives (and vice versa if they are not!). An argument often used here is 'what will happen to the business if we do not invest in improving key operational systems' and therefore 'can we afford the risk of not doing it?'.

The approach that works best for key operational systems is 'monopolistic', which implies a central control and vetting of all applications and enhancements. This enables a standard check-list of questions to be considered in the evaluation of any new project. Factors that are important (other than economic return) from either a business or an IS/IT perspective can be allowed for and, if necessary, changed over time. The centralized approach should also preclude solutions based on only economic expediency rather than business benefits, although it may mean that a particular application may cost more in the short term.

In conclusion, it should be stressed that for key operational systems the business management should be the final arbiter. It is their business which will suffer by lack of investment and they should (provided they can afford to pay) be allocated the necessary resources to meet such systems needs, for whatever reason they feel the case is justified.

Strategic applications

The fact that an application is deemed strategic implies that it is seen as important, even essential, in achieving business objectives and strategies. Obviously, it is important to cost the investment and, where possible, put figures to the potential benefits, even if the latter are only orders of magnitude, not estimates suitable for a discounted cash flow calculation. However, the main reasons for proceeding are likely to remain 'intangible' – expressed as the critical success factors that the application addresses.

The most appropriate approach to managing in this segment is to integrate the planning of the systems with the business plans ensuring that IS/IT opportunities and threats are being considered along with the business issues and strategies. Hence, an application will get the 'go/no go' decision based on whether it is relevant to the business objectives and strategy and likely to deliver benefits in those terms, not as a system in its own right. Whether this will actually happen is partly a question of luck (that the target does not move), partly of judgement (the quality of business acumen of senior managers), and partly good management of the application as and when it is developed.

The key issue is whether the management team, steering group or whatever body makes such decisions, is unified in endorsing the project and that the 'organization' deems the investment worth while. The critical factor is then resourcing the task sufficiently to achieve the objectives in the optimum timescale. This may need repeated senior management intervention to ensure that both user and IS resources are made available. The budget for such investments and then financial control of actual expenditure should perhaps reside with the 'steering group' to ensure that progress and resourcing are centrally monitored as well as planned.

High-potential applications

The very essence of high-potential projects is that the benefits are unknown. The objective in part is to identify the benefits potentially available. It is the R&D segment of the matrix and should be justified on the same basis as any other R&D, and preferably from a general R&D budget rather than IS/IT central funds. In practice, where the money comes from – R&D budget or IS/IT or user budgets – is important but not critical. What does matter is not pouring money down the seemingly bottomless pit that R&D can become if not properly monitored. The idea of 'product champions' to be responsible for such projects, given a budget against agreed general terms of reference, to deliver good results or otherwise, is the most effective way of initiating and managing the 'high-potential' stage in application life-cycles. So whatever the source of the funds, once the project starts the 'champion' has control over the budget, and is accountable for its use.

The word **evaluation** is what the high-potential box is really about – nothing should stay in it too long or have too much money spent on it. When initial allocations are used up, further sums have to be rejustified, not just allocated in the vague hope of eventual success. Clearly this means that the high-potential applications being tested need to be monitored by the business management, both to control overall costs and identify those that have significant potential; so that they can be fully exploited.

The above approaches to application justification in the various segments may lack the precision ideally required. But this is no more than is true of other aspects of research and development, advertising, reorganization, building new plant or facilities, taking on new staff or training people.

IS/IT investments should be considered just as objectively and just as subjectively as other business investments. The portfolio approach allows the balance to vary according to the expected contribution required.

Setting priorities for applications

As mentioned earlier, the mechanisms used to decide whether or not applications go ahead should also be used to set priorities across applications when all cannot be done in parallel. Some priorities are logical – project B cannot proceed before project A has built the data base, etc. – but many more are independent of each other.

It is important to introduce some consistent, rational approach to priority setting if any strategy is to be implemented successfully. Short-term business pressures will change, projects will not proceed as planned, resources will not be available as expected, new opportunities and requirements will emerge. Each of these can change the priorities and unless a consistent rationale is employed, the short-term issues will

Table 4.3 Risk categories and factors affecting success of IT projects

Category	Factors
A. People issues	1. Degree of senior management involvement 2. Business knowledge in the project team 3. Technical skills and experience of project team 4. Coordination between business and technical staff
B. Size	1. Man-years work involved 2. Number of people involved 3. Elapsed time for the project
C. Project control	1. Use of standards and formal development methodology 2. Testing procedures and change control 3. Budgetary and expenditure control procedures 4. Constraints on project team re innovation and change
D. Complexity of system	1. Business complexity of problem 2. Cross-functional business issues 3. Technical complexity of solution 4. Number of system interfaces
E. Novelty	1. Use of new technology (new to the organization) 2. Change to business practices/processes 3. Change to organization
F. Stability	1. Clarity of scope of system and its boundaries 2. Rate of change of business area affected by system

override the strategy. In that short term, resources are limited and must be used to maximum effectiveness. The main constraint is normally skilled IS labour, often in particular skill areas.

Based on the earlier discussion of application evaluation it should be seen that setting priorities across applications of a similar type, i.e. support or key operational, etc., is not too difficult. Other than ranking them on similarly expressed benefits, the remaining parameter is to optimize the resource use. It might also be prudent to modify the final 'score' by consideration of the ability to succeed – the risk of each application – to ensure that not just high-risk projects are tackled, resulting eventually in no achievement! Risk can either be allowed for as contingencies in cost and resources or by reducing the potential benefits or, in some cases, both!

Hence, three factors need to be included in the assessment of priorities:

- what is most important to do   – benefits
- what is capable of being done   – resources
- what is likely to succeed   – risks

Spadaro (1985) shows a matrix-based approach for assessing 'request factors against success factors' to identify a ranking for projects based on importance and risk of failure. The risk factors are classically those which can cause any project to go wrong. Table 4.3 lists a number of major risk categories and factors which can be used to guide the assessment of project risks. The relevance and seriousness of the different risks varies across the segments of the portfolio and hence action to deal with them will also vary. How this can be allowed for is described in detail elsewhere (Ward, 1992).

Priorities need to be set in the short term to enable the best use of resources within the acquisition lead time for further resources, assuming these are actually obtainable.

Support applications

Within the **support** segment setting priorities should not be too difficult — those with the greatest economic benefit that use the least resources should get the highest priority. This will encourage users to express benefits quantitatively and look for resource efficient solutions, such as packages, to obtain a priority. Support applications will tend to be low risk but relative risks may modify the priorities to ensure that an overall return is guaranteed.

Strategic applications

Within the **strategic** segment the basic rationale is equally clear. Those applications which will contribute most to achieving business objectives, and use least resources in the process, should go ahead first. To assess this, some form of simple decision

	APPLICATION CONTRIBUTION		
	High (3)	Medium (2)	Low (1)
OBJECTIVE A CSF 1 CSF 2 etc.			
OBJECTIVE B CSF 1 CSF 2 etc.			
OBJECTIVE C CSF 1 CSF 2 etc.			
OBJECTIVE D CSF 1 CSF 2 etc.			
TOTALS			
OVERALL TOTAL			

Figure 4.5 Strategic weighting via critical success factors.

matrix can be useful in assessing the 'strategic contribution' or weighting of different projects. It produces a strategic 'score' or value for each application or project by explaining in terms of how, and therefore to what degree, it will help in achieving the various success factors. A simple 'high, medium, low' weighting can be used to give some useful perspective that will have potentially the greatest business impact. Figure 4.5 demonstrates the process.

All applications, wherever they fall in the matrix, should be assessed against such a 'strategic weighting' table to help decide or confirm the segment in which they belong. **High-potential** applications should demonstrate some, if as yet unclear, relationship to objectives, whereas **strategic** applications will be more obviously contributing. **Support** systems should show little strategic contribution, otherwise they are more important and **key operational** applications should relate to at least some CSFs.

Key operational applications

Setting priorities among **key operational** systems is more problematic than support or strategic, where the basic rationale is clearer. The arguments for (i.e. benefits of) key operational systems will comprise basically:

- economic
- critical success factors (CSFs)
- risk to current business
- infrastructure improvement.

Each of these issues must be given some form of relative weighting to decide the order of preference before looking at resource constraints.

In each case the cost/resources used by the project should be matched against its importance in each of the four categories to establish overall priorities. Economic benefits are relatively straightforward and business objectives are included via CSFs. The IS/IT view of 'infrastructure' implies providing appropriate hardware/network capacity, implementing coherent architectures, increasing skills, improving the resilience or flexibility of systems, etc., i.e. investments which will avoid IS/IT becoming a business constraint. Risk to current business could be assessed by describing 'what risks are run if the project does not go ahead'.

The types of business risks to be considered (due to poor product/service quality, process failure, loss of control, customer dissatisfaction, etc.) and the links to IS projects are argued in some detail in Chapter 5 and in Chapters 10 and 11.

Applications scoring highly in all four categories are obviously higher in priority than those scoring highly in 1, 2 or 3 categories, and those at each level in the ranking using fewer resources get priority. It is a subjective method but does allow for the strategic, financial, user and IS/IT perspectives to be included.

Buss (1983), who proposed a similar multifaceted approach, also makes an important observation concerning, as he says, the 'misconception' that 'computer steering committee can decide the priorities'. In general he suggests that politics may interfere, that representation in discussion will be unbalanced and the only common ground will end up as economics! He says the best way to set priorities is to make them the product of a formal planning process at corporate or business unit level. The mechanisms to be employed can be agreed by a steering group but they should not be implemented as a meeting-based process.

High-potential applications

These are difficult to prioritize and will tend to be driven somewhat in the reverse of strategic applications: What resource is available to do it and then which application might best employ that resource? If, as is suggested earlier, high-potential applications are 'individually' driven, then, normally a keen champion exists and the secondary resources create the problem. While it sounds wrong to suggest 'he who shouts the loudest', or 'has the most influence' will obtain priority in this segment, it may be the best way to allow priorities to be set because:

(a) the results will depend not just on the value of the idea, but also on the force with which it is pursued;
(b) setting objective priorities on scanty evidence is not very reliable anyway.

If the idea potentially impacts many CSFs it clearly stands out from others and should be elevated above the general scramble for R&D type resources. In the discussion below, high-potential applications are not considered as being in competition for IS/IT funds, but are funded from R&D general budgets. But, of course, they may compete for certain key skills or resources.

Resourcing the various applications

The remaining task is to set priorities across the segments of the portfolio to decide how much resource to devote to the different types of applications. This is not simple since the rationale for investment in each is different, as shown above. However, the approach recommended for key operational applications can be extended out of the key operational domain. The problem is that strategic applications will score heavily on 'critical success factors' whereas support applications will score heavily on 'economics'. Management must decide the weighting they wish to attribute to each type of benefit and then rank the systems.

The relative weighting given each will depend on a number of factors, but in general the greater trust the management have in their own judgement relative to the need to be reassured by figures, and the trust they have in the user's understanding of the business and in IS in developing effective systems the greater the weighting placed on the CSFs etc., relative to financial aspects. In a way this is a sign of maturity of the organization and how it plans and manages IS/IT. It also tends to reflect on the strength of the company within its industry. The stronger the position the less IS/IT investments are expected (like other investments) to prove an economic case in advance, and a short-term payback, as opposed to providing long-term business development benefits and opportunities.

If the overall plan is developed and maintained in a priority sequence that reflects the ratio:

$$\frac{\text{Benefits to be achieved (adjusted for risk)}}{\text{Limited resource consumed}}$$

then it helps both in short- and long-term planning decisions because:

(a) resources can be reallocated where necessary from lower to higher priority applications on a rational basis, with the agreement of users;

(b) appropriate resourcing levels for the future can be set, and action taken to obtain the right type of resources to meet the demands, expressed as a consensus view of the benefits available.

It is quite possible then to produce a 'planning system' which should keep the plans and resource utilization up to date. It is important to 'report' the current plan to **all** involved to aid understanding of the reasons for the ranking of any particular user's project. Mystery or uncertainty is far more destructive of plans than the discussion and reconciliation of real problems.

Again the above arguments may lack the precision ideally required for setting priorities. Much subjective judgement is inevitably involved, but rules for the various factors can be sensibly established, rather than make each priority decision on a different set of criteria.

In both the evaluation of projects and setting priorities, one aspect must not be ignored – 'after the event'! Some form of review/audit (not a witch hunt!) must be carried out on a high percentage of projects to identify whether (a) they were carried out as well as possible and (b) the benefits claimed (and possibly different benefits) were achieved or not.

One of the factors that differentiates successful from less successful companies in their deployment of IS/IT, according to a survey by the Kobler Unit (1987) is the management resolve to evaluate IS/IT investments **before and after** they occurred.

However this, in itself, is fraught with many problems in evaluating the benefits of any system after it is installed – since it will depend on the type of contribution expected, the timescale used and whether the system is viewed in isolation or in the context of other investments. These problems are described by Huff (1990) who concludes 'it appears as if we may never have a complete understanding of the entire costs and benefits of IT'.

Conclusions

Evaluating IS/IT investments is clearly not a simple task. It requires a combination of management perception of the overall nature of business improvements that can accrue plus realistic appraisal of each investment, to ensure that maximum benefits can be realized at an acceptable cost. At the same time consistent criteria must be applied to both the evaluation of investments and the setting of priorities across the variety of investments. This chapter attempts to bring these threads together via the concept of the applications portfolio, which helps management develop a coherent vision of IS/IT investments and thereby the means of adopting a consistent strategy for their management.

References

Brunel University/Kobler Unit of Imperial College (1987) *The Strategic Use of IT Systems* (a survey), Kobler Unit, Imperial College, London.

Buss, M. D. J. (1983) How to rank computer projects. *Harvard Business Review*, January–February.

Huff, S. L. (1990) Evaluating investments in information technology. *Business Quarterly*, Spring, 42–5.

Kobler Unit (1987) *Does Information Technology Slow You Down?*, Kobler Unit, Imperial College, London.

McFarlan, F. W. (1984) Information technology changes the way you compete. *Harvard Business Review*, July–August.

Parker, M. M., Benson, R. J. with Trainor, H. E. (1988) *Information Economics*. Prentice-Hall, New Jersey.

Peters, G. (1988) Evaluating your computer investment strategy. *Journal of Information Technology*, **3** (3), 178–88.

Spadaro, D. (1985) Project evaluation made simple. *Datamation*, 1 November.

Ward, J. M. (1988) Information systems and technology application portfolio management – an assessment of matrix-based approaches. *Journal of Information Technology*, **3** (3), 204–15.

Ward, J. M. (1992) *Assessing and Managing the Risks of IS/IT Projects*, Cranfield Working Papers, Management School, Cranfield.

5

Evaluating your computer investment strategy

Glen Peters

Introduction

Expenditure in computerized information systems continues to rise as a percentage of a company's income. The increasing encouragement given by the information systems industry to regard this expenditure as a business opportunity has made CEOs regard this expenditure less as a necessary operational cost and more as an investment. However, the 'post-crash' environment from 1987, and the 1990–93 recession have brought to business a new atmosphere of cost justification in information technology (IT) expenditure, and managers are seeking a realistic benefit evaluation to accompany computer investment submissions to the board.

The problem is not simple. Assessing the value of investing in new projects has become progressively more difficult, whereas 10–15 years ago computerization was mainly concerned with replacing manually intensive administrative tasks and cost justification was relatively straightforward. Put simply, it was cheaper to do it by computer. By the early 1980s the computer vendors, in a bid to stimulate new products and markets, began to promote concepts such as the electronic office. Paper was going to be replaced overnight. The information age was here. Better information planning techniques were promoted by academics and consultancies. In

Information Management: The evaluation of information systems investments.
Edited by Leslie Willcocks.
Published in 1994 by Chapman & Hall. ISBN 0 412 41540 2.

journals we have read about the strategic use of IT such as American Hospitals Supply Corp. and American Airlines reservation systems (McFarlan, 1984; Porter and Millar, 1985; Benjamin *et al.*, 1984). Many experienced executives today, however, question the validity of current IT planning methodologies. Researchers such as Earl (1988), who have conducted extensive surveys, conclude that many of the frameworks entering information systems discourse are superficial, the strategy formulation techniques are jejune, some of the prescriptions too generalized and many expectations are over-optimistic.

Research and findings

It is against this background that the author conducted a review of over 50 IT projects, mainly in the UK, in a number of different industries. Many of the projects overlapped each other in functionality and scope and a summary of their generic categories is given in Table 4.1. The objectives of this research were to determine how executives evaluated investment in IT and to develop a method for evaluating computer system investment strategies.

The study provided a number of insights into how some of the world's leading companies evaluated their IT investment strategies, and adds to the picture developed in Chapters 2 and 3.

Benefits

The benefits to the organization appeared as one of the most frequently requested attributes of the investment. Clearly some managers were more preoccupied with the identification of hard benefits, while others were prepared to sanction investment on the understanding that some advantage to their organizations would eventually result. This attitude was generally a function of the degree of pressure on cost structure imposed by the market.

Benefits fall into three categories on a continuum. At one end of the continuum benefits associated with **enhancing productivity** provided impetus for sanctioning investment. Examples included logistics systems to reduce distribution costs or systems integration projects which eliminate the need for double handling or the manual entry of data.

At the other end of the continuum benefits are associated with **business expansion** associated with innovative ways of creating new products or ways of doing business, or providing services. Generally, initiatives in this category are closely allied to overall business initiatives and are frequently the result of innovation in the use of technology to aid product differentiation or solve business problems.

Take as an example an initiative involving the automated retailing of motor insurance. Most oil companies retailing gasoline are seeking new and innovative ways of increasing the profitability of their outlets. The core business (motor fuel) is generally low-margin, high-volume business and many would agree that demand is now relatively stable. New products which share commonality with the existing customers would provide the opportunity of creating additional sales per square foot and may also help to consolidate gasoline sales as a side-effect.

Table 5.1 Summary of generic categories

Generic projects examined	Examples
Client support software. Value-added software to assist in product differentiation or locking in customers	Client access to estimating databases. PC-based diagnostic tools which require reference to supplier
Electronic retailing. All applications of IT involving the progressive automation of existing manual retailing functions (e.g. stocktaking) or creation of new retailing channels (e.g. electronic mail order)	Electronic point of sale, electronic mail order. Automated share retailing
Electronic banking. Projects were concentrated in the area of cashless methods of payments	Credit cards. Debit cards. Intelligent compact devices (e.g. SMART cards)
Electronic data interchange (EDI). Mechanisms for displacing paper-based interfaces between suppliers, customer and intermediaries	Oil company joint interest billing exchange. Construction management data interchange
Logistics. Automating business logistics and providing decision support capabilities	Distribution planning and scheduling. Production planning
Manufacturing. Systems which either result in yield improvements or enable advantageous supply or demand opportunities to be taken	Computer integrated manufacturing and advanced manufacturing technology
Order processing. Systems supporting order taking, stock planning/scheduling including trading exchange	International order-taking system. Commodity trading systems
Finance and accounting. Systems to prepare financial statements, monitor profitability, financial performance and provide statutory reporting	General ledger. Direct product profitability reporting
Marketing. Support for special campaigns and market analysis	Data-driven marketing
Office systems. Systems to automate office functions	Electronic mail, wordprocessing, desktop publishing
Engineering. Advanced tools for supporting design and construction of facilities	Computer-aided design. Project control
Software/hardware environments. Initiative to migrate from one environment to another	Migration to 4GL environment. Migration from vendor A to vendor B
Vendor/system integration. Linking together a number of previously unconnected systems	Integrated marketing and distribution systems. Integrated engineering design systems

Most motorists require motor insurance, which is normally retailed through brokers, either over a telephone or after having filled out and posted appropriate documentation. Today's technology can provide end-user machines enabling insurance quotations to be offered directly to customers and paid for in one complete operation via a credit or debit card. The oil company therefore has the opportunity to offer a fully automated insurance retailing service at a service station. The product, by nature of the retailing outlet (24-hour availability, 7 days a week) and its delivery, is totally unique.

The above illustrates a typical case of an IT investment which would fall into the category of **business expansion** through innovation.

Between these two extremes is the category of **risk minimization**. A good

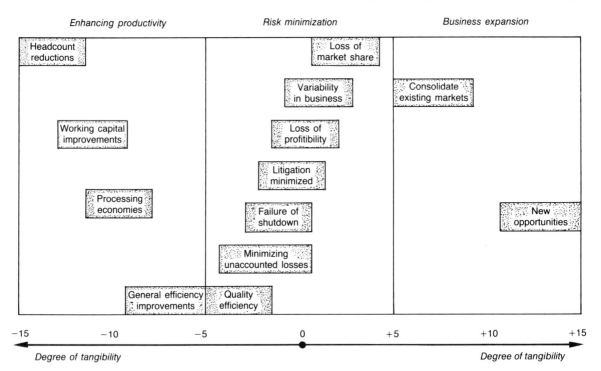

Figure 5.1 Position of investment attributes used to identify the range of anticipated benefits for an IT investment. (Note that '−' does not denote a negative benefit.)

example of this is with many statistical quality control systems (SQC) which are fast becoming commonplace in the chemical, pharmaceutical and process industries. SQC systems monitor historical trends in the quality and consistency of every stage of the manufacture of a product, and give early indications of degradation of plant performance, thereby minimizing the risk of unscheduled failures of either the product or manufacturing plant.

The nature of the continuum enables investments to frequently span across more than one category, and Figure 5.1 enables an assessment to be made of the position that a specific investment may have. The reader will observe that a null point exists in the middle of the scale. Clearly many risk minimization applications will have no identifiable hard benefits but are necessary to insure against serious failure.

Enhancing productivity

The investments that contributed to enhancing productivity fell into the following categories, illustrated in Figure 5.1.

Headcount reduction. The savings identified from headcount reductions represented one of the easiest identifiable savings resulting from the implementation of systems. The savings identified here include those associated with clearly understood productivity gains, such as the elimination of data entry by key punch operators or the elimination of administratively intensive clerical tasks.

Working and capital improvements. Working capital is represented by inventories of finished goods, work in progress and raw materials or interest charges resulting from debtors, which are also clearly identifiable as costs to the organization.

Processing economies. At the core of most enterprises is a facility associated with the production of the eventual product or service. In a refinery it is the plant which processes crude feedstocks to produce fuel. In the insurance company it would be the claims department which processes accident claims, and in the computer bureau it would be the hardware which processes applications. Some investments are targeted directly at obtaining benefits or improving utilization. Better production planning and scheduling systems, for example, can help to improve utilization and produce efficiencies.

General efficiency improvements. By being able to react better to changes in supply and demand through improved information, the organization should benefit from general efficiency improvements and better margins for its products. Better margins may also be gained by people being more effective in their workplace or by avoiding costs paid out to third parties for services. Personal computers with communications devices have enabled salespeople to be more effective by making more calls per day. By integrating a trading system with a refinery production system an oil company was able to take better supply opportunities and increase its refinery margins.

Risk minimization

Risk minimization benefits from IT investments occur in the following areas:

Minimizing risk through improvements in quality. The operational efficiency of an organization is greatly improved when the risks of errors occurring are reduced. Most of the benefits arise from quality improvements which manifest themselves in fewer product failures. A computer-aided design system reduced the number of construction errors by a factor of 10. A direct data entry to an accounts receivable system from a cash book reduced manual entry errors, saving up to 10% of the accounts department's time.

Minimizing unaccounted losses. Unaccounted losses result from either undetected fraud or a lack of knowledge of product movements. Systems which reduce the risk of unaccounted losses, such as an undetected leakage in a process plant or credit misuse, can provide benefits by reducing the level of write-offs. The growth of intelligent credit cards and sophisticated stock movement systems provide benefits here.

Reducing the risks of failure or shutdown. All processing facilities, be they plant, machinery, communications or computer-processing hardware, run the risk of total or partial failure. Partial failures or shutdowns can do significant damage to business. Maintenance management systems, or the reinforcement of a telecommunications network between two operational points, are examples where risks of failure may be minimized.

Minimizing the risk of litigation. Some organizations are particularly vulnerable to risks of litigation or claims for damages. Systems such as a project control system used by one construction company reduced the risk of liquidated damages for failure to complete facilities on time.

Loss of profitability. Information systems which provide management with performance reports on company or sector performance minimize the risk of loss of profitability in unattractive areas. In the same way budgetary and cost control systems also minimize similar risks.

Variability in the business profile. Variability in market demand or supply patterns is generally unfavourable to the running of the modern-day business. Companies have sought information systems either to predict those trends more accurately or to smooth variable demand patterns. Data-driven marketing systems, which provide better information on customer buying trends by product grouping or by geographic area, are an example of such systems. There are also other examples such as automatic ordering systems in customers' premises which help to generate delivery orders once stocks fall past a predefined minimum.

Loss of market share. Market share is important to leaders, followers and new entrants. Systems which minimize the risk of losing market share can have potential benefits in that they protect the company from potential loss of income. Executive information systems can provide management with an update on company performance versus competitors. Systems which add value to the product are usually a more proactive way of minimizing the risk of loss of business to the competition.

Business expansion

Under the heading of business expansion the following categories apply:

Consolidating existing markets. Systems which help to consolidate existing markets can be provided by better customer service, maintaining quality or adding value to the existing product. Improved distribution scheduling systems can, for example, cut the delivery lead times to customers, and on-line access to statistical quality information on products can also help to add value to products in which quality is important.

Creating new opportunities. Systems which help to create new products and new markets through innovation provide benefits through business expansion. Such systems as Reuters' attempt to provide the ability to track and process transactions all on one screen, are clearly unique and lead to more financial institutions buying their devices. Systems such as automated insurance retailing by a fuel retailer, mentioned earlier in this chapter, are a complete departure from its existing fuel-based market and thereby create new opportunities.

Investment orientation

Benefits were not the only criterion used to appraise the value of an IT project. The relationship or orientation of the investment towards the business was also frequently used in evaluation. Various comments such as 'an act of faith' or 'we need it to survive' were made by managers to express the importance or relationship of a planned investment to the business.

The orientation of the investment fell into three broad categories and, like the benefit factors discussed above, also formed a continuum. At one extreme, investments were targeted specifically at **market influencing** initiatives, while at the other extreme the focus was aimed at supporting the technical **infrastructure** such as telecommunications, computers, software environments and data storage. Between these two extremes, applications were designed to process the normal **business operations** of the organization.

Invariably market-influencing applications received the greatest attention in companies with a strong marketing ethos. These initiatives were attempting to change customer buying patterns or attitudes, creating new distribution channels by bringing products or services closer to the end-customer.

Take, as an example, the use of value-added networks (VANs) for booking business travel and accommodation. By bringing the three major components of business travel – airline reservation, hotel accommodation and car hire – directly on to screens in the executive's office, the VAN provider is able to eliminate a number of intermediaries in the supply chain. The service can also give the user guidance on a number of cost options depending on affordability and flexibility of travel arrangements in an environment which is fraught with complex discounts and special deals. The application is therefore influencing business travellers to arrange their own travel and accommodation directly with the providers of the service and, in the process, reap some cost, convenience and time advantage.

Infrastructure projects, on the other hand, are often less glamorous to the approvers of expenditure. Frequently, infrastructure projects are hidden within a market-influencing investment to make them look attractive in a traditional payback investment analysis. This can have long-term deficiencies, as illustrated in the following example.

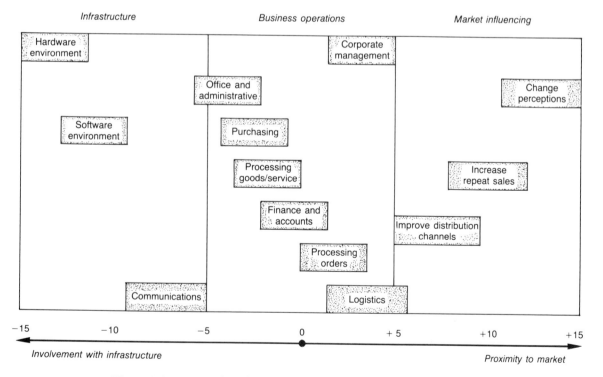

Figure 5.2 Position of attributes used to identify the range of orientation for an IT investment. (Note that '−' does not denote a negative benefit.)

A company wished to implement an international order-processing system to take advantage of a worldwide network of production and warehousing operations. In addition to the new systems that needed to be developed the company included the cost of a network to carry the data traffic between its diverse locations. Growing internationalism within the company meant that there had been several proposals to put in place an effective office systems communications network but the cost justification of this had always been a problem. The implementors of the order-processing system sought approval within the context of the overall investment to install electronic mail facilities to enable the project teams to communicate with each other. The network was therefore designed to take a small amount of this traffic with order transactions being the primary purpose of the eventual network. It may come as no surprise to many that the electronic mail traffic grew exponentially and soon caused substantial performance problems to the main network operation application. In the absence of a clearly acknowledged office systems investment strategy, the transfer of electronic mail was in turn executed inefficiently and cost substantially more than comparable systems in other organizations.

Infrastructure investments therefore need to be considered in their own right and as supporters of other initiatives which form the company's overall investment strategy.

Between the two opposites of infrastructure and market-influencing categories, investments orientated towards business operations occupy the middle ground of investment orientation. These are generally systems primarily concerned with supporting the regular processes of the organization such as order-processing, office and logistics systems. Figure 5.2 gives guidance on how investments may be evaluated for their orientation towards the business.

Business operations

The business processes, as illustrated in Figure 5.2, have IT investments targeted at the following areas:

Finance and accounts. Systems to support the productivity of a regular set of accounts as statutory reporting purposes are considered by many to be mandatory for any sizeable business. The systems provide management information on performance to budgets and targets.

Corporate management. Systems which are aimed at providing information to management on the performance of their company or group are generally for the purposes of longer-term planning.

Processing orders. Systems which support a fundamental business process for receiving enquiries from customers, processing them and organizing for their despatch, frequently also include an element of maintaining existing records on customers.

Production and distribution logistics. These are systems which are primarily orientated towards automating distribution schedules, or providing customers with an improved service. Examples include fleet management systems or customer call-back facilities to support maintenance of plant or machinery.

Processing goods or services. Systems are targeted at the processing of goods or services such as in a production plant (for a manufacturer) or by a clearing system in a bank.

Purchasing or procurement. Systems which support the business processes of bought-in goods or services may be orientated towards either giving the buyer better information to support purchasing decisions or providing administrative support.

Office and administrative. Most companies have substantial office administrative support functions. Facilities which support these administrative activities, such as word-processing, electronic mail, payroll and personnel management, are included here.

Infrastructure

Infrastructure-orientated investments are included in the following categories:

Telecommunications. Telecommunications can be provided either by third party networks or via networks dedicated to the company. Some of these can be geared towards providing greater security, such as upgrading of the telephone-switching system or providing a value-added network to link customers and suppliers.

Software environment. A software environment incorporates operating systems, databases and programming languages to support the applications demanded by the company. Typical investment initiatives include the installation of a fourth-generation language programming environment to assist productivity, speed and quality of new developments, or to provide a uniform relational database to integrate data from different company sources.

Hardware environment. Investments orientated towards hardware are concerned mainly with the efficient and secure running of the company's information processing. Some investments, such as vendor migration, may be embarked upon for greater security while others involving, say, the upgrading of a processor, may be relieving a capacity constraint.

Market influencing

The market-influencing category is composed of the following groups towards which an investment may be orientated.

Improving distribution channels. The phrase 'channels of distribution' is used to describe the number of ways in which a product or service can be delivered to the customer. In the example of automated automobile insurance retailing, the oil company sought to make insurance services available at the garage forecourt. Its all day 24-hour access improved availability to the end-user compared with what was currently available. Another way of improving distribution channels is by merely increasing them such as, say, more phone booths at bus stops, railway stations, restaurants, etc., where people spend time waiting.

Increasing the percentage of repeat sales. Investments targeted at influencing customers to gain repeat business either may be aimed at encouraging greater brand loyalty or locking in customers so that switching costs make it unattractive for the customer to purchase elsewhere. Examples of these include in-store credit cards or various value-added software services being provided by banks for their major account holders.

Changing customer perceptions. Investments aimed at influencing customers by changing their perceptions can be orientated towards altering attitudes to a product from 'a

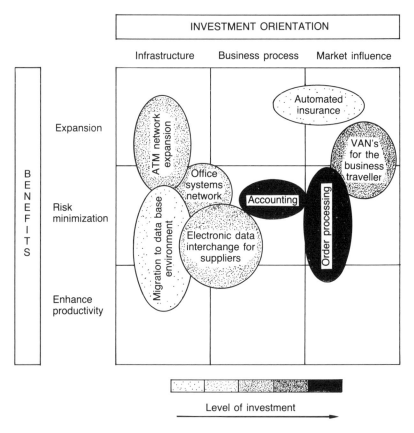

Figure 5.3 An example of an application map to evaluate IT investments.

nice to have' to 'a need to have' perception. Alternatively, the company may provide the opportunity of purchasing these services at unorthodox locations. Other initiatives may be targeted at enhancing the customer's image of the product. The launch of debit cards has been a concerted attempt by the banks to change customers' attitudes on payment by cheque to more cost-efficient electronic means. IT investments frequently span more than one of these categories. Order-processing systems support the business operations of stock allocation, invoicing and delivery scheduling and can be the primary point of contact for customers with telesales, for example. Systems integration projects, primarily orientated towards infrastructure, can produce benefits in enhancing productivity of computer staff, minimizing risks of data errors and creating new business opportunities by setting up links with other parts of the organization or external agencies.

The fact that most IT systems cover a range of benefit and investment orientation categories gives rise to the concept of mapping these systems on a grid composed of the two parameters. This also recognizes the interrelationship of each investment attribute, and Figure 5.3 illustrates how a company could plot its investment strategy. Different levels of shading are applied to indicate high, medium and low expenditure areas. The use of colour coding has also been helpful in highlighting levels of expenditure. In Table 5.2 a number of IT investments have been scored

Table 5.2 Scoring table for mapping IT investments

Planned investment	Orientation		Benefits	
1. Automated motor insurance retailing	+5	+12	+10	+5
2. International office systems network	−5	−11	+4	+7
3. VANs for the business traveller	+7	+15	+12	−7
4. International order processing	+2	+5	+6	−6
5. Migration to common database	−13	+9	−7	+4
6. Accounting systems upgrade	−3	+3	−4	+4
7. Electronic interchange with suppliers	−10	−3	−10	0
8. Expansion of ATM network	−15	−7	+10	+3

using the position of attributes described in Figures 5.1 and 5.2. These investments have been plotted in Figure 5.3, showing an application map.

Emerging themes in investment maps

When maps of several companies were drawn, there appeared to be a clear correlation between an investment map and a company's business strategy. This was

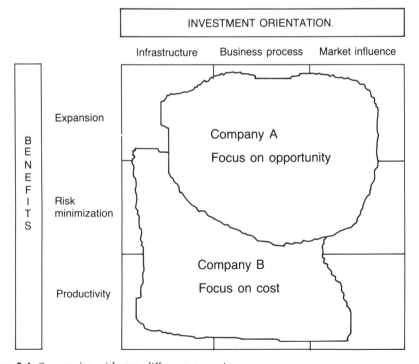

Figure 5.4 Companies with two different strategies.

best illustrated by two companies operating in similar markets with similar products and both occupying strong positions in the world's top 100 companies.

Company B considered its product portfolio to be concentrated clearly in volume–commodity orientated markets where there were few opportunities for competing on a basis other than price. Company A regarded its products as maintaining volume characteristics but with some opportunity for specialization. There were therefore greater opportunities for adding value through innovation and this company created a business strategy focused on product differentiation.

When the IT maps of these two companies were drawn, they reflected the business strategies of the respective organizations. The first company, with the conservative price-led strategy, concentrated on IT investments which cut costs and improved efficiency. The other company's investment was concentrated in the area of innovation and business expansion. This is illustrated in Figure 5.4.

Evolution towards market orientation and innovation

Another phenomenon also observed was that in some cases a company matured in its use of IT as it progressed up the matrix. Presumably this was as a result of automating most of the business process activities in early years and gradually moving on to addressing the more market-related applications.

There were instances when companies supplying information services reflected this increase in market-influencing applications. Reuters, for example, had been steadily progressing in this direction since the early 1970s. Prior to 1971 Reuters marketed a computerized stock-price transmission device called Stockmaster which replaced cumbersome stock tickers on brokers' desks. This improved the productivity of brokers, reduced paperwork and provided improved access. The mid-1970s saw the increasing use of Monitor, a new product which provided foreign exchange information and was targeted directly at the risk minimization and business processes of user organizations, gaining it monopoly status. In the early 1980s Reuters added a dealing system and by doing so was seeking to add value to an existing product and influence customers to buy integrated systems. This new development allowed dealers to communicate with each other, conduct a trade and instantaneously receive printed confirmation. Today Reuters products have reached even higher levels of sophistication in market innovation (Figure 5.5). Their Global Supermarket concept for financial services aims at gaining additional revenue from the existing client base and at providing new products to consolidate existing markets.

Using the maps

IT investment maps can be an effective way of representing an information systems development plan and organizations have found it a useful means of conveying an investment strategy to senior executives. Maps allow managers to compare one investment with another and assess their contribution to providing benefits and their orientation to the business supply chain.

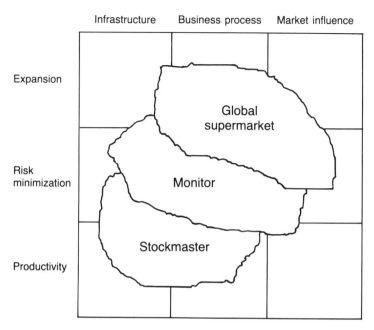

Figure 5.5 Reuters IT products evolution.

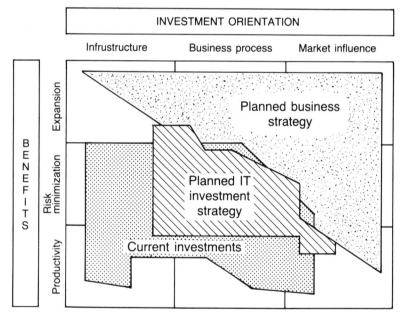

Figure 5.6 Using IT mapping to compare a company's planned investment strategy with its planned business strategy.

As Figure 5.6 illustrates, a map would enable a company to assess its planned IT investment strategy with its current strategy. These comparisons would be made within the context of the firm's business direction. For example, a company with a clearly defined, product-differentiated strategy of innovation and market-influencing initiatives would do well to reconsider IT investments which appeared to show undue bias towards a price-differentiated strategy of cost reduction and enhancing productivity. Investments which fall into favourable areas should be promoted to include a broadened scope of benefits and investment orientation.

Maps can also be used to carry out a competitor analysis of the way in which other companies use IT. The two opposing maps illustrated earlier correspond to two of the world's leading oil companies. Both companies compete vigorously in nearly every major market in the world and they are both regarded as being successful. However, an independent assessment of their investment maps, with only a few exceptions, would reveal consistently opposite ways in which they spend their money on IT. One company pursues a highly opportunistic and market-led IT investment strategy while the other engages in a more conservative price-led, cost-conscious strategy. Both companies are successful in the way they use IT because they have been effective in aligning their system investment with their business direction, culture and management ethos.

Comparisons with competitors' maps are a useful means of being able to understand competitor strategies. This can be achieved surprisingly easily via astute observation by a company's salesforce, surveying company magazines in the public domain and reading trade journals. This, perhaps, illustrates the need for IT professionals to be closely allied to the commercial business of a company rather than mere providers of computing or telecommunications services.

IT investment mapping is already being used by some of Britain's largest companies and early indications are that it is an effective tool for assessing IT investment strategies, presenting them to top management and disseminating the overall framework to key personnel.

References

Benjamin, R., Rockart, J., Scott-Morton, M. and Wyman, J. (1984) Information Technology: a strategic opportunity. *Sloan Management Review*, 3–10.

Earl, M. (1988) *Management Strategies for Information Technology*, Prentice-Hall, London.

McFarlan, F. (1984) Information technology changes the way you compete. *Harvard Business Review*, July–August, **62** (3), 98–103.

Porter, M. and Millar V. (1985) How information gives you competitive advantage. *Harvard Business Review*, July–August, **63** (4), 149–60.

6

The real value of strategy formulation for information technology

Malcolm Iliff

Introduction

This chapter considers the advantages to be gained by an understanding of the significance of developing a strategic view of IT and the contribution this can make to corporate effectiveness. It looks at the place of IT in the broader context of an information management strategy and the interaction of the related components of a well formulated strategy. It considers the role that some analytical techniques can play in its development. Prescriptive ideas are presented for ensuring success in the evaluation, formulation and the implementation of the strategy and the use of a Portakabin type approach to application projects.

The value of strategy formulation for IT can only be achieved when IT issues, that is the technological issues, are viewed in the wider context of the organization where they are to be applied. Developing what will here be called an **Overall Information Management Strategy** is an activity that covers systems and management, as well as the technological, strategies and considers them together. A framework for achieving real value from strategy formulation for IT therefore includes this

Information Management: The evaluation of information systems investments.
Edited by Leslie Willcocks.
Published in 1994 by Chapman & Hall. ISBN 0 412 41540 2.

wider reference. The approach advocated here also copes with the need to reconcile the responses required to immediate business imperatives with the need to focus on the longer term.

The development of an overall information management strategy breaks down into consideration of three manageable sets of issues. These components, which make up a fully formulated corporate strategy on information handling, have been described by Earl (1988) as

- information technology (IT) strategy
- information management (IM) strategy
- information systems (IS) strategy.

When these components are subjected to closer examination it will be seen that the dimensions or subcomponents that can be used to described each of these three strategies are not unique. Study will show, for example, that management, cultural, and organizational dimensions cut across all three. Nevertheless, the distinction between IT, IM and IS strategies is usefully maintained to enable the formulators of strategy to recognize the limitations as well as the strengths they may have in researching the subject, or the extent to which they will have to probe elsewhere within the corporate environment and enlist assistance in order to do justice to the broadly defined task of information management strategy formulation.

The three components and their interactions are addressed in more detail later in this chapter.

The contribution of IT to corporate success

It is well appreciated and widely documented that the sensible use of information technology contributes significantly to the achievement of corporate efficiency and, in many instances, towards corporate profitability. The elements in corporate existence that can be affected by the use of IT include:

- competitive advantage
- cost base efficiency
- product delivery
- operational feasibility
- capacity to manage.

It is interesting that the competitive advantage aspect of IT is now being seriously questioned within the context of the more mature IT environment as, at best, of transitory relevance (see, for excample, Ciborra, 1991). Recognition of the principles outlined in this chapter can enhance the likelihood that all these benefits can more certainly be achieved.

Businesses are made up of a variety of functional activities: information technology, finance, marketing, manufacturing, personnel policies procurement, outbound logistics and sales activities are often seen as critical (Porter, 1985). It cannot be disputed that having thought-out, coordinated strategies to support these aspects of an organization is of significance in preserving a healthy corporate operating environment over time. The alternative option open to a company's management is to operate on a day-to-day basis with little strategic backbone to management decision making. The consequences of this are an approach which favours short-termism, the development of divisional or localized suboptimal policy and an increased risk of failure in the medium to longer term. Sadly, there is much evidence of lack of application of strategic thinking in the remaining shadows and skeletons of companies that are now being administered by receivers and by liquidators and reviewed by the unfortunate creditors who had no say in how their customers were managing their operations until it was too late. Maybe this is painting too pessimistic a picture of the consequences of ill- or un-considered strategic thinking. But there are many shades of inefficiency and missed opportunities which have resulted from the failure to plan long term and to appreciate the wider context in which IT should be managed. There is no claim to the presence of IT-related strategies being the *unique* requirement of corporate management policy for survival in an increasingly competitive environment. The need for coordinated strategic thinking should pervade a company's management culture and be applied as much to other domains as to information management and technology. Marketing, personnel, finance, sales and organizational strategy should be progressed in parallel with the IT strategy if there is to be a balanced corporate development. It is unusual, for example, to find a sales-oriented company which has no sales or marketing strategy. Nevertheless, despite the fact that information and the underlying data form part of the most valuable assets a company has, they are frequently the victims of ad hoc planning and piecemeal development rather than being incorporated into strategic thinking. Perhaps the present concern and enthusiasm in some circles for executive information systems (EIS) is founded on a realization that coordination of information storage, gathering, presentation and manipulation is crucial to a company's efficient and timely response to market and other commercial pressures. EIS respond to the need for senior management to have corporate-wide data at their fingertips and an effective mechanism for accessing and coordinating management information across divisional boundaries. However, even executive information systems need to be viewed in a broad information systems planning and processing context. They cannot easily be divorced from the selection and planning of individual divisional application systems.

The contribution of an information management strategy

Having an overall information management strategy in place implies satisfaction of the need for **long-term confidence** in the direction of development. It implies coincidence with and **support for long-term business goals and targets**. Strategic thinking implies that **cost-effectiveness** is measured over the longer term and that there is a significant element of **stability in the infrastructure** of the corporate being and its operations. It also implies that development is also not confined to the short term, but allows for continuing **incremental improvement** of systems, products and operations, built on a sure base and a solid systems architecture.

If there are so many claims for the beneficial consequences of a well thought-out and confidently embraced strategy, it is necessary when attempting to define an information strategy and deliver the benefits in the real world, to ensure that the process of strategy formulation is well understood. If it is not, the consequences can be negative rather than beneficial. A misdirected strategy, based on insufficient analytical work, lacking realism, or narrow in its genesis but too broad in its application, can cause conflicts of interest, confusion or, at worst, corporate disaster. There are a number of causes that lie behind the provision of poor strategic deliverables, some of which will be referred to later in this chapter. The main problem, however, is that the concept and scope of strategic formulation is incompletely understood. Alternatively, it is recognized but not addressed. A strategy for IT is best developed when the process is linked, as should be the outcome, with other management strategies.

An international organization employed consultants to advise on a new information systems strategy after three previous failed and incomplete attempts. Although the proposals for the new IT strategy were well researched, well argued, plausible and appreciated by the board, the board were reluctant to link the recommendations into the strategies for other aspects of the business. They were unwilling to address the need for a radical change in personnel policies, and the need for a shift in the culture to match the increasingly competitive environment in which they existed. Delays in implementing the strategy were immediately evident and it is unlikely that the IT strategy and operational policies will ever be translated into reality.

It is worth pausing here to touch on a problem of semantics. There tends in practice to be confusion and overlap in the meaning attributed to IM strategy, IT strategy and IS strategy. In this chapter I have used the following approach. The most general level of consideration is referred to as information management strategy (spelt out in full). The more specific 'IS', 'IM' and 'IT' initials are prepended to the term 'strategy' in the more specific contexts which I have considered below. So it can be seen that information technology and its application in business enterprises is wrapped up in the wider issue of information systems and information management. As suggested in the Introduction to this book, IS and IM may be more, or less, IT-based.

A recent survey by Canmore Consultants of what senior managers understood by information management strategy revealed almost as many variations as respondents. Where the differences arise is not so much in the identification of the components of an overall information management strategy (though some respondents chose to ignore certain issues in their analyses) but in the variation of emphasis that is placed upon even the most significant factors. Experience would suggest that unbalanced views of what comprises an information management strategy can lead to difficulties, usually discovered in the longer term when the shortcomings in the original analysis become apparent. There is therefore a need to recognize and apply oneself to a whole range of factors. That is, those factors which (a) ensure optimal choice of target applications, (b) impact on the chance of successful applications implementation, and (c) provide the opportunity for the long-term realization of the full benefits from the chosen developments. It is therefore beneficial to have a framework, and understanding by all involved, of the scope and aims of the strategic planning exercise. At the simplest level this may be achieved by the use of a checklist against which one can test the completeness of the information management strategic planning exercise. However, such a basic approach often proves inadequate.

In terms of the formulation exercise itself there are a number of practical issues. The 'who?', the 'when?' and the 'how?' of the formulation are as crucial as the components of the framework. For example, choice of the person who will conduct the formulation exercise is critical. Constraints may be imposed on the project manager in charge of the strategy research and formulation which may be related to rank, sphere of influence, or accessibility to vital facts or opinions. This can happen even if sponsors of strategy exercises are IT directors with a place on or near the company board. If the task is to be completed successfully, it needs to be managed by someone with a broad range of competences, and by a person with wide access to the organization at all levels. The candidate may well need to be a consultant from outside the organization, though such a candidate can never be a total substitute for internal involvement.

Inadvertent and initially unrecognized constraints may be imposed which will restrict the scope of the findings and recommendations or the value of the plan in the broader corporate context. This may be due to poor choice of project managers, poor terms of reference, or lack of adequate sponsorship or understanding by senior management in user divisions. The extent to which these factors impinge on the information strategist will, of course, be a function of many things. The size and organizational complexity of the company and the industrial sector in which it operates will be significant factors.

The three components of an information management strategy

The relationship between the IT, IM and IS strategies, the three components of the overall information management strategy (Figure 6.1), is bi-directional. In different organizations, different flows will predominate. In some organizations decision making about systems tends to be top-down (IS to IT). That is to say, wish lists are presented to IT functionaries by board members or members of senior management, often without serious consideration of the benefits that can be gained from systems integration, the use of new technologies, and development of long-term architectures. A contrasting scenario can be seen where bottom-up initiatives predominate. The board leave it up to the IT department to initiate and control IT development plans and concern themselves only with the approval of incremental budget submissions. There is here an element of abdication by the board, of policy development

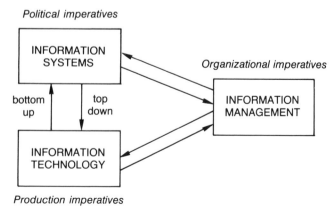

Figure 6.1 Components of a strategy in IT (adapted from Earl, 1988).

in the IT environment. In the more balanced scenario the top-down initiatives are mixed and combined with technical initiatives, innovation and bottom-up product development and an iterative exchange of views takes place.

There are many situations where the corporate IT function, fully integrated into the planning process, can significantly influence the way a company is able to develop its customer service relationship, its position in the market *vis-à-vis* its competitors, or the company's ability to withstand or go along with economic pressures in the wider market place. This may be through the presentation of timely financial data, the ability of the company to maintain a cost base advantage through efficient processing or information systems, or through the ability to provide products with a technological edge over competitors.

The relationships between the IS and IM components, and between the IT and IM components, are generally to do with issues of absorption of policy directives into the organizational structure; the cultural impact and the cultural constraints on new systems; the impact on, and the impact of, management in the organization. IS to IM involves consideration of the impact of application systems on organizational topology, management relationships and roles, whereas IT and IM interact at the level where IT and the IT functional area is itself folded and incorporated into the organization. Is it a federal structure? Is it centralized? How is it monitored and controlled? Where is IT represented and how does IT respond to and provide day-to-day and longer term input to business units?

So what are the definitions of these three strategic components? **Information systems (IS) strategy** describes the relevance of the corporate business direction, the corporate culture, targets, the economic and competitive business environment to the development of information systems. It is most closely allied to, and should be aligned with, corporate strategy. It is influenced by the positioning of the corporation *vis-à-vis* its competitors in terms of efficiency, product range, product development and culture, size, and the manner in which these are dealt with from a managerial and information management point of view. It is formed on the basis of perceived opportunities, short and longer term. It should be part of the catalyst which facilitates the link between political vision and operational activity. The emphasis in determining IM strategy is at the corporate (or divisional, in a large organization) pinnacle. Nevertheless, this top-down perspective must not be divorced from the bottom-up analysis and contribution based on presently perceived capabilities and resource availability. Information systems strategy formulation is not the sole remit of the boardroom, nor, at the other extreme, can it be successfully researched without good access to those who determine the corporate direction, be it the chief executive or the whole board. Organizational topology will obviously influence the identification and impact of this aspect of the input.

Those who, at board level, determine the direction in which a company will develop, will be imposing their political will on the organization. It is a group of executives who, in many companies, are also involved in exercising that will in an operational sense. Information systems strategy is associated with the interpretation of political imperatives and conversion of these into operational activity. IM strategy is very much related to the thinking of this group, their modus operandi, and to the top-down influence which they exert.

The second component, **information management (IM) strategy**, is, on the other hand, to do with management and staff operational control activity, organizational structure *per se*, and planning. IM strategy is related to the topology of management; that is to say, the relationships, manner and scope of IT operational control and the way in which IT affects or will affect the corporate operations. However, this strategy is not restricted to its impact on the IT department (or IT departments) alone, but also applies to consideration of the shape and management procedures in the user departments where IT has its impact. IT, particularly in service companies (but not being restricted to them), has to be seen as impacting on and fully integrated with the operational and managerial controls in marketing, sales, production and so forth. Formulating the information management strategy can therefore result in the re-evaluation of existing departmental and operational responsibilities, organizational structures and procedures, interdepartmental boundaries, channels of communication, job-descriptions and responsibilities. The long-established and accepted epithet that one does not generally computerize what one has but rather what one *should* have, goes further than definition of a fresh system application specification. It can challenge organizational structure, existing methods of control, managerial responsibilities and departmental protectionism. How desirable changes can be identified and how they take place is a matter of planning and management involvement which cuts across divisional boundaries and goes well beyond the confines of the IT department.

The third component, **information technology (IT) strategy**, describes the IT department operational imperatives. It is concerned with the 'boiler-house', the deliverables and the mechanisms that lie behind them. It includes consideration of the computing facilities, the 'data-processing' department, communications and the IT applications themselves. Such a brief (and incomplete) listing does scant justice to the complexity of the issues that are raised in IT strategy determination. But again, the exercise must go beyond departmental confines for completeness. Supplier security, technological futures, security and the channels of communication with users are part and parcel of the debate.

The IT strategy is also deeply concerned with data; its definition, its flows, utilization, value, availability and security. It is strange that data, its characteristics and usage, is so casually considered and handled in so many corporate environments, not to say so many IT departments. After all, MIS reports support many corporate decisions these days, even where it is only the accounting systems that are automated. These may be operational decisions, production schedules, investment decisions, funding decisions and customer-related decisions. Yet despite the impact all these matters may have on corporate health, there is frequent evidence of inconsistency in data definition (ask two bankers from the same organization how many 'customers' each believes he has), presentation and storage of this elemental matter which underlies and underpins the reporting systems which contribute to corporate success or failure.

Historically, there has been a tendency to identify IT strategy as **the** information management strategy, with consideration of manufacturer, software supplier, operating system, communications protocols and other technical matters being at the forefront of management planning. Crucial though these matters may be, they form just one part of the whole.

Strategic significance

Having then briefly described the three components behind strategy formulation, are they of significance in the real world? They are in several ways. First, they allow students of strategy formulation to understand the **scope** of the exercise with which they are faced. Secondly, they provide a **framework** for the application of real and worthwhile analytical techniques that are both top-down and bottom-up in their approach. They provide the **check-list** for the practitioner. They indicate some of the **interactions** between the conventional IT domain and the users that should be studied and managed in the migration process from system concept through to implementation.

Re-engineering is a term in common use for the process of modifying, updating and replacing information systems. A recent conference on 'Re-engineering the Insurance Industry' (Computers in the City, London) addressed the far-reaching beneficial impact of new processes, new structures, new opportunities, and new attitudes that resulted from a recognition that the technology is only part of the re-engineering process. It also addressed the **problems** of re-engineering – most of which were not technological issues, but those of change management, education and attitudinal development in all parts of the organization. Massive changes are taking place in this industry. What contributors all agreed on was the need for clear corporate leading (the IS component), the huge organizational and managerial impact (the IM component), and the close relationship to these of the technology architectures and development policies which were mainly handled within the IS or IT department. It is not simply a matter of technology upgrade in the re-engineering task; the impact is to be recognized as corporate-wide.

The lessons that can be drawn from the move from the steam-driven charabanc to the use of the internal combustion engine are not too remote to apply to the changes taking place in commerce and industry as new technology and new techniques of handling information are introduced. It is not a matter of actual or potential speed, or engine horse-power in the modern automobile. The concerns we address today are much wider. The social and environmental consequences of the internal combustion engine were hardly foreseen by the inventor of that technology. The least that can be done in the information systems arena is to ensure that those factors which we can already identify as affected by technology applications, play a part in our thinking in the longer term plan. For example, data that contributes to decision making on markets, investment, delivery mechanisms, manufacturing control and so on. A strategic framework provides some chance for identifying and addressing those areas for change before they begin to slow down and threaten the very improvements we are intent on introducing. One is reminded of that early lesson in physics, that the very act of measuring an object causes change in the object being measured. In information technology, one is not fixing a systems template to a static corporate body; one is involving and modifying the very stuff of which the corporate being is made, its personnel policies and practice, its history, its image. And one is changing many aspects of its internal as well as its externally perceived character through the introduction of more and more significant systems.

The important conclusion is, that by determining the strategy for an IT department – the hardware architecture, the communications facilities, application priorities, data definitions and so on – one is not, by that alone, presenting a comprehensive strategy for the handling of corporate information systems. There is much more to it.

Historically, there has been at least a partial overlap between IT application selection and the need to support corporate objectives. The evidence in these situations is that there has been a clear and acceptable projection as to the payoff, the return on the investment or the payback period. In the 'initiation' phase of IT evolution, such benefits are often immediately obvious, and need relatively little

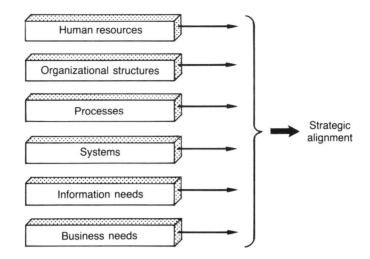

Figure 6.2 Coincidence of business and IT strategy in investment in IT project.

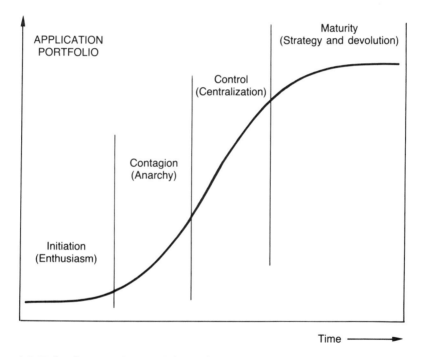

Figure 6.3 IT development S-curve (after Nolan, 1979).

elucidation. However, as the impact of technology becomes more pervasive and systems become more sophisticated and the benefits begin to be described by the harassed accountant as 'intangible', the need for overlap or, preferably, the coincidence of business and IT strategy is more relevant as a justification for proceeding with the investment in an IT project (Figure 6.2). Alignment of information systems development with corporate direction has long been carried out on an opportunistic basis with a looseness of direction which is probably entirely appropriate when a company is on the lower slopes of the S-curve of IT growth (Figure 6.3). (In Figure 6.3 'spend' has been crossed through to show the revision from the original graph by Nolan (1979).) As a company achieves success in IT, the problem changes. As information technology begins to impact and even underpin a company's operations, it becomes that much more critical to

(a) achieve **marginal** increases in efficiency;
(b) avoid expensive or even catastrophic discontinuities either in processes, technological upgrading or communications;
(c) introduce stepwise or incremental advantage over competitors without the technology being a constraint; and
(d) ensure business and systems alignment.

Opportunistic development at an early stage can be a tremendous motivator and an introduction to the advantage of information technology in a company that has not experienced in any depth, its potential contribution to corporate success. However, the advantages reduce as organizations reach IT maturity.

A large public service company, faced with the problem of introducing a significant set of re-engineered information systems, found itself in the middle of an unwelcome takeover bid and, at the same time, a two-stage relocation exercise. These events had a major impact on the company's effectiveness in the introduction of new systems. The coincidence of the changes in the information systems and these other events turned out to be very fortunate. It focused management attention on organizational, personnel and communication issues which otherwise may not have had the attention they merited. It was clear to all concerned that these events should not have been relied upon to drive the changes that would have had to take place when the re-engineered systems were being introduced. Processes were redesigned and organizational changes introduced. Management took a far shorter time to achieve the changes than would have been the case had there been no relocation and no takeover of the company. Strategic planning of information systems removes, or at least reduces, the need for beneficial 'chance elements' to be present to spur a project to success. In the strategic environment, one is better able to steer around some of the traditional stumbling blocks to successful IT implementation.

Advantage over traditional approaches

How does information systems strategic formulation differ from the traditional approaches to the selection of applications, their evaluation and implementation? In one sense it does not, since it builds on traditional techniques of identifying applications and evaluation. Porter's value chain analysis, other comparable and related techniques, or even common sense, can continue to be used for the identification of potential applications.

Traditional approaches to the use of financial-based evaluation procedures for the assessment of system proposals can continue to be used. ROI, NPV, payback periods and other more sophisticated analyses can continue to be applied. However, the strategic approach demands more than these. An approach is needed that is holistic in nature. An approach is needed that recognizes the interaction over time of the technology, organization, staff and management, and corporate direction. These are matters which will not show up in formal economic assessments or IRR calculations (Hochstrasser and Griffiths, 1990; see also Chapter 1).

A bank embarked on the development of a sophisticated new MIS because the board recognized the need to take a defensive approach to the niche competitors and to enhance its own ability to cross-sell between previously uncommunicative divisions. The accounting NPV calculation was carried out, but the real justification was seen by the board to be related to enhanced business development opportunities.

There are parallels in the holistic approach to medicine. In a similar manner to an enlightened approach to health, no single analysis is considered adequate; few diseases demand a single remedy. Psychotherapy, surgery, radiotherapy, occupational therapy and even religion each have relevance to regaining a healthy body. They may be considered with different emphases depending on the diagnosis of the problem and the wisdom, experience and power of the healer. In a similar way the narrow-minded approach labelled 'computerization' has quite rightly given way to 'systems development' where the technology plays only one part; the systems that involve human resources, organizational issues and the corporate and business environments now comprise the other parts.

A planning model

A structured model of the strategic planning process is helpful in describing the way that the process of information systems development can be aligned to the business goals. This is a model which was successfully applied in a large financial services company when it was decided to undertake a major strategic review of the information management support systems. The model (Figure 6.4) is on two levels. The first refers to the corporate dimension; the second, the operational or departmental level. For an organization that has many levels of hierarchy, one is split into autonomous divisions, or one that cannot be pigeon-holed into this simplistic view, the readers can develop their own paradigms. The principles remain consistent whatever the corporate topology. The timescale will be dependent on many factors, not the least being the willingness of senior management to recognize the need for

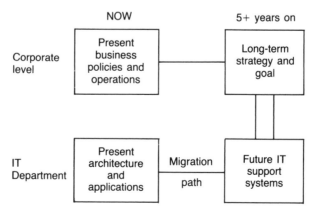

Figure 6.4 Strategy model.

long-term thinking, the relevance of utilizing new technologies in the business as they appear, and the pace of change typical for the industry sector being considered. The route through the model is straightforward.

First, there is the need to understand, at the corporate level, the present activities of the company, its strengths, weaknesses, the environment in which it operates, the culture, functions and products; the top-down (IS) approach. This is not as easy as it may sound. Secondly, with the help of the corporate plan, understanding of unwritten and documented corporate aspirations, projections and a view of the external influencing factors, a scenario needs to be painted of what the organization wants to be. The model requires an analysis of where it is intent on being in its chosen market, what its growth pattern is to be – organic or acquisitive, well defined or poorly defined. The more weakly defined the targets, the greater difficulty there will be in defining the eventual supporting technological and systems architecture to support the business. This is even more difficult to achieve with any significant consensus view. Then one reaches the third stage; defining for five or more years hence, the operational systems that will be required to support the chosen scenario or the range of options that have been defined at corporate level for the same time horizon. Here one can provide a lot of bottom-up (IT to IS) input to the process. Again, in the ideal environment a parallel activity has to take place in the domains of personnel, marketing, sales, finance and so forth. Finally, the migration path needs to be defined; taking us from the present sets of applications and architectures to the scenario that supports and aligns with long-term corporate aspirations.

The last three stages are part of an iterative process which needs to consider the strategic components referred to earlier. Each point on the model needs to be revisited until a feasible set of options can be derived. The alignment, after all, is not only of technology with corporate plans; it is also of technology with sales plans, with product development plans and so on. Indeed, there is in this model the opportunity for the systems options to feed into the corporate targets as well as vice versa. Technology is as likely to facilitate higher volumes and new delivery mechanisms as product development plans are likely to determine systems facilities that are to be put into place. The important thing here is that the participants in this exercise of corporate planning recognize the contribution that can be gained by incorporating bottom-up initiatives, as well as being aware of the need for corporate aspirations to be articulated to those who prepare the system architectures. There is, of course, input to the systems level from outside, from suppliers, competitors, software developers and researchers.

The essential output from the model is the migration path. But this has to be recognized for what it is. It can best be described as a cone (Figure 5.5) – starting from a well-defined point which defines the present set of systems, the existing organization and management characteristics. It broadens out over time – yet with a consistent architecture underpinning the options that lie *in extremis*. Not only is the migration path more flexible in its definition as one progresses through time but it also has to be responsive as the model is revisited year after year. An information systems strategy is not static; it has to be revisited in order to update the assumptions and to respond to internal as well as external changes. The frequency of revisiting the strategy should not need to be more frequent than annually. What should happen, though, is that there should be few surprises, few massive changes in direction in the information systems arena if the planning of the migration path, the alignment of information systems and corporate strategic direction have been thoroughly considered.

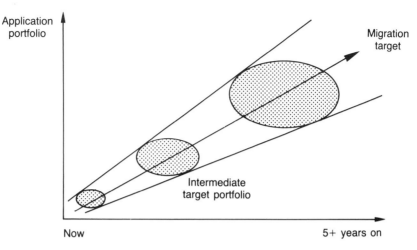

Figure 6.5 The need for early delivery on the migration path.

Scoping the strategic planning exercise

What is involved in scoping an information systems strategy? There are three factors that should be recognized by the individual or group charged with the analysis and preparation of the strategy. They are:

(a) the components of the IS, the IT and the IM strategies referred to earlier;
(b) the need for certain skills to be present in the strategy team itself, which will facilitate the presentation and ultimate acceptance of the plan by sponsors, users and technologists alike, and ensure a recognition of the interaction of the various issues which stretch beyond simple consideration of the technology alone;
(c) the need for recognition of an increased level of risk associated with any systems investment if any of the component issues are not addressed during the strategy formulation exercise.

The process of strategy formulation requires a broad management perspective of the activities of the company within and outside the information systems function. It will probably involve the secondment of individuals who can be least spared from their normal duties. The team needs high-level sponsorship – preferably at board level, and with secondees of merit. In one company, membership of this team was seen as a near essential staging post *en route* for a directorship. Most strategies cannot be developed on a two-hours-per-week basis involvement from user departments. The battle to achieve such commitment from users is not an easy one unless another factor is adequately dealt with – that is, the educational requirements of those who regard the whole exercise as over-kill or irrelevant. Research by the writer has identified a number of companies where this last point has never been totally solved. Maybe there will always be the sceptics whose conversion to the benefits of strategic planning will only come when they are touched by the improved quality of the deliverables. That is a serious point and is a factor to be borne in mind by planners. It is crucial that if a strategic plan and those who deliver the technology are to have and retain credibility, then there should be identifiable islands along the migration route; islands which represent solid advantage-producing deliverables to the users. The intention of a long-term information systems plan is not, after all, to deliver the all-singing, all-dancing fully integrated system in ten years' time. The plan has to be able to cope with short-term business imperatives, windows of opportunity, pre-existing business needs and 'mandatory' projects of a regulatory or defensive nature that cannot wait for nirvana.

Flexibility and adaptability

Flexibility and adaptability are two key attributes to be associated with successful execution of strategic planning exercises and their deliverables. There ought to be flexibility and adaptability in three senses.

1. The manner in which the strategic planning exercise is conducted should be carefully considered. There is no fixed formula or methodology applicable to all companies.
2. The deliverables should incorporate a flexibly designed set of proposals which will permit adaptation to business imperatives and changes in emphasis and design over time.
3. The infrastructure or architecture presented at the end should be such that it is not invalidated by any predictable changes in company strategic emphasis or foreseeable developments in technology.

These are expanded on below.

It is often asked whether there is a methodology one can utilize for undertaking this important task. There are a number of learned texts on the issues to be addressed but the author is presently unaware of any comprehensive published methodology that has wide application. There is no fixed methodology for achieving a comprehensive information systems strategy. There are a number of guidelines and some techniques one can employ for different purposes. In practice, all sorts of factors come into play, not the least of which are the size, industry sector and cultural characteristics of the organization being addressed. At a micro level the approach will depend on the extent to which good user liaison and understanding of the issues across all potential users can be established.

The strategy team should be sensitive to detail, but avoid the danger of becoming so concerned and overwhelmed by it to the cost of a long-term view and the need for objective and lateral thinking. The information systems manager of a brewery highlighted this when explaining why one apparently major area had been cut out of the long-term planning exercise. The reason was that the excluded area was such a political hot-potato that, had it not been excluded, no significant progress would ever have been made on any other information systems matter within the brewery complex. That was considered too high a price to pay. Nevertheless, it was anticipated that this matter would at some future point be reintroduced into the debate. Hence, the plans for the rest of the organization were drawn up so as to permit later linkage to the contentious area.

There should be what can be termed 'discrete' use of analysis techniques such as data modelling and data flow analysis. Yet these and other tools should only be utilized at this stage to the extent that they provide an input to strategic thinking. They may be utilized to a higher level of refinement in the context of systems development itself, but should be limited in this first stage.

Data modelling, for example, can provide some valuable insights into the scope for product development and customer-based service relationships, which feed into the high-level consideration of product strategies and the extent to which the IT can contribute to competitive advantage. A further technique that can be applied in the strategic planning phase is that of 'goal decomposition'. Here, the analyst identifies, at each level of an organization, the way that the functional activities in that division, department or functional area directly contribute towards achievement of the corporate goals. In this analysis, one considers not only the processes that are undertaken in each area and their relevance to the overall (top level) goals. The analysis will also review, for example, the extent of duplication of effort, situations where there is interruption of communications without adding value and the appropriateness of tasks to functional area (should they be carried out elsewhere?), and there will be a search for situations where functional activity actually works against the corporate goals. Examples of the latter category might be where there are particular inefficiencies of processing or where limitations are placed (by dint of historical practice) on targets ever being achieved. Thus, in the use of techniques, there should be flexibility in the choice and a pragmatic approach to the depth of analysis required for this early stage in the development cycle of application selection, development and implementation.

A second aspect of the flexibility factor needs to be seen in the design of the infrastructure, the architecture, the technological groundwork. As has already been observed, the migration path can be said to exist within a cone (Figure 6.5); that is, the long-term scenario is a fuzzy picture which will only pan out with clarity at some point along the development path. In the meantime, there will be technological changes and environmental changes which will impact on developments and application selection. At a recent seminar given by one of the major manufacturers of hardware, a six-month lead time for the introduction of major new functions into personal systems was suggested to be the norm. The lead times are getting shorter. Perhaps the most difficult aspect of the strategy determination for IT is the laying down of an architecture or a series of linked architectures which are neither likely to become redundant, nor be inadequate to cope with these changes. For example, an open systems architecture is, for many companies, still too immature for consideration at the present time as a base for technical development. Nevertheless, a legitimate view may be that it will, within the next five years or so, become sufficiently attractive to justify a technical migration from a proprietary architecture. In this case, the strategic migration path and the attendant rules should permit developments that are capable of being transferred, in due course, to the preferred long-term technical base without inordinate further disruption or cost.

The 'Portakabin' approach

It is not unusual for company management to say that today is not the day for initiating a strategic planning exercise for information systems. The reasons are legion, but the most common is that there are too many other things to do which take higher priority. Is it ever the best time? The decision would be a great deal easier to make if it was not felt that the very act of strategic planning held up projects that were already underway. It is a little bit like trying to stop busy shoppers in the High Street by giving away £10 notes. People do not think, or perhaps do not recognize, that it is worth them stopping! One method of overcoming the problem is through better senior management education into the benefits that can be gained through strategic alignment of systems with corporate goals. Another way is to reassure senior management that putting a strategic plan into operation does not mean that all the presently urgent projects will be postponed for another 12 months (at the least). The Portakabin approach to systems management describes the parameters that have to be in place in order to allow existing projects to keep moving without holding up the strategic planning or pushing it off the rails.

The sales director of a financial services organization, having had the outline plan for the implementation of systems over the following five years explained to him, expressed in his broad Australian accent that it seemed like 'An answer to a maiden's prayer'. It is imperative that a strategic approach to information management systems does not paint so idealistic a picture that it loses credibility before it has begun, or before the first line of code has been written. The need for a progressive delivery of applications over time has been noted earlier. There have to be islands to identify and land on in the long sea crossing of the total migration path. More than that, there has to be a capacity within a strategic plan to be able to cope with immediate business imperatives. It is in response to this last issue that the concept of the Portakabin approach to IT systems has been developed (Figure 6.6).

It would be most unusual if, in an organization that was developing a strategic plan for information systems, there was not a residue of existing projects in varying states of completion, and a portfolio of applications-in-waiting. Sometimes it is the sheer weight of outstanding projects and historical delays that have given rise to the making of a strategic plan. Almost certainly, the portfolio of existing projects will include some applications which are urgent, long promised but not delivered, or mandatory. How does one treat these applications? Or, more critically, how does one treat the users whose expectations are about to be dashed as the strategic plan introduces a yet longer delay to their fulfilment?

There will inevitably be application development projects that require to be progressed while the longer term projects are prepared. The danger that arises when the pressures are put on the IS department to deliver short term, is that short-term

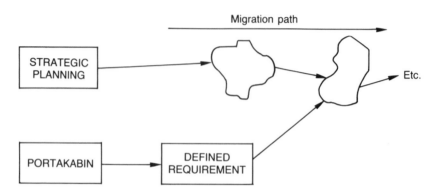

Figure 6.6 Portakabin redundancy.

projects becomes the norm. When one short-term project is finished, another is waiting. Resources become diverted from the mainstream, strategic direction. Interest in a long-term architecture and the need to develop an integrated and solid base infrastructure becomes subordinated to a short-term project culture. This results in the organization being back where it started, with 'He who shouts loudest gets his way'; sometimes known as 'decibel planning'.

In the building world, the Portakabin provides a temporary home for the displaced department, the overflow from the expanding office, and while former buildings are demolished and the new ones are made ready. Following the Portakabin approach in building is one way to overcome the inevitable conflict between the need to respond to business imperatives and the need to work along a well-thought-out, consistent migration path that is aligned to long-term business goals. However, the Portakabin is not designed to facilitate wholesale avoidance of the strategic imperatives. It is designed as a drug to relieve short-term symptoms of distress. It must be administered under supervision or it can become addictive. A problem exists when short-termism becomes the norm and the migration path, if it can still be called such, is neglected. If this problem becomes a real danger, then there is a need to call into question the quality of the analysis and conclusions from the strategic planning exercise, and whether the scoping of that exercise was adequately stated.

It may be useful to take the analogy of the Portakabin further. If the buildings are to stay for more than a brief period then they will be fitted out with mains electricity, plumbed in, and will be operated in 'house style'. Only in that way will the eventual migration back to the mainstream operational environment be easily, cheaply and successfully accomplished.

There are a number of principles that can be applied to the Portakabin approach. They are not mandatory, but the consequences of modification or ignoring them should be appreciated.

1. There must be a business imperative that overrules the priority accorded the related project within the strategic plan. Alternatively, the strategic plan may not yet be prepared and/or there are business or regulatory reasons for not holding up the development any longer.

2. Portakabin-type projects should be largely resourced without disturbing the pace of progress on the migration path for all other applications. This can sometimes be achieved by buying in resources, outsourcing and by the use of packages where, in other circumstances, in-house development might have been the norm.

3. Portakabin-type applications, if they do not have a built-in total redundancy, should be developed or implemented in such a way that they can, in due course, be brought back into the strategic architecture. This has to be planned to take place with the minimum disruption. Factors that can help here are the use of common data definitions in line with strategic projects, the use of a common hardware or systems base, and the use or availability of interfaces which will permit exchange, uploading or downloading of data to and from the strategic systems platform.

4. Finally, short-term Portakabin-type projects should never provide the basis for selection of a new systems architecture.

If the conflicts between the strategic planners and the advocates of the Portakabin applications become too great, then there may be only one conclusion. Rework the strategic plan.

Prioritizing projects

Finally, what is the relationship between the strategic planning of information systems and the problems of selecting and prioritizing applications for development? Evaluation of projects was the topic of the survey reported in Chapter 3 where the general conclusion was that most organizations assess or evaluate projects on too few criteria. Over 60% of respondents used cost–benefit analysis as their first priority, but more than 60% only used one or two criteria for their evaluation (see Willcocks and Lester, 1991). Hochstrasser and Griffiths (1990) found that limited criteria pointed a majority of investments in IT into improving the efficiency of internal operations.

How then does evaluation of projects and the methods used tie in with strategic planning?

When a strategic planning exercise is undertaken, there are a number of methods for identifying applications and projects that should or could be part of the eventual strategic plan. These have been referred to earlier. Having completed the selection of applications that will support corporate goals and which are aligned with the corporate objectives, one has in effect already carried out much of the evaluation that is required to allocate a priority on the migration path. The more strongly a particular application underpins the strategic aims of an organization, the higher up the priority list it should be. Each of the criteria listed above forms part of the **strategic** evaluation exercise and to that extent helps determine what priority should be accorded a particular application.

There are other criteria that can be used for assessment (see also Chapters 4 and 5, and Ward *et al.*, 1990):

1. Is the project mandatory, either in regulatory terms (e.g. to meet the requirements of a Statutory Regulatory Order) or in defensive terms (as a response to competitive pressures)?
2. Is it providing the infrastructure for other parts of the strategic plan?
3. Are there internal dependences that should be recognized in the ordering of projects?
4. Are organizational changes anticipated or required which require system developments?

None of these evaluation criteria feeds directly off the result of an ROI or NPV calculation. Nonetheless, the accountant's method of evaluating projects still has its place, though it is further down the ranking of evaluation criteria than has been the case in the past. Strategic planning is not the same as ranking the costs of boxes, software and personnel against quantifiable benefits. One might venture to suggest (and research supports this view) that too many financial evaluations are less than scientific, often being designed to present the desired result rather than a totally unbiased conclusion based on consideration of **all** the costs and **all** benefits. The motive underlying many presentations of financial justification is that the project will be 'good for the business', whatever precise(?) ROI comes out in the wash. This must not be seen as an argument against an accountant's approach to project evaluation. It is making the point, as argued throughout his book, that, with strategic justification for a project, measures such as payback periods, ROI, IRR and NPV become of less significance than accorded them in the past. Matters of strategic alignment should take on a more significant role. These matters are in turn, and as has already been described, associated with organizational, management, competitive and cost-base issues to list but a few of the considerations which determine the place of a project in the strategic plan and its priority within it.

Conclusions

The real value of strategy formulations for IT is to be found in the context of the corporate information management strategy. The overall message of strategic planning in the information systems arena is the need to take an holistic view of the role and impact of the technology. There has to be a recognition that when one talks of the benefits from alignment of information technology with corporate goals, one is talking about alignment of policies of organizational shape, human resource management, sales, marketing, finance and production. The analytical techniques for examining data and its flows no longer form the sole province of technologists – they can contribute to the strategic formulation. The formulators of strategies can usefully apply themselves to the three sets of components, each of which interacts with the others. IT, IS and IM strategies each need to be considered if the strategy is to have chance of long-term validity in its development into practical working systems. The users are not just the recipients of new applications – they are party to application planning and development and will be affected directly by organizational changes and management restructuring that may need to flow from these developments. Priority setting, evaluation and ranking of projects is no longer the sole remit of the accountants or any other party – they are to be set in response to corporate direction and corporate priorities. And finally, even within the strategic framework, short-term business imperatives have to be handled constructively. Strategists need to be able to deliver, and, when necessary, they need tools such as the Portakabin-type approach to help them deliver early.

References

Ciborra, C. (1991) From thinking to tinkering: the grassroots of strategic information systems. In *Proceedings of the Twelfth International Conference on Information Systems*, 16–18 December, New York, pp. 283–91.

Earl, M. (1988) *Management Strategies for Information Technology*, Prentice-Hall, London.

Hochstrasser, B. and Griffiths, C. (eds) (1990) *Regaining Control of IT Investments: A handbook for Senior UK Management*, Kobler Unit, Imperial College, London.

Nolan, R. (1979) Managing the crisis in data processing. *Harvard Business Review*, March–April, 261–5.

Porter, M. (1985) *Competitive Advantage*, Free Press, New York.

Ward, J., Griffiths, P. and Whitmore P. (1990) *Strategic Planning for Information Systems*, Wiley, Chichester.

Willcocks, L. and Lester, S. (1991) Information systems investments: evaluation at the feasibility stage of projects. *Technovation*, Autumn, **11**, (5), 283–302.

7

Assessing the value of strategic information technology investments

Brian L. Dos Santos

Introduction

Today, information technology (IT) is extremely important to the smooth operation of many organizations. Firms in many industries would be seriously affected if their IT-based systems failed even for short periods. In addition to being important to operations, IT-based systems are just as important in the control and planning functions (Bruns and McFarlan, 1987). There now is a growing awareness that IT investments can be of strategic importance to a firm, that is, IT investments can improve a firm's competitive position or allow the firm to become more vulnerable to competitive forces (Parsons, 1983; Benjamin *et al.*, 1984; Cash and Konsynski, 1985; Clemons and Row, 1988). The list of publicized cases where IT investments have enabled firms to gain a competitive advantage includes investments by such firms as American Airlines, American Hospital Supply Corporation, Avis, Bank America, Citicorp, Digital Equipment Corporation, and General Electric (Cash and Konsynski, 1985; Ives and Learmonth, 1984; Porter and Millar, 1985; Strassmann, 1988; Wiseman, 1985).

Information Management: The evaluation of information systems investments.
Edited by Leslie Willcocks.
Published in 1994 by Chapman & Hall. ISBN 0 412 41540 2.

A number of frameworks have been proposed to help managers identify strategic IT (SIT) applications (Clemons and Row, 1987; Ives and Learmonth, 1984; Porter and Millar, 1985; Vitale *et al.*, 1986). The conceptual frameworks that allow managers to identify IT applications which *may* lead to firm-specific strategic advantage opportunities, do not help managers make these investments decisions. Recently, senior managers in many organizations have begun to question whether information technology (IT) investments add value to the firm (Bittlestone, 1990; EDP Analyzer, 1985; Strassmann, 1988). To add to the problem, investments in strategic systems tend to be large and risky (McNurlin and Sprague, 1989).

Justifying IT investments has been and continues to be a serious problem (Bittlestone, 1990; Dos Santos, 1991). It is widely recognized that traditional capital budgeting approaches are not easily used to justify IT investments and, therefore, alternative approaches have been suggested (Gremillion and Pyburn, 1985; Keen and Scott-Morton, 1978; Keen, 1981; Clemons, 1991). Corporate financial theory predicts that managers make investment decisions to maximize the value of the firm. Most of the recommended approaches, however, do not explicitly consider this objective.

Today, discounted cash flow (DCF) techniques are widely used to make capital investment decisions (Mason and Merton, 1985). However, as argued in earlier chapters, DCF techniques have been criticized because of their inability to properly value investments that are strategic in nature (Gold, 1976; Hayes and Garvin, 1982) and, consequently, it has been suggested that 'gut feel' or 'intuition' be used (Cash *et al.*, 1988). Failure to use financial techniques, however, means that SIT investments will be *ad hoc*. Besides, frequently, senior management insists that financial analysis be conducted for large capital outlays. In this chapter we assume that financial analysis must be used to justify IT investments.

Finance academicians have taught the net present value (NPV) method as the correct procedure to use in making capital budgeting decisions. The NPV approach is described in most introductory finance and capital budgeting textbooks (e.g. Brealey and Myers, 1988) and will not be discussed here. The theory suggests that only positive NPV projects should be funded because a positive NPV project will increase the value of the firm. However, using the NPV approach to evaluate strategic investments presents a number of problems that we shall discuss later. As a result of these problems, SIT investments frequently will not have a positive NPV, yet, they may be valuable investments for the firm.

To add to the approaches developed in earlier chapters by Ward and Peters, we show how financial analysis can be used to evaluate investments in IT that could have a strategic impact on the firm. In the following section the key characteristics of strategic IT projects that are relevant to the investment decision are discussed. We then discuss why NPV analysis is not always appropriate for assessing SIT projects, and in the next section, we show how options-pricing models can be useful in conducting a financial analysis of SIT investments. A case where one of these models was used is described and the use of these models is demonstrated with a numerical example. The impacts of project characteristics on SIT investment decisions are discussed and conclusions are presented in the final section.

Characteristics of strategic IT investments

IT investments can have a strategic impact on the firm by enabling the firm to obtain higher returns than its competitors; that is, these investments can enable a firm to gain competitive advantages. Throughout this chapter the terms IT and IS are used interchangeably. An IT investment can provide a firm with large returns by enabling it to develop new products (e.g. Merrill Lynch's use of IT in developing its Cash Management Account), or enabling it to develop or maintain any advantages it currently enjoys. There are numerous examples of the latter type of IT investment in the information systems literature (e.g. Citicorp's ATM network (Glaser, 1988); American Airlines' SABRE system (Copeland and McKenney, 1988)). These investments may provide a firm with competitive advantages only until competitors are able to develop their own systems. Impediments, faced by competitors, that make rapid imitation of the investment difficult, determine the length of time early investors obtain competitive advantages (Feeny and Ives, 1990). Timing may or may not be important, depending on the size of the advantage and how difficult it is for competitors to gain the same benefits from the investment. For example, early investments in automated teller machines (ATMs) in the United States enabled banks that were early adopters of ATMs, and large banks, to gain competitive advantages (Dos Santos and Peffers, 1991a).

Strategic IT investments have the following characteristics.

1. Only the first firm, or the first few firms to successfully complete the project will gain large returns from the investment (Dos Santos *et al.*, 1991; Dos Santos and Peffers, 1991b). With such projects, there may be large learning curve effects, so that by investing early, the firm stays ahead of its competitors for a long time; or, by investing early, the firm is able to capture other assets that are not easily available to followers. For example, the firm might be able to capture the best customers or the most desirable locations or markets. With these projects, if the investment is delayed, the opportunity may be lost irretrievably. We refer to such projects as **now-or-never** projects. With a 'now-or-never' project, timing is critical. A delay in the decision to develop and implement the system is likely to greatly reduce the benefits that are obtained. American Airlines' investment in the SABRE system is an example of a 'now-or-never' project (Copeland and McKenney, 1988).

2. The investment will enable the firm to take advantage of unique firm characteristics, allowing the firm to gain a long-term advantage because structural differences among competitors are such that competing firms are unable to obtain the same benefits even if they implement similar systems (Clemons and Row, 1987; Dos Santos and Peffers, 1991b). In this case, a delay in the development and implementation of the system may not have a dramatic impact on the value of the system. In this chapter, by value, we mean economic value. For example, American Hospital Supply's ASAP order entry system took advantage of the firm's centralized structure, which was different from that of its major competitors (Vitale, 1986a). Otis Elevators' investment in OTISLINE is another example of such a SIT investment (Stoddard, 1988). Frequently, such projects are not 'now-or-never'.

In most cases, investments in strategic systems are large and the amount to be invested is difficult to estimate accurately because the costs are affected by the capabilities provided by the system, and these capabilities are seldom known in advance. Besides, the technologies used to develop the system also affect costs. If the technologies are ones with which the firm has little or no experience, it is difficult to predict development costs accurately (Dos Santos, 1991). Another important aspect of development costs is how these costs are spread over the development period. In some cases, a large portion of the costs must be committed early. Such is the case when new hardware, software or communication technologies must be acquired in order for the project to proceed. In other cases, development can proceed with existing assets, requiring any new acquisitions to be made at a later date. Large expenditures early in the development process can have a significant effect on the viability of the project, particularly so if the investment is in assets that are not easily sold or deployed elsewhere.

Strategic IT investment decisions

The nature of a project's benefits and costs may require that managers make a commitment to the project immediately. In the case of 'now-or-never' projects, it is frequently necessary to make such a commitment, because it is important to complete the project quickly. Also, in cases where a large portion of a project's costs are incurred at an early date, managers effectively make a commitment to the project with the initial investment. This is because, after the large initial outlay, future funding for the project is assured since the incremental costs are less than the projected benefits, even though the project as a whole may lose money.

Owing to the uncertainty associated with SIT projects, these investments should only be made after careful and thorough investigation. Vitale (1986b) suggests that understanding the risks inherent in SIT projects is critical if these investments are not to have a negative impact on the firm. McNurlin and Sprague (1989) suggest that since SIT projects result in a new product or service being provided, traditional project management techniques do not work. They suggest that a strategic system must first be created in prototype form, tested on a small scale by the users, and only then must full-scale development be undertaken. We refer to the initial investment (for example, investment in a prototype) that a firm may make prior to deciding on full-scale development as a preliminary investigation (PI).

A PI could help management decide whether investment in a full-scale system is warranted. A PI may involve the development of a prototype to help estimate the benefits and costs of a full-scale system, or a PI may involve almost complete development of the actual system, to determine its impact over a limited time period or on a limited set of users (McNurlin and Sprague, 1989). Conducting a PI will reduce cost and/or benefit uncertainty. The remainder of this chapter describes how financial analysis of SIT projects should be conducted.

Financial analysis

Adding to the criticisms expressed in earlier chapters, there are two major problems that arise in using the NPV approach to evaluate strategic projects:

1. It is difficult to estimate a project's cash flows (Clemons, 1991). Some project benefits are difficult to quantify, while others are difficult to estimate accurately.

Consequently, discount rates chosen are high. Most of the past literature has dealt with the evaluation of systems that affect the performance of individuals or small groups within the organization (Keen, 1981; Gremillion and Pyburn, 1985). The effects of such projects are primarily observed on individual and small group processes. With SIT projects, the impacts are frequently at the firm or strategic business unit level. This should make it easier to estimate benefits in terms with which managers are familiar. In the case of *ex-post* evaluation studies, IT investments are now being evaluated using such measures as return on investment, changes in income, stock prices and market share (Banker and Kauffman, 1988, Harris and Katz, 1991; Dos Santos *et al.*, 1991). Hence, for SIT projects, it may be easier to estimate the financial impact of the resulting system. Of course, future cash flows from these projects are likely to be highly uncertain. This, as we discuss later, does not mean that NPV analysis can or should always be used to make these decisions.

2. The project is treated as a black box and, therefore, ignores the fact that future management actions can significantly affect the value of the project (Kester, 1984; Myers, 1984). During the course of a SIT project, for example, management may make decisions to expand or reduce the scope of the project, abandon it, etc. In the case of SIT projects, management may decide to undertake a PI and, based on the results, determine whether a full-scale project should be undertaken. The PI could be treated as another project. However, its value cannot be computed using the NPV approach because its value is determined by the full-scale project, which may or may not be undertaken. The NPV approach does not consider the decisions that managers can make during the development life of the project.

As a result, the NPV approach undervalues the project.

'Now-or-never' projects

From here on, a distinction is made between the costs incurred to develop and implement a system (referred to as the **development costs** of the project) and the **benefits** of the resulting system. The development costs include all the expenses incurred in getting the system up and running. The benefits are the net cash flows after the system is in use. The costs incurred while the system is being used are included in determining benefits. Therefore, here, benefits include all costs incurred while the system is in use, including maintenance costs.

For 'now-or-never' projects, the decision to invest must be made immediately, because most of the benefits go to 'early movers'. Financially, a 'now-or-never' project is one that has a positive NPV if undertaken right away, and a negative (or zero) NPV if delayed; i.e. by not investing now, the opportunity to invest in the project disappears. For 'now-or-never' projects, it is appropriate to make decisions using the NPV approach, i.e. the net present value must be positive for the project to be funded. The project NPV is determined by the expected development costs and benefits of the projects.

Frequently, it is difficult to estimate the development costs and the benefits with reasonable accuracy. Many costs are difficult to anticipate, much less quantify. For example, the human and organizational costs incurred in making the changes necessary to take advantage of the new system are difficult to anticipate and quantify. Anticipating the benefits and quantifying them also poses many problems because the organization may have little relevant experience to draw upon. For 'now-or-never' projects, when development costs and benefits are difficult to quantify, non-financial methods may have to be used. Numerous approaches have been suggested in the literature (Parker *et al.*, 1988; Silk, 1990; Strassmann, 1988). They will not be reviewed here; the reader is referred to the original sources, and other chapters in this book. It should be noted, however, that financial analysis methods, because they explicitly consider project risk, could be helpful, together with other methods.

Projects that can be delayed

For projects that can be delayed, however, decisions based upon NPV analysis may not be appropriate. Let us assume that a NPV analysis is conducted and that the project has a positive NPV. Hence, investment in the project is justified. However, we know that although the project has a positive NPV, because the development costs and benefits are uncertain, the project could actually turn out to be a loser if development costs turn out to be higher than expected and benefits lower.

For projects that can be delayed, a positive NPV does not necessarily mean that management should go ahead and invest in the project. Delaying such a project typically means a temporary loss in benefits that the firm would have received if the project had been undertaken sooner. However, delaying the project may prevent taking on a bad project. Therefore, when projects can be delayed, it might be prudent to delay investment if, by doing so, management could avoid making a bad investment.

In most instances, however, SIT projects will have negative NPVs. Negative NPV estimates are common for strategic investments for a number of reasons, including the fact that when these projects are treated as black boxes the high-risk nature of the investment results in the use of very high discount rates (Myers, 1984; Hayes and Garvin, 1982; Kester, 1984). However, SIT projects that have a negative NPV should not be rejected right away. Future uncertainties mean that negative NPV projects could turn out to be valuable if events turn out favourably and, therefore, may turn out to be good investments.

For projects that can be delayed, regardless of the outcome of NPV analysis, cost and benefit uncertainties may be reduced by undertaking a PI. By conducting a PI, management may be able to mitigate losses and take advantage of good fortune as uncertainty is resolved. Frequently, however, a PI may generate little tangible value on its own. Therefore, the NPV of a PI as a separate investment would be negative. However, a PI could be very valuable if it affects the decision to undertake investment in the full-scale system. The real value of a PI, therefore, is determined by its impact on the decision to invest in the full-scale project.

Conducting a PI can be viewed as follows: instead of investing in the project (i.e. the benefit-producing stage) right away, the firm can choose to invest in a PI which will enable the firm to invest in the project if it appears that it will be profitable to do so and to abandon it if it appears that it will not be profitable. The choice faced by a manager making a SIT investment decision is similar to the choice faced by a stock market investor. An investor can choose to buy a firm's stock or a **call option** on the firm's stock. A call option is a 'contract that conveys a right to buy a designated stock at a designated price (i.e. the **exercise price**) during a stipulated period'. The buyer of a call option obtains the right to buy the stock, but is not obliged to do so. The option will only be exercised if events turn out favourably, i.e. the stock price exceeds the exercise price.

Conducting a PI provides management with an option to invest in the project at a later date, if it appears to be a profitable investment at that time. A difference between owning a stock and a call option is that stock owners are eligible to receive dividends (and other payouts) from the firm while owners of a call option are not eligible to receive these payouts. Similarly, completing the full-scale project results in benefits (i.e. cash flows) while completing a PI may not result in any 'real' benefits. Hence, direct investment in the project is similar to investment in the stock, while investment in a PI is similar to investment in a call option on the stock.

The price of a firm's stock is determined by the present value of the expected future cash flows to stockholders. By investing in stocks an investor obtains the right to future cash flows. Hence, DCF models can be used to price stocks. DCF models, however, are inappropriate for pricing options. The models that have been developed to price securities options are quite different from DCF models. Options-pricing models have recently been proposed to determine the value of investments that are strategic, or investments where there is considerable management flexibility in the way the project proceeds (Myers, 1984; Kester, 1984; Mason and Merton, 1985; Dos Santos, 1991). These models may be useful in determining the value of a PI . The use of options-pricing models is discussed in the next section.

For projects that have a positive NPV, there is a temptation to immediately invest in the project. However, by delaying investment, the firm may avoid making a bad investment. Assume that the project can be delayed by a year, during which time a PI will be conducted. Then management should delay investment in the project and invest in a PI if the following relationship holds:

$$V_{pi} - C_{pi} > NPV \quad \text{for NPV} > 0$$

where: V_{pi} = value of a preliminary investigation
C_{pi} = present value of the cost of a preliminary investigation
NPV = the net present value of the project if investment in the full-scale system is made today.

For projects that have a negative NPV, investment in a PI is justified if the value of the option generated by conducting a PI is greater than the cost of the PI. Hence, management should invest in a PI, if the following relationship holds:

$$V_{pi} - C_{pi} > 0 \quad \text{for NPV} \leq 0.$$

In the next section, we describe how V_{pi} can be determined for SIT investment projects.

Using options-pricing models

The term **exercising** a call option refers to the act of trading in the option for the stock on which it is written, by paying the exercise price. Black and Scholes (1973) are responsible for the options-pricing model upon which most of the literature in the options-pricing area is based. In order to price a stock option using the Black and Scholes model, it is necessary (and sufficient) to have reasonably accurate estimates of the following variables: (1) the current price of the stock; (2) the time before expiration of the option contract; (3) the instantaneous variance rate of the price of the stock; (4) the exercise price; and (5) the risk-free rate of return (Sharpe, 1985).

By analogy, to determine the value of a PI (V_{pi}), reasonably accurate estimates of the following are needed: (1) the present value (PV) of the expected benefits from immediate investment in the project; (2) the time beyond which the benefits of the investment are expected to change significantly (i.e. the time before which the investment decision must be made); (3) the instantaneous variance rate of project benefits; (4) the expected development costs for the full-scale project; and (5) the risk-free rate of return.

The model developed by Black and Scholes to price (value) a call option is:

$$V_{pi} = P\,\mathbf{N}(d_1) - X\,e^{-rt}\,\mathbf{N}(d_2) \tag{7.1}$$

where: P = the current price of the stock. Here, it is the present value of the expected benefits (i.e. cash flows after the system is implemented) of the project if it is undertaken today. It is what the firm would be willing to pay today for the implemented system. The present value of the development costs may be more (or less) than what the firm would be willing to pay today

X = the exercise price of the option. In this context, it is the expected development cost of the full-scale project

$\mathbf{N}(\bullet)$ = the cumulative normal probability density function, and

$$d_1 \quad = \frac{\ln(P/X) + rt + \sigma^2(t/2)}{\sigma\sqrt{t}}$$

$$d_2 \quad = \frac{\ln(P/X) + rt - \sigma^2(t/2)}{\sigma\sqrt{t}}$$

t = time to exercise the option. In this context, it is the time the firm has to develop the system, without the benefits being greatly reduced

r = the risk-free rate of return, normally assumed to be the rate of return on government-backed securities

$\ln$ = natural logarithm function

σ^2 = variance per period of the rate of return on the stock. Here, it is a measure of the uncertainty of the rate of return on the project.

This model, or one of its variants, can be used to determine the value of a PI. In the next section, we describe an actual IT investment decision where this model was helpful in getting a PI funded.

An application

A large firm in the agricultural products industry was contemplating the development of a system to support its telemarketing function. In addition to a regular salesforce, the firm operated a telemarketing salesforce. The telemarketing salesforce dealt with the smaller accounts, while the regular salesforce was responsible for the large accounts. Although the individual accounts that the telemarketing group dealt with were small, they accounted for a sizeable percentage of sales (the actual numbers are confidential). Among the customers supported by the telemarketing salesforce, some were much larger than others and the products and quantities purchased by different customers varied considerably.

The IT project being contemplated would enable the telemarketing salesforce to target their sales calls more effectively by enabling them to determine whom to call, based upon such factors as customer buying behaviour, local weather, the firm's product promotions, etc. The cost of the system was relatively easy to estimate since the bulk of the anticipated expenses were on new hardware and software that would be purchased from vendors. This firm currently is the only firm in the industry with a telemarketing function. Consequently, it was felt that the sales growth potential for the telemarketing salesforce was great since this firm was the only one that directly serviced these customers. However, because competitors did not have such a salesforce, it was felt that the project was not a 'now-or-never' project.

The telemarketing group had a problem getting this project approved. The benefits were very difficult to estimate accurately. If everything worked out very well, it was felt that the system could help the group's sales to increase by 150%. However, if their worst fears were realized, the system would have no effect on sales and, instead, would simply increase the time per sales call. These were believed to be extreme outcomes. In the former case, this would result in benefits of $75 in each of the next three years, while in the latter it would result in a loss of $10 in each of the next three years (figures and indicative only). The cost of implementing this system was estimated to be $90. NPV analysis indicated that the project should not be funded.

Because the project was not 'now-or-never', a possible alternative was to implement a prototype that would be tested in one sales region. This prototype could be easily implemented and, for one region, could be run on existing hardware for a short period of time. The incremental cost of the prototype was estimated to be $16. This prototype, it was believed, would provide a much better indication of the benefits of the complete system. However, the tangible benefits of the prototype itself were not sufficient to allow the prototype project to be funded on its own. Its contribution to the decision on the full-scale system was necessary to gain approval for the prototype. In this case, the value of the prototype was estimated using an options-pricing model. Its value as a call option, using estimates provided by managers, was shown to be much greater than $16. After management was convinced that the analysis was carried out properly using the options model, the prototype project was funded. In this case, the value of the prototype as a call option was considerable because there was a high probability that the full-scale project could prove to be a mistake, i.e. to have a negative NPV. This project would never have been approved without valuing the PI as a call option.

An alternative options model

In many instances, prior to undertaking a PI, the cost of a SIT project is difficult to estimate accurately. This often is the case when the project involves a new techology for the firm. In such cases, there is a difference between a stock option and an option on future investment in a SIT project. The development cost, X, is uncertain. The exercise price of a stock option is fixed at the time the option is purchased while the development cost of the project is uncertain at the time investment in a PI is being considered. Development costs are affected by the outcome of a PI, market conditions, etc. In such cases, the Black and Scholes model and most of its variants are not useful in determining V_{pi}. Undertaking a PI gives a firm the option to exchange risky development costs for risky benefits. Based upon the pioneering work of Black and Scholes, Margrabe (1978) developed a model that determines the value of an option to exchange one risky asset for another. For SIT projects involving risky costs and benefits, Margrabe's model will provide a more accurate estimate of the value of a PI (Dos Santos, 1991). Using Margrabe's model, the value of the option to delay investment in a SIT project is computed as follows:

$$V_{pi} = B\,\mathbf{N}(d_1) - C\,\mathbf{N}(d_2) \tag{7.2}$$

Where: B = present value of the expected benefits of the project if it is undertaken today

C = present value of the expected development cost of the project if it is undertaken today

$d_1 = \dfrac{\ln(B/C) + \sigma^2(t/2)}{\sigma\sqrt{t}}$

$d_2 = d_1 - \sigma\sqrt{t}$

σ^2 = instantaneous variance of the ratio, B/C

$\quad = \sigma_B^2 + \sigma_C^2 - 2\sigma_B\,\sigma_C\,\rho_{BC}$

σ_C^2 = variance of the rate of change of development costs for the project

σ_B^2 = variance of the rate of change of benefits for the project

ρ_{BC} = the correlation between development costs and benefits for the project.

Although options-pricing models are computationally more complex than DCF models, it may not be too difficult to obtain reasonable estimates of a model's parameters. In model (7.2), B and C are estimates of the PV of benefits and costs of the project before a PI is undertaken. B and C have to be estimated to determine the NPV of the project. The variances of B and C can be determined by estimating the probability that the values of B and C will lie within some percentage of their expected values. A numerical example will be used later to help clarify how this can be done. The correlation between development costs and benefits (i.e. ρ_{BC}) is determined by the degree to which the project's benefits are dependent upon the development costs. If benefits are dependent upon the features that are provided by a system (as is often the case when a system is custom designed), development costs and revenues may be highly correlated since, presumably, adding features will increase both development costs and benefits. Development costs and benefits will have a low correlation if benefits depend upon the acceptance (or penetration) of the system, and acceptance is primarily affected by factors that do not add to development costs. For example, when software packages and hardware costs comprise a large portion of the development costs, benefits may be determined by what portion of a system's capabilities are used or by the actions taken by a firm's competitors.

How long the benefits from the project are available will depend upon project characteristics and the PI that is conducted. The information and experience gained from a PI will only be useful for some time. Technological changes, personnel changes, and other environmental factors (e.g. competitors' actions, economic conditions, etc.) will not allow management to delay the decision to invest in a SIT project beyond some point. Thus, the time for exercising the option (i.e. t) on a project is not likely to be very long. However, the time available to exercise the option will vary for different projects.

A numerical example will help demonstrate how this model can be used. Assume that the present value of the expected benefits (B) from a project is $2 000 000 and the present value of the expected costs (C) for the project is $2 500 000. In this case, the project would be rejected. However, since both the costs and benefits are uncertain, the project may still prove to be profitable. If this project can be delayed without the benefits being greatly affected (it is not a 'now-or-never' project), undertaking a PI may still be a good decision. In order to determine whether investment in a PI is justified, we need to estimate the other parameters in model (7.2). We briefly explain how the other parameter values may be estimated.

Let us assume that there is approximately a 2/3 probability (normal distribution is assumed) that the revenues will fluctuate within a range of 60% above or below the expected value in one period. Business and/or environmental conditions may be the cause of this uncertainty. Then, the standard deviation of the rate of change of benefits (σ_B) over one time period of the option's availability is 0.6. Similarly, if there is approximately a 2/3 probability that the development costs will fluctuate within a range of 40% above or below the expected value during one period, then the standard deviation of the rate of change of development costs (σ_C) over one time period of the option's availability is 0.4. The development costs may be uncertain because the requirements of the system are uncertain and/or new technologies are being used.

Assume that the correlation coefficient between the rates of change of revenues and development costs (ρ_{BC}) is 0.5. This also has an intuitive interpretation. About 25% of the variation in the development costs is determined by factors that also affect benefits. For example, increasing the features provided by a system might increase benefits, but will also increase costs. The rest of the variability in revenues is due to other factors, e.g. different levels of acceptance of the technology, competitors' actions, etc. Finally, assume that the option is available for one time period (e.g. one year). During this period, management must decide whether the full-scale project should be undertaken. Development of the project cannot be delayed beyond one year without being greatly affected by factors that management cannot control.

Using the above assumption in model (7.2), the variance, σ^2, is:

$$\sigma^2 = (0.6)^2 + (0.4)^2 - 2(0.6)(0.4)(0.5) = 0.28.$$

Then, d_1 and d_2 are -0.1571 and -0.6863, respectively. Hence, the option value is:

$$V_{pi} = 2 000 000 * \mathbf{N}(-0.1571) - 2 500 000 * \mathbf{N}(-0.6863)$$
$$= 2 000 000 * 0.4326 - 2 500 000 * 0.2464$$
$$= \$249 200.$$

Hence, although the full-scale project currently has a negative NPV, a PI that costs less than $249 200 is justified. For projects with a negative NPV, the costs of a proposed PI should be compared to V_{pi}. If they are larger than V_{pi}, a PI should not be funded. This example shows that it may make sense to conduct a PI even if the project has a fairly large negative NPV because of benefit and cost uncertainty. It may also be useful to delay investment in the project and conduct a PI when a project's NPV is positive.

It is easy to see from this example why managers often choose to ignore the results of traditional NPV analysis and invest in projects that have a negative NPV (Hayes and Garvin, 1982; Myers, 1984; Raho *et al.*, 1987). Investing in a prototype system, for example, may be justified even if the NPV of the project is negative.

Furthermore, managers may choose not to go ahead with full-scale development, even though the project NPV is positive; instead, choosing to conduct a PI. Options-pricing models can be useful in determining whether a proposed PI is worth undertaking. In the next section, we discuss the impact of project characteristics and business conditions on the value of a PI and, therefore, on SIT project decisions.

The impact of project characteristics

SIT projects can differ in many different ways, such as: the type of system (e.g. inter- vs intra-organization); the technology used (e.g. new vs established); the degree of change in the way the firm operates (e.g. major vs minor); the size of the investment necessary; how benefits are determined (e.g. competors' actions vs employee acceptance of the system); etc. Here we discuss how differences in project characteristics affect SIT investment decisions. This discussion is based upon insights provided by model (7.1).

Project scale

Competing firms differ in many ways, such as in size, organizational structure, degree of centralization, etc. Consequently, investment in a system could be strategic for some firms but not for others, depending upon firm and system characteristics (Dos Santos and Peffers, 1991b). For example, certain types of IT investments might have economies of scale, while others allow scaled expansion. Investments that exhibit economies of scale or enable scaled expansion, favour large firms.

Consider a project where the benefits are uncertain and the firm is considering a PI for example, an office automation (OA) project involving the automation of document handling and processing in the office. The benefits of such a project are difficult to estimate accurately. They are dependent upon the degree to which the employees accept and adapt to the new environment. Such projects may not be 'now-or-never' projects. Arriving late means that the firm will receive benefits at a later date. A PI could be undertaken to determine more accurately what the benefits are likely to be. The PI will be more valuable to a large firm than it is to a small firm if the large firm can, because of its size, make greater use of the system, should there be substantial benefits to automating these tasks. Scaled expansion means that P and X may be increased proportionally. If P and X increase proportionally, V_{pi} increases. If an IT investment allows scaled expansion, the value of a PI to a large firm is likely to be greater than the value of the same PI to a small firm; a large firm may be able to undertake a PI, while the same PI may not be justified for a small firm. Therefore, **the value of a preliminary investigation increases if the scale of the system can be increased**.

Benefit uncertainty

It is the uncertainty of the benefits (and possibly, cost uncertainty) of a SIT project that is the major reason for conducting a PI. Were it not for this uncertainty, these investment decisions would be easy. Intuitively, it seems obvious that the more uncertain the benefits, the greater the need for a PI, since a PI can reduce uncertainty and therefore, reduce the likelihood of making a bad investment. From model (7.1), we can see how the value of a PI is affected by benefit uncertainty. As benefit uncertainty increases, σ^2 increases, resulting in an increase in V_{pi}. This is due to the fact that a large σ^2 means that there is a higher probability of P minus X taking on large values and, therefore, the likelihood that the full-scale project will be very profitable is higher.

For many SIT investments, the benefits, P, may be determined by the timing of competitors' investments in systems that provide similar benefits. In a competitive market, if all firms invest in similar systems at the same time, competition within the industry will not allow any firm to benefit greatly from the investment. For example, if a firm develops a system that provides better customer service, the firm will be able to raise prices (or increase market share) if other firms do not provide similar service. However, if competitors also provide similar service at the same time, no firm will be able to raise prices as a result of the investment. The more innovative an IT application, the less likely it is that competitors will develop similar systems at the same time. However, the impact of innovative IT applications is more difficult to predict accurately and, therefore, there also is considerable uncertainty as to the benefits. Innovative applications could also result in large losses, should the benefits not materialize. Therefore, **the more innovative the project, the greater the value of a preliminary investigation**.

Project and firm characteristics

How long a full-scale project can be delayed has an impact on the investment decision. If investment can be delayed for a long period of time without a large decrease in benefits, there is a greater likelihood that the investment will be profitable. If the benefits of a SIT investment are greatly affected by other assets that the firm owns (complementary assets) and competing firms differ in terms of their access to these assets, a firm may be able to delay investment in the project for some time and yet obtain most of the benefits. When the benefits of SIT investments are primarily the result of differences among competing firms, delaying investment may be possible. In such cases, it may be helpful to delay the decision to begin full-scale development so that the firm can learn from other firms' mistakes. However, if there are large learning curve effects associated with the project, delaying investment for a long time may mean that the firm will continue to lag behind the early adopters (Dos Santos and Peffers, 1991b). Large learning curve effects exist if it takes a long time for the firm to learn to use the new system properly and, therefore, to gain maximum benefits from the investment. Therefore, **the value of a preliminary investigation increases if the firm controls complementary assets that competitors cannot easily obtain and if the learning curve effects are small**.

Conclusions

Recently, we have been made aware of the potential importance of information technologies to the firm; beyond their traditional role of providing management information and decision support. Firms can use information technologies to gain competitive advantages. Many conceptual models have been proposed to help firms identify IT investments that provide firms with competitive advantages. However, management has been provided with little help in determining whether these investments are financially justified. Most of the literature dealing with justification of strategic IT investments suggests alternatives to financial analysis. However, managers frequently insist on using it. Moreover, IT projects compete for scarce resources with other projects that are justified using financial analysis. It may therefore be necessary to justify IT investments using the latter.

Investments in IT that can have a substantial impact on a firm's competitive strategy typically are large and risky. As a result, risk-reduction methods are recommended when developing these applications, e.g. prototyping. In such cases, financial analysis based upon options-pricing models can be used to aid in these decisions. An advantage of the options approach is that senior managers are likely to be quite familiar with these models, since in many large corporations, a significant portion of senior management's compensation package may be stock options. Hence, presenting the results of such an analysis should meet with much less resistance than if the approach were entirely foreign to senior managers.

References

Banker, R. D. and Kauffman, R. J. (1988) Strategic Contributions of Information Technology: An Empirical Study of ATM Networks, *Proceedings of the Ninth International Conference on Information Systems*, Minneapolis, Minnesota, pp. 141–50.

Benjamin, R., Rockart, J., Scott-Morton, M. and Wyman, J. (1984) Information technology: a strategic opportunity, *Sloan Management Review*, Spring, 3–10.

Bittlestone, R. (1990) Computerization: out of control? *Computerworld*, 12 March.

Black, F. and Scholes, M. (1973) The pricing of options and corporate liabilities. *Journal of Political Economy*, **81** (3), 637–54.

Brealey, R. and Myers, S. (1988) *Principles of Corporate Finance*, 3rd edn, McGraw-Hill, New York.

Bruns, W. and McFarlan, F. (1987) Information technology puts power in control systems. *Harvard Business Review*, September–October, 89–94.

Cash, J. and Konsynski, B. (1985) IS redraws competitive boundaries. *Harvard Business Review*, March–April, 134–42.

Cash, Jr J. I., McFarlan, F. W., McKenney, J. L. and Vitale, M. R. (1988) *Corporate Information Systems Management: Text and Cases*, 2nd edn, Irwin, Homewood, Illinois.

Clemons, E. K. and Row, M. C. (1987) Structural differences among firms: a potential source of competitive advantage in the application of information technology. *Proceedings of the Eighth International Conference on Information Systems*, Pittsburg, PA, pp. 1–9.

Clemons, E. K. and Row, M. C. (1988) McKesson Drug Company: a case study of Economost – a strategic information system. *Journal of Management Information Systems*, **6** (1), 36–50.

Clemons, E. K. (1991) Evaluation of strategic investments in information technology. *Communications of the ACM*, **34** (1), 22–37.

Copeland, D. G. and McKenney, J. L. (1988) Airline reservation systems: lessons from history. *MIS Quarterly*, **12** (3), 353–70.

Dos Santos, B. L. (1991) Justifying investments in new information technologies. *Journal of Management Information Systems*, **7** (4), 71–89.

Dos Santos, B. L. and Peffers, K. (1991a) The effects of early adoption of information technology: an empirical study. *Proceedings of the Twelfth International Conference on Information Systems*, New York, December, pp. 127–40.

Dos Santos B. L. and Peffers K. (1991b) *Rewards to Investors in Innovative Information Technology Applications: A Study of First Movers and Early Followers in ATMs.* Working Paper, Krannert Graduate School of Management, Purdue University, West Lafayette, Indiana 47907.

Dos Santos, B. L., Peffers, K. and Mauer, D. C. (1991) *The Value of Investments in Information Systems: An Event Study.* Working Paper, Krannert Graduate School of Management, Purdue University, West Lafayette, IN 47907.

EDP Analyzer (1985) *Six Top Information Systems Issues,* Canning Publications Inc., **23** (1), January.

Feeny, D. F. and Ives B. (1990) In search of sustainability: reaping long-term advantage from investments in information technology. *Journal of Management Information Systems,* **7** (1), 27–46.

Glaser, P. F. (1988) Using technology for competitive advantage: the ATM experience at Citicorp, in *Managing Innovation Cases from the Services Industry* (eds B. R. Guile and J. B. Quinn), National Academy Press, Washington, D. C.

Gold, B. (1976) The shaky foundations of capital budgeting. *California Management Review,* **19** (2), 51–60.

Gremillion, L. L. and Pyburn, P. J. (1985) Justifying decision support and office automation systems. *Journal of Management Information Systems,* **2** (1), 5–17.

Harris, S. E. and Katz, J. L. (1991) Organizational performance and information technology investment intensity in the insurance industry. *Organization Science,* **2** (3).

Hayes, R. H. and Garvin, D. A. (1982) Managing as if tomorrow mattered. *Harvard Business Review,* May–June, 71–9.

Ives, B. and Learmonth, G. (1984) The information system as a competitive weapon. *Communications of the ACM,* **27** (12), 1193–1201.

Keen, P. G. W. (1981) Value analysis: justifying decision support systems. *MIS Quarterly,* **5** (1), 1–15.

Keen, P. G. W. and Scott-Morton, M. S. (1978) *Decision Support Systems: An Organizational Perspective,* Addison-Wesley, Reading, Mass.

Kester, W. C. (1984) Today's options for tomorrow's growth. *Harvard Business Review,* March–April, 153–84.

Margrabe, W. (1978) The value of an option to exchange one asset for another. *The Journal of Finance,* **33** (1), 177–86.

Mason, S. P. and Merton, R. C. (1985) The role of contingent claims analysis in corporate finance, in *Recent Advances in Corporate Finance* (eds E. I. Altman and M. G. Subramanyam), Irvin, Homewood, Illinois.

McNurlin, B. C. and Sprague, R. H. Jr (1989) *Information Systems Management in Practice,* 2nd edn, Prentice-Hall.

Myers, S. C. (1984) Finance theory and financial strategy, *Interfaces,* **14** (1), 126–37.

Oster, S. M. (1990) *Modern Competitive Analysis,* Oxford University Press.

Parker, M. M., Benson, R. J. and Trainor, H. E. (1988) *Information Economics: Linking Business Performance to Information Technology,* Prentice-Hall, Englewood Cliffs, New Jersey.

Parsons, G. (1983) *Information Technology: A New Competitive Weapon,* Harvard Business School Case Services, Boston, MA.

Porter, M. and Millar, V. (1985) How information gives you competitive advantage, *Harvard Business Review,* July–August, 149–60.

Raho, L. E., Belohlav, J. A. and Fiedler, K. (1987) Assimilating new technology into the organization: an assessment of McFarlan and McKenney's model, *MIS Quarterly,* **11** (1), 47–58.

Sharpe, W. F. (1985) *Investments,* Prentice-Hall, Englewood Cliffs, New Jersey.

Silk, D. A. (1990) Managing IS benefits for the 1990s, *Journal of Information Technology,* **5**, 185–93.

Stoddard, D. (1988) *Otisline,* Harvard Business School Case Services, No. 9-186-304, Boston, MA 02163, January.

Strassmann, P. A. (1988) Management productivity as an IT measure, in *Measuring Business Value of Information Technologies,* ICIT Research Study Team #2 (ed.), ICIT Press, pp. 93–120.

Vitale, M. R. (1986a) *American Hospital Supply Corp. (A): the ASAP Systems*, Harvard Business School Case Services, No. 9-186-304, Boston, MA 02163, March.

Vitale, M. R. (1986b) The growing risks of information systems success. *MIS Quarterly*, December, 327–36.

Vitale, M. R., Ives, B. and Beath, C. M. (1986) Linking information technology and corporate strategy: an organizational view, *Proceedings of the Seventh International Conference on Information Systems*, San Diego, CA, pp. 265–76.

Wiseman, C. (1985) *Strategy and Computers*, Irwin, Homewood, Illinois.

Part Three

Techniques

8

Justifying IT investments

Beat Hochstrasser

Introduction

To justify IT investments, solid procedures to evaluate, prioritize, monitor and control IT investments have first to be put in place. During a three-year study at a research centre, the Kobler Unit at Imperial College, guidelines for good practice were identified that address both the primary objectives of systems, and the inevitable human and organizational second-order effects of working with IT. Based on these guidelines, a framework for justifying IT investment has been developed that concentrates on critical success factors, on risk assessment, on business performance indicators, and on strategic alignment while offering at the same time a mechanism to monitor and evaluate the investment over time.

Companies are often surprised to learn that researchers into the effective use of information technology regularly report failure rates of up to 60% – in the sense that, three years after installation, an IT project has either been discontinued or falls well short of delivering the benefits aimed at. According to practitioners, the reason for such a high failure rate is that solid but easy to use management tools for evaluating, prioritizing, monitoring and controlling IT investments are hard to come by – at least, in an easily accessible form that industry can readily use. Evidence for this lack of practical control and evaluation methodologies can be found in numerous studies; for instance, research at the Kobler Unit, Imperial College, London, involving 60 managers from 34 British companies over a period of three years, has shown that only 16% of companies use rigorous methods to evaluate and

Information Management: The evaluation of information systems investments.
Edited by Leslie Willcocks.
Published in 1994 by Chapman & Hall. ISBN 0 412 41540 2.

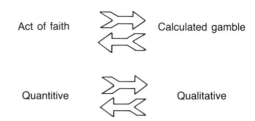

Figure 8.1 A range of approaches.

prioritize their IT investment. However, if these high failure rates are indeed attributable to the lack of suitable management tools, the development and validation of such tools is to be taken more seriously. Industry must work more closely with research centres to specify how decisions concerning IT investments can evolve from being based on 'acts of faith', entailing a high intensity risk, to a calculated gamble where the odds are increasingly known (Figure 8.1). IT investments can only be justified when solid procedures are in place to evaluate, prioritize, monitor and control IT investments at pre-implementation and post-implementation stages. In this chapter we present an IT justification framework, a management tool in the form of four modules, within which such procedures can be successfully implemented.

Difficulties with current evaluation and prioritization procedures

Traditional evaluation and priority setting procedures for controlling IT investments are based on accountancy frameworks and are often implemented under the auspices of the finance director. The procedures are specifically designed to assess the bottom-line financial impact of the investments by setting total costs against all financial benefits actually achieved or accurately predicted to be achievable.

In contrast, today's IT projects are often designed to support and improve the medium- to long-term business scenario based on a variety of business goals. Typically, such goals are formulated in both quantitative and qualitative form. For instance, while the benefits of a system designed to 'cut costs' is immediately quantifiable in financial terms, other projects aiming to 'improve customer support' or to 'offer better market information' might, in the short term, be impossible to quantify.

As more and more IT projects fall into the latter category, there is now often a mismatch between the problem of 'evaluation and priority setting' and the solutions at hand. In particular, there are conflicts in assessing the value of investments designed to support or enable medium- to long-term business strategies by procedures concentrating on measurable short-term financial returns; conflicts between quantitative methods in use and qualitative benefits to be achieved; conflicts between the security of numbers and the inherent nature of risks in IT investments; and conflicts between the concentration on costs and the efforts to achieve value.

But how can we evaluate investments that are medium- to long-term, risk intensive and aimed particularly at qualitative improvements?

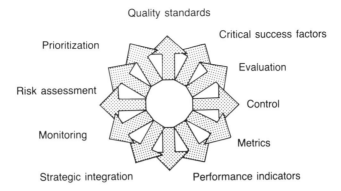

Figure 8.2 Issues in IT evaluation.

To justify IT investments, we need to evaluate; we need to assess the business value IT investments, monitor the performance of the investment over time, and keep IT aligned to the business. Similarly, we need to set priorities; we have to choose between alternative investments by addressing the most promising business opportunities, and we want to allocate our resources in the most effective way.

To deal with the inherent risks of IT investments we need to make sure that we choose the best investment opportunities available, and that we effectively control and monitor the chosen investment on as large a number of relevant key variables as possible (Figure 8.2). The limitations of the accountancy framework can only be overcome by complementing financial analysis with a structured use of business metrics, by complementing objective measurements with informed judgements, by complementing the view of business analysts and IT providers with the view of IT users, and by complementing a one-off stocktaking exercise with regular assessments. We believe that good, solid judgements by people in the know are infinitely more useful than the practice of simply measuring what is easy to measure but irrelevant.

Evaluating and prioritizing infrastructure IT projects

While the main thrust of this chapter is to present a framework for non-infrastructure projects, other work at the Kobler Unit concerning infrastructure projects is relevant. Infrastructure projects are hardware or software systems installed to enable the subsequent development of front-end systems. As such, infrastructure systems are one step removed from making a direct business impact. This makes a standard evaluation procedure for infrastructure projects impossible, particularly as the exact nature and evaluation of the front-end systems subsequently to be developed are often still in the early planning stages. Examples of infrastructure projects are the installations of networks, servers, extensive integrated programming environments, CASE tools or multi-user operating systems. The indirect link between such projects and business impact means that infrastructure projects can therefore not be evaluated in terms of directly quantifiable business benefits achieved. However, examples of good practice have shown that an evaluation is still possible if a company carefully plans its IT involvement in terms of the three- to five-year business scenario to be

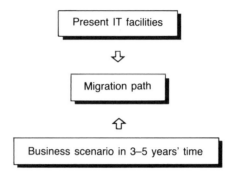

Figure 8.3 Evaluation along the migration path.

realized. Such a medium-term business scenario can be constructed by laying down the role and impact of the business on a designated market environment within an advocated time-frame. Presented with a favoured business scenario of where a company would like to be in the medium term, it is then possible to analyse the necessary IT infrastructure to support these aims. A migration path can then be defined from the present IT facilities and systems to the facilities and systems required to support the strategic vision (Figure 8.3). The evaluation of infrastructure projects can then be achieved by establishing how closely an infrastructure project is to this migration path.

A framework for evaluating and prioritizing non-infrastructure IT projects

In consultation with industry and based on three years of extensive data gathering at the Kobler Unit, a framework for evaluating and prioritizing non-infrastructure IT investments can now be proposed. The framework is divided into four main modules, to be applied in a sequential fashion (Figure 8.4).

The first module addresses a wide range of corporate standards that must be adhered to when proposing new IT initiatives; the second is designed to raise the

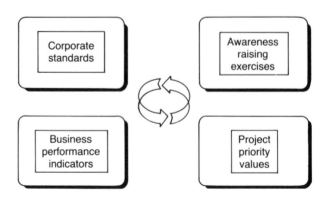

Figure 8.4 Framework for evaluation and prioritization.

awareness of the wider implications – particularly with respect to costs – of IT projects; the third specifies measurable business performance indicators for different classes of IT projects; and the fourth amalgamates the lessons learned and calculates an explicit value – the project priority value – of new IT initiatives. By working within this broad framework, a company can specify concrete procedures and evaluation methods that can provide a solid basis for the justification process of new IT investments. The framework is particularly designed to address IT projects where a straightforward quantitative cost–benefit analysis is not possible and where management is concerned about the existence and extent of claimed 'soft benefits'.

How to apply the framework

The framework is best applied not by a single IT or business manager but by a strategic management group comprising IT professionals, business managers and users. To work in a small group setting is particularly useful as a number of judgements to assess the relative technological, organizational and human risks are necessary. This strategic management group can then report back to the senior manger in charge who might well have additional criteria (e.g. of political nature) to assess new IT proposals. However, by first applying the framework to every new IT proposal, the senior manager will be presented with better quality proposals where hidden flaws and weaknesses have already been exposed. He or she will therefore have a better informed view when deciding how limited resources are to be allocated.

Module 1: Corporate standards for new IT initiatives

The first module, corporate standards for new IT initiatives, can be regarded as a set of critical success factors that all have to be addressed before the proper process of evaluation can even begin. The standards in the worksheets presented prescribe a number of individual investment factors that our research found to be particularly important in distinguishing success from failure. For instance, successful projects are typically guided by a business sponsor; valuable business benefits of the investment are explicitly specified and monitored; the responsibility for both data-ownership and data-feeding is clearly established; the experience of other divisions in similar projects is made use of; training needs are strongly coordinated; systems are designed to be user friendly; the interface often conforms to other corporate systems; users are involved at all stages of the systems specification and implementation process; data-security and data-backup are planned for; and most importantly, the transition period from old paper-based systems to new electronic systems is well planned for. Individual market sectors and particular types of companies have additional specific sets of criteria that must be explicitly elicited and taken into account.

Module 2: Awareness of potential wider effects

The second module consists of a number of submodules designed to raise the awareness of the steering group on a number of potential wider effects resulting from systems implementation. In particular, a need has been identified to be better aware of the true costs of IT projects, so that costs can be better controlled. Researchers are consistently pointing out that most companies tend to underestimate the total costs of IT projects. Comparing the projected costs at the pre-implementation stage with subsequent post-implementation reviews, differences in the costing structure of up to 50% are regularly encountered. Even the costing structure itself is not clear: according to our experience, an average of 30–50% of IT costs occur outside the official IT budget. If companies do not engage in rigorous cost analysis they tend to be unaware of the true costs involved of deploying IT. As a consequence, companies find themselves in a position where the extent of their IT investment is not known and cannot be evaluated.

The true costs of IT projects can be divided into direct costs and indirect costs. Direct costs are often underestimated owing to unexpected additional hardware accessories (e.g. secondary data storage devices), installation and configuration costs (often needing expensive outside consultancy), environmental costs (e.g. underfloor wiring, air conditioning, new lighting or additional furniture), running costs (the power consumption of colour screens, laser printers and plotters is considerable), maintenance costs (service contracts for software – systems engineers spend up to 70% of their time trying to understand code already written before being able to install new functions), systems breakdown (can seriously harm ongoing business), security costs (e.g. protection against systems abuse and viruses), networking costs (e.g. access times to external information systems can be expensive), training costs (consistently underestimated) and the costs of phasing a system out at the end of its lifespan.

Even more importantly, case studies have shown that, as a rule of thumb, indirect human and organizational costs might well be four times as high as direct costs. One of the largest human costs is management and staff time spent on successfully integrating a new system into current work practices. Senior managers will spend time devising, approving and subsequently amending IT strategies; planning, explaining and implementing IT-related policies; and on security reviews and audit verification. Middle managers will spend time discovering the business potential of the new systems and experimenting with new structures of information flows; on novel ways of manipulating information; and on alternative divisions of business functions and processes. Line managers will spend time absorbing the transition from traditional to new work practices. Everybody will spend time being trained and training others. Another example of human costs often forgotten is the effect of new salary structures resulting from training a sophisticated workforce able to handle the new technology. Additionally, as well-trained staff recognize that their new skills are very marketable, staff turnover might increase and there might be a recurring cost of training new personnel.

Organizational costs are caused by the transition from old to new work practices. At first, a temporary loss of productivity is often experienced as learning and integration take place. Once the basic functions of the system are in place, further organizational costs occur as management attempts to capitalize on the wider potential of information technology. Alternative, extended and better integrated information flows are being introduced with the result that traditional divisions of basic business functions and processes no longer reflect the company's ability to manipulate and share information. The need will be perceived that organizational functions, processes and reporting structures must be redesigned to exploit new opportunities. As was pointed out by Hochstrasser (1987), companies with extensive IT installations in place tend to change their corporate shape by reducing the number of management levels, by redefining the role of middle management and by exposing more surface to their market environment. The costs of organizational restructuring can be extensive, particularly if isolated groups within a company resist change and are unable or unwilling to make the transition.

Module 3: Business performance indicators

The third module, measuring business performance indicators (BPI), specifies measurable business metrics. There is a very clearly identified need that companies ought to measure more, and that more business metrics are needed to assess the impact of new investments on a variety of business goals. The main reasons for this need are three-fold: first, by specifying concrete metrics before implementation begins, a company is forced to look at current business practice with the view of what it wants to improve and postulate the required improvements needed. The focus is therefore shifted from the technology to business issues, and one of the main dangers of systems developments – technology-push – is thereby reduced. Secondly, by assessing performance on a variety of business metrics at the pre-implementation stage, a foundation is put into place for subsequent post-implementation comparison. Thirdly, by concentrating at the outset on the dynamics of change, justification and evaluation processes are now regarded as ongoing processes, not as mere one-off exercises. This has the beneficial effect that any improvements can now be monitored over time against well defined goals, and, if things go wrong, early action can be taken to rectify the situation. If no valuable and measurable BPI can be found for new IT proposals, the investment purpose may not be aligned to the company's business aims. However, the application of BPI demands that management agree on a consistent and relevant set of business criteria. To facilitate the generation of evaluation criteria and to standardize evaluation procedures across the whole organization, examples of good practice suggest that individual IT initiatives can be classified into larger project groups that share similar business objectives. An eclectic set of evaluation criteria can then be developed for each class of business objective supported by a particular IT system. A number of (overlapping) project groups suggest themselves:

1. *Internal projects*

IT systems introduced to increase a company's internal efficiency are basically designed to save the company money by streamlining internal operations. To assess the effectiveness of an IT system in this area, a number of variables can be identified that are actually measurable – not in terms of dollars and pounds, but in terms of effective work practice. For instance, it is not very difficult to measure the time spent on both core and support activities, and to measure how the ratio between the two is shifted after the introduction of the new system.

Similarly, it is possible to measure time/costs spent within core/support functions before and after systems implementation.

2. *External projects*

IT systems introduced to increase a company's external effectiveness are designed to make money. Effectiveness goals can be measured on a wide variety of business performance indicators such as market share, revenue, knowledge of market opportunities, frequency of contacts with external agencies, knowledge of the company by the market, and the perception of a company's image over time.

3. *Cost replacement projects*

IT systems introduced to automate manual activities related to information processing, e.g. optical character recognition (OCR) or basic word processing (WP), can often be evaluated by a simple or extended cost–benefit analysis like the Index Group's stages survey (Gibson and Jackson, 1987) or AT Kearney's direct labour cost substitution (AT Kearney, 1987). In its simple form, these methods are based on a quantifiable correlation between the cost of the system and some organizational or management costs saved as a result of introducing the system. For instance, the elimination of direct labour costs can be employed to evaluate OCR and some forms of WP systems. Similarly, the upgrading of an existing information system by a new system can be quantified either by the new system being cheaper to run while offering the same functionality, or by the new system costing the same but offering an increased functionality. Often, however, additional factors have to be taken into account. An extended cost–benefit analysis will have to be employed for more sophisticated forms of WP that might not only save labour costs but also offer additional facilities, e.g. mail merge or an increase in the quality of finished documents. The evaluation procedure therefore has to measure business performance indicators (BPIs) by attempting to quantify the effectiveness of these additional facilities. For instance, various levels of document quality can be assessed by monitoring the effectiveness of differently produced sales brochures. Similarly, while the benefits of an automated payroll system can partly be quantified in terms of staffing levels, an additional benefit of the system is better money management. An attempt must therefore be made to evaluate not only the direct labour costs saved, but to measure additional BPIs, for instance the new ability to increase the control on cash flow.

4. *Economy of scale projects*

IT systems introduced to allow a company to handle an increased volume of data, e.g. systems allowing electronic data interchange (EDI), point of sale systems (POS) or just-in-time manufacturing (JIT), can be evaluated either by a company's increased ability for capacity handling with the same level of resources or by a company's increased ability to speed up the business cycle. For instance, introducing EDI can remove bottlenecks in order processing or in tendering for new contracts. Such a system can then be evaluated by an increase in business turnover without employing and training new staff. Similarly, POS and JIT manufacturing systems will strengthen a company's control over resources thereby enabling the evaluation of these systems in terms of a faster business turnaround while using the same level of resources.

5. *Economy of scope projects*

IT systems introduced to allow a company to perform an extended range of tasks, e.g. sophisticated relational data bases (RDB) or integrated help desk (HD) facilities, can be evaluated by a company's ability to expand the business horizon with the same level of resources and by an increased flexibility to change products and services rapidly according to specific market needs. For instance, the integration of a marketing database into a corporate database showing the profiles of established customers can make it possible to offer not only a more individual service to different market segments, but also additional services as and when market opportunities arise. Evaluation can then proceed by establishing the payback of these additional services. More complicated systems designed to increase the economics of scope allow a company to extract information from their already existing customer data to branch out into adjacent market areas. For instance, in the banking community, systems are introduced to offer banking-related activities like insurance cover or mortgages. These activities can then be performed with very few new resources and an evaluation of these systems can be obtained by measuring the actual market impact of the new business activities.

6. *Customer support projects*

IT systems introduced to offer better services to customers can be evaluated by methods derived from the Customer Resource Life Cycle as described by Ives and Learmonth (1987). The rationale behind this approach is based on research results showing that it is five times more expensive to gain new customers than it is to keep existing ones, and on the observation that, as customers are the life-blood of a company, they demand full attention and optimal service. It has been shown that customers perceive a company's products differently over time. This perceptual change is locked into a life-cycle of several distinct stages. The method can be used to evaluate the degree to which the system to be installed will fulfil critical needs of customers throughout this life-cycle. For example, an integrated customer enquiry facility can be justified by the critical need that new customers expect such a service when they first start dealing with a company. Evaluating a possible installation of extensive communication links with existing customers can proceed by establishing the relative need, as perceived by customers, that such installations are indeed critical for securing their continued loyalty at more mature stages of their life-cycle, by the opportunity of 'locking in' customers by creating switching costs, by the positive effect of differentiating a company from its competitors, and by the relative success of carving out niche markets.

7. *Quality support projects*

IT systems introduced to increase the quality of the finished product, for instance knowledge-based systems (KBS) or production-modelling systems (PMS), can be evaluated by Porter's (1980) value chain analysis, value linking and value acceleration. These techniques serve to establish the value of IT to transform both the internal and external value chain to a firm's advantage. They are extensions of traditional value-added methodologies, and assess the benefits of quality support systems by identifying beneficial changes in the product quality at each node of a product's value chain from the raw material obtained by the supplier to the finished product sold to the customer. Additionally, value acceleration measures the timescales involved at each node of production. For instance, a KBS might offer advice to workers on the shop floor on how to dynamically optimize a particular manufacturing function either to achieve a better quality product or to shorten manufacturing time while adhering to the same level of quality. Similarly, a production-modelling system might allow a company to model different combinations of its manufacturing processes and to compare these new combinations with current practices. Both of these systems can be evaluated by identifying their effect on quality and speed of production.

8. *Information sharing and manipulation projects*

IT systems introduced to offer better information sharing and information manipulation – for instance, office automation (OA) systems, decision support systems (DSS) or management information systems (MIS) – can be evaluated by relating the system to a thorough information flow analysis of key business goals. A recent study (Hochstrasser and Griffiths, 1990) observed that while there is a growing consensus that information will be **the** key commodity in the coming 'information era', 70% of companies report that they suffer from a **lack** of accessible information. Typically, information needs have been neglected or have been analysed on a simple piecemeal basis, thereby losing any strategic coordination and control. As a result, two main problems arise: either a company suffers from information starvation where not enough shared data is available to allow individual divisions and senior management to operate effectively, or a company suffers from information overload where too much data is available, but salient information is so hidden that it is simply not accessible. An information strategy is therefore needed that lays down a clear structure for corporate information flows and manipulates these flows into specific levels of detail at different levels of management. The objective of the exercise is to increase the quality of horizontal cross-divisional communications, to install effective cross-functional linkages between overlapping activities, and to ensure that vertical information flows reflect the practical information needs at each level of management. At the Kobler Unit, an information strategy framework has been devised that identifies the necessary elements underlying the strategy and offers planning tools to generate and analyse a set of management goals in terms of information needs. Systems introduced to share and manipulate information can then be evaluated by the degree of alignment to information flow analysis of key business goals.

9. *New technology projects*

IT systems introduced, strategically, to exploit the business potential of the new technology to do things that were not possible before – for instance, introducing home banking or smart cards – can be controlled by the risk minimization strategies described by Peters in Chapter 5, and can be evaluated by risk evaluation techniques. These techniques take into account an investment that may be insecure but promises a potentially high payoff, and is ultimately justified by having a strategic advantage over competitors, or by having a greatly increased market share. The nature and definition of risk taking is such that a bottom line quantification based on a cost–benefit analysis is not possible at the pre-implementation stage. To evaluate risks, informed judgements will have to be made. To facilitate the process, the overall risk can be broken down into smaller risk components. One particular technique is to denote individual risk elements as the cells in a conventional spreadsheet. These cells can then be linked to individual probability ratings showing a manager's trust in the validity of each cell's value. When subsequently manipulating the values of a combination of cells, the associated probabilities are also manipulated to give a much more accurate picture of the distribution of risk faced. By combining probabilities with individual risk elements, a sophisticated model of different kinds of risks facing a project at different points in time can then be built. It is important to realize that the association of probabilities to risk elements involves an informed judgement and can therefore only be made by someone understanding the dynamics of the market and not, for example, by a professional IT evaluation team. The risk of the investment has therefore to be evaluated by those actually taking the risk. Risk receives more detailed treatment in Chapter 11.

The objective behind module 3 is therefore born out of the need to ensure that the newly introduced technology impacts favourably on the business aims of a company and is therefore aligned to real business objectives. This can be done by specifying measurable business performance indicators in the form of concrete metrics that can be monitored over time. By classifying individual projects into larger generic project groups, this process can be facilitated. The groups suggested here include internal projects, external projects, economy of scale projects, economy of scope projects, customer support projects, quality support projects, information sharing and manipulation projects and new technology projects.

Module 4: Project priority value

The fourth module, calculating the project priority value (PPV), is an exercise designed to assess the relative merits of individual projects against one another. If several projects compete for limited resources, a project priority value can be established by translating the perceived value and risk of the project on a variety of complementary dimensions into concrete figures that can subsequently be combined into the PPV. If only one project is to be assessed, the exercise is still valid and offers the opportunity to study the proposal through a number of complementary investment factors of importance. Lessons learned from applying the previous three modules are applied – particularly lessons learned about cost issues, about the awareness of the potential wider human and organizational impact, and about the awareness of the alignment between the project and the business objectives through the process of specifying performance indicators. But, more importantly, this module is designed to continue and to deepen the discussion – possibly within the framework of a strategic management group – of the actual business value of the proposed investment.

To calculate the PPV, a company first weighs the relative importance of a number of investment factors against one another, in the light of the company's overall business objectives. This is similar to generating a company profile. Each of the IT proposals competing for limited resources is then measured against this company profile. The project with the highest PPV is most closely aligned to what the company is trying to achieve. Of course, a strict application of this procedure might well reveal that none of the proposed initiatives deserves funding at a particular point in time. Alternatively, it might reveal that the business benefits of several projects are indeed so substantial that the framework for evaluating and prioritizing IT investments will form the foundation for arguing a business case that additional funding for new IT should be released.

The module combines the following four dimensions: the primary objectives that the proposed system is designed to achieve; the potential second-order effects (both opportunities and potential barriers) resulting from the human impact and organizational change of installing sophisticated IT; the strategic integration into both business and technology architecture; and the assessment of a wide range of risks involved.

To evaluate the primary business objectives of IT initiatives, an overall judgement of the relative value for money of different IT initiatives must first be made by comparing the various projects competing for the limited resources. Work done in module 3, specifying business performance indicators, will assist in this process by making the link between the investment and business benefits more explicit. In the case of projects that lend themselves readily to a strict cost–benefit analysis, the actual return on investment can be calculated. In other projects – and the majority of today's IT investments fall into that category – a well-informed judgement by the steering group is necessary. To achieve an even stronger link to explicit and well-defined management goals – and to allow a subsequent weighting and prioritizing of projects according to business aims – the primary objectives are then subdivided into the areas of internal efficiency, external effectiveness and new business opportunities. The application of this module demands that management must agree on a consistent and relevant set of management goals – a common explicit or implicit business strategy – and a set of business criteria against which the investment is to be measured.

To evaluate the second-order effects of IT initiatives, both additional opportunities presented by the system envisaged and potential barriers to success have to be taken into account. The social and political implications of IT deployment cannot be avoided and must therefore be assessed as early as possible. While a report from OECD (1988) strongly argued the need for larger investments in money, effort and time to integrate IT with important wider environmental and societal considerations, a more recent study by the British Institute of Management (BIM, 1989) concentrated on the need to integrate IT with the social and political processes inside companies. The BIM study points out that introducing IT into a company always requires a substantial additional investment in continuous management education, development and reaction to social and political change. Similarly, at the Kobler Unit it was noted that large-scale deployment of IT always brings about wide-ranging changes in the way a company is structured and in the way people work. These effects can result in radical shifts in job descriptions, salary structures, the role of middle management, and in traditional divisions between functions. Introducing IT often forces a company to redesign the shape of its organization. It was also noted that some organizations have been vulnerable to hijacking by small but strong interest groups seeking power and status. Evaluations of IT initiatives have to take these potential effects into account by judging a company's ability to control the internal dynamics of organizational change. In practice, such evaluations can be based on instituting regular discussions between all groups affected by the introduction of IT. The backdrop to these meetings has to be a climate where open debate is possible, and where the discussion is not couched in the technical terms of the system provider, but in the language of the information user.

Often the payback from an IT system depends on successful mediation between groups of people who have different interests, particularly when changes are proposed in the distribution of corporate power relating to the control of vital information. A good case study is the service company that introduced a sophisticated distributed customer database containing both 'hard' data (contacts, purchasing history, reliability ratings, etc.) and 'soft' data (purchasing preferences, plans, rumours, etc.). Top management was then urged by line managers of other departments to make this new information available across the company. However, that proposition was strongly resisted by the small team who currently controls access to the data – partly for security reasons but also partly out of fear that to release control on the data might weaken their own political position within the company. This situation was eventually resolved by a strong CEO who forced the current holders of the data to participate in a corporate team spirit and to understand the business needs of their colleagues. To sweeten the pill, the CEO increased the status of the department by expanding the size and extent of the data collection process, and by putting the current team in charge of the operation with the additional responsibilities over security arrangements and over the accuracy and timeliness of the data.

Similar case studies contribute towards the perception that the level of commitment of all users to a particular IT system has to be established before the system is deployed. Running or introducing an expensive IT installation which, according to technical specification, could save the company money or offer potential business benefits can be very cost ineffective if the system is not used to its full potential by all parties concerned. A low level of commitment is particularly conceivable if large-scale retraining, redundancies or redeployment of staff are involved and if certain groups resist change and misuse facilities.

To evaluate the strategic integration of IT investments, the system needs to be assessed in relation to a company's business strategy. According to our research, such a strategy can take the form of an explicit document but is more likely to consist of a consensus based on an understanding and sharing of common business goals by senior management. The proposed IT investment is assessed both from the point of view of medium- to long-term strategic direction and from the point of view of offering short-term tactical benefits. Again, this distinction allows companies to 'weigh' their preferred method of operation at any one point in time.

A further class of strategic integration is concerned with effective information and technology management. Information strategies and IT strategies are therefore needed. Based on discussions with 60 senior managers, a strategy framework has been assembled. Its main components are the dynamic unification of business mission, competitor modelling, market performance indicators, customer feedback, operational needs, and IT opportunities into a consistent and relevant set of management goals. Once such a set of goals has been agreed upon, it can then be analysed in terms of general information needs and concrete information requirements as a basis for generating effective corporate information management – and, subsequently, an IT strategy to implement the needed information flows.

As changes in market conditions accelerate, the need for an information strategy becomes more prominent. Without clearly defined processes for updating the information that is critical to competitive success, companies are finding that they have vast resources committed to keeping out-of-date material accessible. A formalized information strategy enables flexibility to be built in so that the needs of the company and of managers are always the main focus. Having better access to information allows managers to do their jobs more effectively. The formulation of an information strategy does not include prescribing any technical implementations. Indeed, not all information needs are best fulfilled by technical means. There is a need for informal channels of communication where 'soft' data can be freely circulated. Non-IT-based information exchange – like company specific 'grape-vines', social meetings, or regular gatherings outside company premises – do exist and have to be acknowledged as an integral part of an organization's information infrastructure. Attempting to formalize these processes more rigidly does, however, lead to wasted resources and increased distrust among employees. The essential function of an information strategy is to facilitate the flow and exchange of business relevant information.

While the information strategy delineates those information needs that are critical for a company's success, an IT strategy specifies how some of these needs are to be fulfilled. It is important to realize that the main thrust of an IT strategy is to plan the implementation of the information strategy, and that an IT strategy can therefore only be specified if an information strategy has first been put into place. If implementation is not preceded by a comprehensive IT strategy, as is regularly found in the majority of cases, a company will subsequently experience a strongly increased number of IT-related difficulties. This suggests that the relation between strategic planning and business success is a major hallmark distinguishing successful from less successful companies.

Conclusions

An eclectic approach to justifying IT investments is proposed which reaches far beyond the current but limited practice of cost–benefit analysis. The framework is presented in the form of a set of four modules, to be applied in sequential fashion, that offer a comprehensive way of evaluating and justifying sophisticated IT projects. While the first module specifies quality standards in the form of a set of critical success factors, the second module is designed to raise the awareness of decision makers on a variety of relevant topics – for instance, the awareness of the true costs involved of deploying IT, or the awareness of the social and political impact of IT. The third module shows how to specify measurable business performance indicators by combining IT projects into larger generic project classes. Finally, the fourth module combines the lessons learned and amalgamates the individual investment factors into a comprehensive whole by calculating a concrete project priority value.

Owing to the dynamic factors inherent in IT investments, evaluation must be regarded as a continuous process which needs to be kept under review at regular intervals. It cannot be tenable to justify a policy proclaiming a single one-off evaluation procedure. Without regular re-evaluation, potential further benefits can be missed on several counts: the technology itself may develop to a stage where cheaper technical solutions become viable, users may outgrow the current system, or the demands of the market environment in which a company operates may change so that older systems no longer address current needs. The lack of relevant and regular evaluation procedures leads to loss of control of IT investments. Without relevant evaluation procedures, the introduction of IT is based on an act of faith – without repeating these procedures at regular intervals, benefits once achieved may no longer be realized. As such, the development of a comprehensive programme is not an overhead, but an investment in a valuable tool for supporting a company's strategic IT deployment.

References

AT Kearney (1987) *Corporate Organisation and Overhead Effectiveness Survey*, AT Kearney, London.

BIM (1989) *The Responsive Organisation – People Management: The Challenge of the 1990's*, British Institute of Management, London.

Gibson, C. F. and Jackson, B. B. (1987) *The Information Imperative: Managing the Impact of Information Technology on Businesses and People*, The Approach of the Index Group, Lexington.

Hochstrasser, B. (1987) *Assessing the Effectiveness of IT: Groundwork for a Knowledgebase*, Imperial College, London.

Hochstrasser, B. (1987) *Does Information Technology Slow You Down?*, Kobler Unit, Imperial College, London.

Hochstrasser, B. and Griffiths, C. (eds) (1990) *Regaining Control of IT Investments: A Handbook for Senior US Management*, Kobler Unit, Imperial College, London.

Hochstrasser, B. (1990) Evaluating IT investments – matching techniques to projects. *Journal of Information Technology*, **5** (4), 215–22.

Hochstrasser, B. and Griffiths, C. (1991) *Controlling IT Investments: Strategy and Management*, Chapman & Hall, London.

Ives, B. and Learmonth, G. P. (1987) The information system as a competitive weapon, in *Towards Strategic Information Systems* (eds E. Somogyi and B. Galliers), Abacus Press, Tunbridge wells.

OECD (1988) *New Technology in the 1990's: A Socio-economic Strategy*, Organization for Economic Co-operation and Development, Brussels.

Peters, G. (1988) Evaluating your computer investment strategy, *Journal of Information Technology*, **3** (3), 178–89.

Porter, M. E. (1980) *Competitive Strategy*, Free Press, New York.

Scott-Morton, M. (ed.) (1991) *The Corporation in the 1990s*, Oxford University Press, Oxford.

Strassmann, P. (1990) *The Business Value of Computers*, The Information Economic Press, New Canaan.

Wilson, T. (1991) Overcoming the barriers to the implementation of IS strategies. *Journal of Information Technology*, **6** (1), 39–44.

WORSHEET 1: Corporate standards for new IT initiatives

Investment factors*	More work needed	Yes
Has the project got a business sponsor?	. . . . .	. . . . .
Are there valuable business benefits from the investment?	. . . . .	. . . . .
Is the responsibility for data-ownership established?	. . . . .	. . . . .
Is the responsibility for data-feeding established?	. . . . .	. . . . .
Is the experience of other divisions in similar projects made use of?	. . . . .	. . . . .
Are training needs coordinated?	. . . . .	. . . . .
Is the proposed system user-friendly?	. . . . .	. . . . .
Does the user interface conform to other corporate systems?	. . . . .	. . . . .
Are users prepared to accept the new system?	. . . . .	. . . . .
Are data-security and data-backup planned for?	. . . . .	. . . . .
Is the transitional period from old to new system well planned for?	. . . . .	. . . . .
Have the wider cost issues been taken into consideration?	. . . . .	. . . . .

Only proceed with the project evaluation process if all investment factors can be answered with 'Yes'.

WORKSHEET 2: Awareness of the true costs of IT projects

1. **Hardware costs** (incl. backup and accessories) . . . . .

2. **Software costs** (incl. updates and operating systems) . . . . .

3. **Specification costs** (incl. revisiting users as needs change) . . . . .

4. **Programming costs** (incl. environments, 4GL, CASE) . . . . .

5. **Installation costs** (incl. time spent inputting current records) . . . . .

6. **Environmental costs** (incl. wiring and furniture) . . . . .

7. **Running costs** (incl. power consumption and access charges) . . . . .

8. **Maintenance costs** (incl. service contract and emergency backup) . . . . .

9. **Security costs** (incl. data backup and storage) . . . . .

10. **Networking costs** (incl. dedicated servers and workstations) . . . . .

11. **Training costs** (incl. retraining and staff turnover) . . . . .

12. **Consultancy costs** (incl. initial help and later emergencies) . . . . .

13. **Transitional costs** (incl. disruption to normal work practices) . . . . .

14. **Management costs** (incl. time to formulate policy and control) . . . . .

15. **New salary structures** (as a direct result of new system) . . . . .

WORKSHEET 3: Business performance indicators

Project type	*Examples of business metrics*
Internal projects	Time spent on core activities Time spent thinking and planning Level of staff satisfaction Level of staff skills
External projects	Knowledge of market environment Frequency of contacts with external agencies Knowledge of company by the market Perception of company image
Economy of scale projects	Turnover and business turnaround Manufacturing times per product Throughput figures
Economy of scope projects	Range of products Range of services Range of business activities Number and quality of innovative ideas
Customer support projects	Survey data on customer satisfaction Time needed to answer customer enquiries Telephone enquiries answered on the spot Judgement of customer loyalty Customer retention rate Level of repeat business by old customers
Quality support projects	Product/service quality measurements Value chain analysis/value acceleration Quality of information security Quality of corporate learning
Information management projects	Decision quality Decision times Degree of information overload/starvation Alignment to ideal information strategy

WORKSHEET 4: Calculating the project priority value

	(A) Scores −5 to +5	(B) Weights 1 to 5	(C) Priorities (A) × (B)
Primary objectives			
1. Perceived value for money	. . . . .	. . . . .	. . . . .
2. Offering better internal efficiency	. . . . .	. . . . .	. . . . .
3. Offering more external business effectiveness	. . . . .	. . . . .	. . . . .
4. Offering new business opportunities	. . . . .	. . . . .	. . . . .
Second-order effects			
(a) *Opportunities*			
5. Social and political implications	. . . . .	. . . . .	. . . . .
6. Impact on job functions	. . . . .	. . . . .	. . . . .
7. Impact on salary structures	. . . . .	. . . . .	. . . . .
8. Impact on organizational structure	. . . . .	. . . . .	. . . . .
(b) *Potential barriers*			
9. Organizational barriers	. . . . .	. . . . .	. . . . .
10. Human barriers	. . . . .	. . . . .	. . . . .
11. Educational barriers	. . . . .	. . . . .	. . . . .
12. Cultural barriers	. . . . .	. . . . .	. . . . .
Strategic integration			
13. Alignment to long-term strategic business direction	. . . . .	. . . . .	. . . . .
14. Offering short-term tactical business benefits	. . . . .	. . . . .	. . . . .
15. Integration into information strategy	. . . . .	. . . . .	. . . . .
16. Integration into technology strategy	. . . . .	. . . . .	. . . . .
17. Offering flexibility to change	. . . . .	. . . . .	. . . . .
Risks			
18. Business risks	. . . . .	. . . . .	. . . . .
19. Technological risks	. . . . .	. . . . .	. . . . .
20. Risk of not investing in project	. . . . .	. . . . .	. . . . .
Total		_____	_____

Project priority value (Total priorities/Total weights employed)   ========

- Allocate weights according to your company's needs before assessment begins (same weights for all projects).
- For each project, only fill in the investment factors that are relevant; leave the rest blank.
- Positive implications for systems development are scored +1 (low) to +5 (high).
- Negative implications for systems development are scored −1 (low) to −5 (high).

9

Information economics: a practical approach to valuing information systems

Devra Wiseman

Introduction

This chapter outlines some early experience gained from using an approach to the evaluation of information systems, called information economics (IE). This has received attention elsewhere in the book, notably in Chapters 3 and 4. The objective here will be to suggest how the IE approach can be operationalized. Two case studies will be used to show and assess the learning points from the IE approach in practice. Information economics was devised by Marilyn Parker and Robert Benson, from the IBM Los Angeles Research Center and Washington State University respectively. Their early work started to enter the professional literature in 1987 and 1988. It was soon taken up in the US and a definitive description appeared with the publication of a book (Parker *et al.*, 1988). Parker and Benson had been greatly helped by Ed Trainor, a practical DP manager, who had been responsible for IT at Amtrak, the US railroad company. His contribution ensured that the IE approach was practical. By 1989, the IE approach was 'sweeping the board' (Strassmann, private communi-

Information Management: The evaluation of information systems investments.
Edited by Leslie Willcocks.
Published in 1994 by Chapman & Hall. ISBN 0 412 41540 2.

cation) in the USA. Some idea of its influence can be gauged from its frequent mention in other chapters of this book.

Parker and Benson were researching the eternal problem – what is the value of computer-based information systems to an enterprise? Given a finite amount to invest, why should an organization choose to put its money into information technology (IT) rather than into other important projects? In order to answer that question, one also had to be able to deal with the problem of prioritizing IT projects. In practice, organizations do invest, and heavily, in IT, whether or not they can make the case for IT as opposed to other investments. Something more explicit is needed when faced with a number of competing IT projects.

In their textbook, Parker and Benson position IE chiefly as a way of prioritizing investments in information systems and technology. So far, the method has been used in two different ways. This is unlikely to have exhausted further possibilities. The approach can be thought of as a general method for putting value on information systems, although prioritization will undoubtedly remain its main use.

A key point that Parker and Benson make is that IE is meant to be adapted to the different organizations using the approach. While their book is certainly a foundation, it should not be fossilized. Parker and Benson themselves are further developing their ideas, as is the author of this chapter.

Current problems

All the contributors to this book make the point that organizations still find it extremely hard to justify their investment in information systems and technology. Many organizations and feasibility studies claim that productivity is improved, yet cannot put figures to it. They talk of unquantifiable benefits. They know they cannot do without computers, but they cannot talk meaningfully about the real value of information systems. 'IT decision-makers are suffering a growing crisis of confidence as the time approaches to authorize new computer-based information systems' (Angell and Smithson, 1990).

A logical approach, which has much appeal to the crisis-ridden executive at the crucial point in the budget cycle, is to think in terms of a comprehensive IT strategy which aligns the information systems with the business goals (see Chapter 6).

In the ideal scenario, the enterprise will have worked out a business strategy. Then it will have decided on the information systems needed to implement that strategy. By definition, therefore, such systems must be valuable. Next, the organization decides on the technology infrastructure to deliver the information systems (IS). It is then a question of prioritizing the IS projects decided on, so that they are developed in the most useful sequence. Even if this logical approach has been followed, prioritization remains a problem. All the systems decided on must be valuable to the organization, as we have said. We have still not answered the question: which is most valuable?

Of course, it rarely, if ever, happens quite like this. Organizations have to start in the here and now. They have existing information systems, paper-based and electronic, and informal verbal systems, as people meet and pass information around. They also have technology which may be non-electronic, but undoubtedly there will still be computers of different generations and types which are incompatible with each other.

The enterprise finds itself in a fast-changing environment. Today, changes in information technology are almost swamped by social, political and legislative change. We may characterize the situation in the phrase 'turbulent times'. The problem that enterprises of all kinds face is how to manage in such times. What happens, as far as investment in IT is concerned, is that a wish list is produced of systems that various managers think they need. There is even less understanding of whether any of the systems are worth while.

Does it matter? It is disquieting to learn that

> There is evidence, in the United States at least, that the investment in the new technologies has coincided with lowered overall productivity and profitability . . . The problem is knowing when to change to using new capabilities and knowing when new capabilities should not be employed even though they exist. The problems are management problems and not hardware or software problems. (Thurow, 1991)

Such a statement is now a truism. It needs some analysis before we can start to form a solution. The technical and human factors are very closely intertwined. The technology changes radically enough and fast enough for the gap in mutual understanding between the business managers and the technology professionals to remain forever too wide. Bluntly, we still face the situation where the technology side perceives that wonderful possibilities exist to improve business performance, but the business side, holding the purse-strings, cannot easily grasp the implications of the technology and is appalled at the cost.

This applies at whatever stage of computer usage an organization finds itself. Thus, an organization which can now afford cheap personal computers will balk at installing a network. Organizations with numerous mainframes in different countries are faced with the need for global networks and will have serious data management problems.

Networks, and all that they imply, have been mentioned deliberately. They epitomize the recurring problem that technology poses to business managers. It is now not so difficult for a business manager to see that information technology can help a business to carry out specific functions; for example, sales order processing or accounting. The manager traditionally looks at the costs and benefits of the 'application system'. However flawed, there is a reasonable basis for decision making. But the business side cannot relax. The new demand is for communications, for office systems, for networks, local or global. In other words, infrastructure projects, rather than application systems, are sought. The problem is not so new. Reviewing the literature, Sullivan (1985) noted that existing strategic information systems planning methodologies do not adequately address architecture issues. 'Furthermore, they do not sufficiently consider the effective use of such new technologies as data communications' (Lederer and Sethi, 1991).

The problem we started with – how to evaluate the worth of an investment in IT – has been exacerbated. It is more difficult than ever to state where the benefits lie. The costs, while not crystal clear, are certainly big enough to be seen. But can a business manager start to talk about the benefits that a network will bring? The answer is probably, yes, if all the strategic thinking has gone on and approaches such as those detailed in Chapters 3 and 4 have been applied. But we are in the vicious circle of having to start in the here and now rather than with the grand strategy. Mintzberg (1987) has put before us the concept of the 'emergent strategy' where strategy evolves from implementation. It is a rare organization, however, that can take on the financial commitment necessary for a major infrastructure project in order to see whether the business will evolve in a desirable way. Nevertheless, infrastructure projects are seen as crucially important to the survival and success of organizations.

Analysing values and risks

The danger is that executives may actually turn against the technology that is costing so much and does not bring the advantages hoped for. There is, more than ever, the need to pause and think. Angell and Smithson (1990) say

> However, our message is not 'anti-technology' *per se*, it is rather that decision makers must re-examine the assumptions under which systems are justified, and they must become aware of the risks inherent in the introduction of information technology and balance them against the benefits.

Is there a way to become more aware, and to carry out the balancing? The approach known as information economics offers some positive advantages. This is because of its rather commonsense and practical view of the situation in which enterprises today find themselves, *vis-à-vis* investing in information technology and systems.

While IE certainly starts from the problem of looking at application systems, even though they are referred to as IT investments, its approach to the analysis of values and risks, rather than traditional costs and benefits, allows it to tackle the further problems of infrastructure projects. It must be said that it is more a question of building on the foundations that IE gives us, rather than finding pat answers in the book.

As Hochstrasser and others suggest in this book, the hard cash benefits of infrastructure projects are virtually impossible to evaluate. They are unlikely to be perceptible. A big new relational database management system may or may not bring hard benefits to the first major project it is used for. It will certainly make a difference to every subsequent project. How do we bring all this into the equation when trying to decide on the investment in the first place?

Much depends on how the IT budget is allocated. It is common to have discrete business units holding their own budgets, with development tools and methodologies decided on at the centre. One key issue, therefore, is achieving consensus among the different budget holders on the benefits that may or may not accrue from major decisions on a new database management system, or an extension to a network, and of course from more commonplace application systems.

There is another aspect to the problem. The temptation to make the figures come out right is irresistible. The politics of evaluation practice received some attention in Chapter 3. No matter how stringent the regulations regarding an acceptable rate of return, somehow the manager with clout finds a financial controller who can show miracles. A company demanding a 30% internal rate of return can be shown that a computer system will bring in a 400% rate. This is not merely personal experience. Angell and Smithson (1990) point out that 'The arbitrariness of cost–benefit studies within the euphoria of computerization provides a golden opportunity for the shrewd political operator'. And Hughes and England (1991) on planning and controlling IT budgets, are disarmingly frank, 'We are all probably guilty of using some dubious means to build budgets. We would be embarrassed if really challenged to justify the adequacy of our planning, or the true business value of the projects and services we provide.'

Information economics offers a way to grapple with these issues by proposing a highly adaptable framework which can guide the various parties to the decision as to whether an IT investment will be worth while, and to what extent. IE looks at how systems will be developed and used, as well as what benefits a system may bring. Thus it encompasses a number of human and management factors, as well as business factors. Since the success or failure of a system largely depends on these human factors, this is a great strength in IE. Within the framework, all the positive and negative impacts that an IT project can have on the enterprise can be discussed by all concerned. Positive impacts we may call values; negative impacts are risks.

Risks have to be taken. Any activity carries risk. However, if we can understand the kind and degree of risk, we can manage the situation so as to minimize it. Clearly, when dealing with information technology, there are major developmental activities and management actions involved. Hence, as suggested in other chapters, there will always be risks to be taken. On the other hand, even with difficult network projects, it is always possible to develop insights into the positive impacts, or values, that such a project may have for the enterprise.

Value or benefit?

We have mentioned positive impacts, or values, that a system may have for an organization. What meaning can we ascribe to the term **values**? The Introduction to this book has discussed terminology in some detail. Information economics distinguishes values from benefits. We do not lose sight of benefits, but value is a larger concept. One may take the view that benefits are what one pays for; value is what one takes risks for. We may note, in this context, that the decline in the productivity and competitiveness of the USA has been attributed, in part, to managers' aversion to risk (Freeman *et al.*, 1991).

One may be able to think and talk about **benefits** using knowledge and logic. If we install an on-line order-processing system, we may be able to be quite accurate in quantifying how many staff we would need and how much faster things would happen. This can then be turned into money benefits. We then write this down and say we have a benefit statement. But in fact, the system will only be developed and installed and used as a consequence of certain human activities. As soon as we do something, we take a risk. We therefore need an approach which goes beyond the logical benefit statement to consider real activities and real risks. One may potentially be able to process orders 20% more speedily and help the cash flow. The really hard question is: How likely is it that this will actually happen? The answer will depend on all sorts of factors. For example, what are the staff attitudes? How committed is top management? What firm plans are there for training? And so on. At the end of the day, there could well be the cash benefit plus extra value. This extra value might be a more satisfied and competent set of employees and a far better perception of the company by customers and the financial sector. But this total value will only have been gained through taking risks.

Value is not directly related to payment. For example, we talk of something having sentimental value. Such an item will almost certainly not be costly, rather the opposite. It is hard to say that it brings benefits. But we will probably fight harder for such an item than we would for something we could go out and buy. Of course, information systems hardly fill one with warm and tender feelings. But think about removing a system that has been in place for some years. The company gained the benefits of it long ago. Yet strong emotions are likely to be generated if it is killed off. It has acquired values. People understand how to use it. They have invested time and effort in it. It is part of the way things are done now, which is probably different from when it was first installed. This comes back to the point that value develops as people do things.

However, we still find it hard to separate the concepts and the terminology of value and benefits. Go to any seminar, and the discussion inevitably centres around benefits. It is agreed that some are soft, unquantifiable benefits. One is thus left with the status quo – if we can quantify the benefits all well and good. That is firm justification. If we cannot, then we simply take things on trust. Often this is accompanied by rhetorical flourishes demanding to know if we still justify the installation of telephones.

Information economics, for its part, offers a means of ascribing value to certain consequences of installing an information system, as well as including hard cash flow, or benefits, analysis.

On the other hand, it must be said that the word 'value' seems to have at least two meanings in Parker and Benson's usage. Value, in the larger sense, is the total positive impact of the information systems on an enterprise. Thus one needs to work out negative impacts as well. Actual money flowing out is negative, so is disruption to the work pattern caused by introducing a new information system, the time spent in learning new skills and working practices, and perhaps, accommodating new technology that does not fit into the old architecture.

But these are risks that often must be taken in order to achieve the positives. New learning, more effective ways of doing business, and an enhanced technology infrastructure to support the development of the enterprise are all valuable. Information economics defines and labels these values and risks, which means that it offers a clear set of concepts that people can begin to discuss.

The 7Cs of information economics

At one level, therefore, the IE approach offers a decision-making process. Interested parties, business managers and technology managers must get together to discuss how the proposed investments – as far as they can determine – measure up against the value and risk factors. This process leads to a number of significant advantages – the 7Cs of information economics.

1. **Comprehensiveness** – all relevant business, economic and technical issues are addressed.
2. **Consistency** – in the decision-making process.
3. **Clarity** – of objectives, values and attitudes.
4. **Communications** – vastly improved across and between functions.
5. **Confidence** – that projects have been thoroughly analysed and justified.
6. **Consensus** – between managers from different business units and functions.
7. **Culture** – gap closing.

These have all to do with human and management factors which, earlier noted, were crucial to the success or otherwise of information systems.

> Organizations have more problems than choice. Another fundamental organizational problem is to achieve co-ordinated collective action...In order to mobilize organizational action, it is important to secure commitment from presumed actors. (Brunsson, 1990)

One reason for IE's strength in helping communications between IT professionals and the business managers, is that it places the broad concepts of values and risks in a model that is clear, easily understood, and applicable to all enterprises using information systems and technology.

The two-domain model

Information economics starts with a simple, but accurate, model of an enterprise in the context of investing in IS. This is called the 'two-domain model' (Table 9.1). These two domains are the business domain and the technology domain. This is the case, whatever the organizational structure, and however systems are run and developed. Even if a company has gone for facilities management, it retains responsibility for deciding on its information systems.

The comprehensive view given in the table immediately goes to the heart of the problem discussed earlier: that is, the gap between the business side and the IT professionals. Somehow, with all the end-user computing and the management education and the power users and the spreadsheets and word processing, there is still mutual incomprehension. Further evidence was produced in the *Information Technology Review* 1991/1992 (Price Waterhouse, 1991).

The key point is that each domain will have its own reasons for thinking that an investment in a particular system would be worth while. These reasons represent the valuable aspects of the system. At the same time, each side will have its own worries that things might not work out as hoped. In other words, each side takes risks. There is more to the relationship between the domains than that of purchaser and provider. Only when the two domains understand each other's values and risks, can they start to solve the problem of information systems that do not bring the expected benefits, or of projects that go over time and budget. Without doubt, the technology side does try to understand the business. It does know that the systems it builds

Table 9.1 The two-domain model

Business domain	Technology domain
	Provides services to create value in business
Value Created by the use of information technology	*Cost* True cost for resources used for services to business domain; includes risk
Cost Technology and business charges for resources used; includes risk	*Value* Costs recovered or investment made in technology domain
Net value produced Business feasibility and economic justification for project, based on business performance	*Net support produced* Technical feasibility and economic viability for project, based on technology viability

should support the business aims. The business side may say that perhaps even more understanding is needed. But do the business managers think of the needs of the IT professionals? Do they think of the technology side as having to take risks?

The whole process of deciding on and justifying IT is highly political. Studies (Guimaraes and McKeen, 1988) have shown the bias displayed by different groups of decision makers as they evaluate proposals for management information systems (MIS). Steering committees apparently liked extremely large projects, which may be high risk and entail a good deal of organizational change, not to mention long development times. User departments, on the other hand, looked for small projects that were quickly developed and had low risk. The information services wanted projects that integrated well with existing systems, matched their skills and were (un-believably) risk free. Top management projects were 'almost totally unremarkable'.

Such a political situation is not to be totally smoothed over by any methodology. However, IE offers a way of getting various groups to understand each other's values and risks, communicate openly and come to a consensus. It presents a means, through a scoring system, to objectively assess feelings and attitudes, and to put a number against the total value. One system can then be compared with another, to produce a list of information systems, in priority order of value.

The second meaning of value

It was remarked earlier that hard cash benefits were not forgotten in IE. These constitute the second meaning of 'value'. The first factor to consider is return on investment. Parker and Benson urge those applying the method to look beyond the obvious cash benefits to the unit for which the proposed system is designed. One is encouraged to look at what they call 'value linkage'. Does another department or area obtain a money benefit from the proposed system? Another way of arriving at a money benefit is called 'value restructuring'. It is possible that a whole department is reoriented to more valuable work through the new system. One is referred to the 'hedonic wage model' which is a way of quantifying the cash benefit of allowing, say, managers, to spend more time doing what they are paid to do, rather than administrative work. There is also the idea of 'value accelerating', that is, quantifying the actual one-time cash benefit of getting something done sooner through the use of the new system.

The point is that IE presses home the importance of working out the hard money benefits, or indeed, the losses, before going on to consider the other value and risk factors.

Business domain: value and risk factors

We have arrived at the basic framework that IE presents of value and risk factors (see Figure 9.1). Within the two-domain model, each side has its own list of value and risk factors. The factors that would lead one to make the investment, the value factors, in the business domain, are:

- Return on investment (ROI) – This can be measured any way a business wishes.
- Strategic match – The degree to which a proposed project supports the strategic aims of the organization.

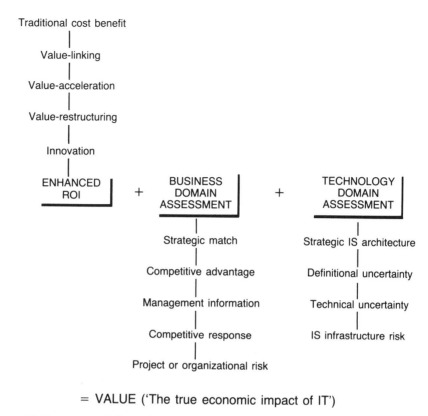

Figure 9.1 Investment: information economics can be tailored to different evaluation needs.

- Competitive advantage
- Management information on core activities
- Competitive risk – This assesses the degree to which failure to implement the system will cause competitive damage to the enterprise.

The risk factor, that is, the reason why the proposed system may not work as it should, and be less valuable, is:

- Organizational risk – This considers the degree to which the business side is prepared for the changes a new or enhanced system may bring. I view this as perhaps the most crucial risk of all.

Technology domain: value and risk factors

In the technology domain we find only one value factor:

- Strategic IS architecture – This evaluates the degree to which the project is aligned with the overall information systems strategies of the enterprise.

The remainder are risk factors.

- Definitional uncertainty – This assesses the degree to which the users' requirements or specifications are known.

- Technical uncertainty – This looks at the readiness of the technical domain itself to undertake the project.
- IS infrastructure risk – This assesses the degree to which extra investment, outside the specific project, may be necessary to accommodate the project.

These factors are first of all weighted to reflect their relative importance to the enterprise, and then proposed systems are scored against them.

Some key points

Experience has shown that these factors cover all the major issues that arise when tackling the question of whether a system is valuable and should be funded. However, as suggested by Willcocks and Lester in an earlier chapter, the model is highly adaptable. This point is particularly important when, as is the case at present, change in IT capabilities and usage is so very rapid.

The ROI factor can be translated by an organization using the IE approach to suit its own methods and culture. A company can use its own measuring techniques. It may choose a highly advanced approach to calculating the financial return on information systems investments, such as that of Paul Strassmann. Or, if this factor is not so highly significant, it can take a simple approach. The important thing is that the hard money side is not forgotten.

Perhaps the most significant factor here is organizational risk. Information economics suggests criteria by which this risk can be assessed. As always, the criteria can be changed. As they stand, they provide a valuable check-list, covering such matters as the commitment of top management to the proposed system; the extent to which working practices may have to change; the attitudes of staff towards change, and so on.

If IE does nothing more than warn managers that they will very likely be wasting their money on a system when organizational risk scores highly, then it will have been worth while using the approach.

As well as warning, IE points to specific areas where managers can take action and minimize the risk. This will help them to succeed next time round.

The value, in technology, is that the proposed project will fit with and further develop the technological structure of the organization. The technology domain itself will be strengthened, and the company will gain as its technical capability is enhanced. However, systems development is a risky process. The key risk, correctly placed in the technology domain, concerns the users. The question is: How far are the IT professionals trying to hit a moving target when they start the system development process? If the users' requirements are unclear and ever changing, then they are likely to end up with a system that does not do what they wanted and is therefore less valuable than it might have been. This is not the place to discuss this complex issue fully; the issue receives detailed attention in Chapter 11. The main point is that the risk needs to be understood and measured.

Weighting the factors

Once the factors have been agreed, the business and technology managers must decide their relative importance to the enterprise, and show this by assigning weights to them. This means getting consensus on what the business's strategic direction and culture are. The weightings reflect a specific organization's outlook and decisions, and constitute a way in which IE is tailored to the organization.

It is extremely valuable for the business and technology managers to pause and clarify just what is important to their business. Is it ROI? Is it strategic match? Should it be? What sort of organization is it when it comes to risk? The point is not to run away from all risk, but to be aware of how the company would react. Is it really risk-averse, or will the chief executive be able to take a robust view? Will the finance director have apoplexy or does the company believe that nothing ventured, nothing won?

We have returned to the earlier comments on value and risk and the feelings that these engender. In the end, we are talking about company culture. The weightings that are applied to the different factors reflect the fundamental approach of the enterprise. Experience has shown that it is important to be very clear about the weights. What is needed is very strong direction. There is no need to weight each factor, nor is there any point in agonizing over whether a weight should be 6 or 7 on a 10-point scale.

Parker and Benson actually go so far as to try to produce some models of likely emphases in the weightings to reflect different organizational types. They imply, undoubtedly correctly, that a finance-oriented enterprise will have a different pattern of weights from that of a market-oriented business. However, there is a danger in trying to generalize and offer a ready-made solution. It is better if the managers confront their own specific situations. It may be that they discover anomalies. For example, they may like to think of themselves as highly strategic, and supportive of a customer-oriented approach. In reality, it may be found that they value a system that gives them management information above one that pushes them towards a more radical implementation of their customer-oriented strategy.

Information economics can, and should, be used as much to educate and enlighten and stimulate further thinking, as to produce a list of projects in a rote fashion.

Adaptability of information economics

A case study casts light on just how adaptable the IE approach is. It was introduced to a central government department. Its use has now been made mandatory. This in itself indicates that it is an effective and easy-to-use method.

Clearly Parker and Benson hardly had a British Government department in mind when thinking through the IE approach. Nevertheless, taking up the cue that they give that IE can be tailored to different users, a team approach was taken with the client, represented by members of the management services group, which had originally requested that the method be introduced, to tailor it for the department.

As is commonly found, the department subsumed a number of different 'business units', in this case, five. While some were clearly in related areas, some were quite disparate. Some were advanced in their use of IT, some much less so. Their IT needs were different. Hence, there was a problem, as they all had to share one overall departmental IT budget. Their differences also meant that it was difficult to prioritize in a way that was seen to be reasonable and fair to all.

Each unit had been asked to produce its business strategy. This was not only to help the units to achieve their goals, but also to help the central IT management group, composed of senior executives from each of the business units, to allocate the budget and give approvals for IT projects.

This approach was new. There was no history of the newly defined units exchanging plans and information. The concept of a corporate entity overarching the units, with its own strategy and needs, was not clear.

In this situation, IE satisfactorily fulfilled its dual role. First, it helped produce an acceptable prioritized list of projects. Perhaps more importantly, it prompted the representatives of the different business units to define the corporate strategic aims, state what was particularly important in terms of what information systems could bring and, above all, to develop a common language and shared views. The mechanics were that primarily information economics factors were minutely gone through to evaluate their applicability and usefulness to the department. During this phase we jointly decided on what to retain and what to change or develop. We also looked at the scoring criteria and adapted them to be, frankly, more anglicized and understandable. Where we developed new factors, we also developed new scoring criteria. An obvious factor to change was competitive advantage. The department is not yet an agency committed to commercial ends. What was more important was the policy analysis and review process. So we substituted this, and developed appropriate scoring criteria.

Sometimes we felt that the terminology used by Parker and Benson could be clarified. For example, we changed 'competitive response' to 'negative response', to underline that we were talking about what would be the consequences of **not** doing the project. While we kept the ROI factor, it was felt that we should also use net present value. This was partly because an NPV calculation is in any case made for each proposed investment in IS. Also it gave a fairer picture between large and small business units. Another organization might want to make its own changes to the factors. The basic model is robust enough for such alterations, and will neither collapse nor turn into something very different.

In a number of instances, we also changed the way in which the scoring criteria were phrased and, indeed, what they should be. Obviously the people who are eventually going to do the scoring have to understand the criteria. These should be changed accordingly. Taking an example from the scoring criteria of negative response (replacing competitive response), the original criterion is, for a score of 3,

> If the project is postponed, the enterprise remains capable of responding to the needed change without affecting its competitive position; lacking the new system, the enterprise is not substantially hindered in its ability to respond rapidly and effectively to change in the competitive environment. (Parker *et al.*, 1988).

That, we felt, was less than clear and helpful. One's respect for our Civil Service must rise when it was robustly decided to go for 'If the proposed project is postponed, there will be severely damaging effects.'

Business managers using the IE approach

Once the factors and scoring criteria had been decided, a meeting was held with a member of the management group to gain his first impressions and to clarify certain issues where we needed guidance from the user side. It was interesting to see that at that very first meeting, the need to confront things in black and white, and make a choice, helped to bring about a change of mind. This was with regard to scoring the ROI and NPV. The user's first reaction was that it was not worth making distinctions between different bands of ROI and giving different scores accordingly. Either the system showed a return, in which case it passed the threshold, or it did not, in which case it would not be, generally, an acceptable project. However, given the possibility of making finer discriminations, and given the fact that his decision would be down in black and white, literally, and would form the only basis of choice for all the other members of the decision-making group, it was decided that the more discriminating approach was better.

The next step was to prepare an explanatory document, showing the factors and scoring criteria. This was sent in advance to all the members of the management group. They were also invited to a presentation of the approach, where their questions could be answered and they could express their views.

This meeting was particularly positive. They found the IE method easy to understand and use. The terminology, as adapted, was familiar to them. It spoke of their business, not technology. The approach brought them together and gave them a positive goal to aim for. They could also view their own business area in the context of others and of the department as a whole – something that it is not easy to do without a helpful framework. The management group members were pleased that they now had a mechanism to help them clarify their respective situations with regard to information systems.

The final step in this phase was for the management group members to weight the factors. The process of coming to a consensus about which factors were most significant to the department as a whole was stimulating and helpful. However, it became clear that in actually deciding on numbers, the key aspect of weighting – that is, giving a very clear direction on what is, and what is not, important – was rather lost sight of. The management group decided to use numbers from 1 to 20 rather than 1 to 10. There is no particular merit in this. The members then became somewhat embroiled in making fine distinctions between say, allocating 14 or 15 to a factor. This makes no useful difference at all in the final scoring. Nor is it essential to weight every factor.

This step marked the end of consultancy involvement. The management group, supported by management services, started to use the IE approach. Its use is now mandatory to prioritize investments in information systems. The department is considering extending its use at different points within the systems development cycle.

Valuing a system

Information economics in a major company

The case of a US government department is perhaps an extreme example of the adaptability of the model. There is another way of using IE, which shows its flexibility. A major organization wanted to see whether IE could be used to arrive at a value for just one important system.

The system had been developed, over some years, with different groups within the organization being involved. A considerable amount of money had been expended.

The system was viewed as one which provided management information, not one which of itself could bring a cash return. While it was clearly a large and important system, its use within the organization was limited. The underlying question was typical: Is it worth spending more money on this system?

The client understood that the use of the IE approach in order to value just one system meant it had to be applied in a rather different way. We therefore defined the assignment as a prototype approach. However, since we were neither developing a system nor seeking to involve a number of business unit managers in a total prioritization exercise, the client's requirement was that a minimum of client time was to be devoted to this. The consultant was to do as much work as possible, consistent with essential input from the client side.

It was decided to use the basic, unchanged IE model. It is noteworthy that the factors, when applied to a system within a private sector company, were relevant and useful and did not need to be altered. One interesting point was that while it was agreed that the ROI factor was important, it was felt that it could not be applied in this instance. The system under consideration was characterized purely as an information giving system, not one designed to produce a return. The ROI factor was therefore left out. However, as an unforeseen result of applying the IE approach, the organization did in fact start to make a case for the system based in part on the financial return it had undoubtedly made.

The method decided upon was to go through the exercise of using the IE approach, with members of the technology and business domains, to weight the factors and score the system. In so doing, a good deal of information was collected about the business and about the system, its development history and the role it currently played in the organization. The score was then compared with a theoretical but realistic maximum. However, a score as such – while indicating whether or not the system was valuable, as compared with an optimum-scoring one – was not the most useful piece of information to be gained.

Balancing values and risks

What was enlightening, was being able to look at the value as against the risk scores. The system scored quite highly on value. In particular, it was excellent at delivering the management information and was certainly an obviously important system. So why was there a question about its value?

Looking at the risk factors allowed us to see why the organization was not getting as much value as it could. The organizational risk was high, and there was also a technical risk. The organizational risk was that there was not an obvious system champion. This led to limited use. Another major factor was that there was no ROI score, as this aspect had been viewed as being of no relevance to the system. In turn, this meant that even those who were using the system were not seeking hard business benefits.

The technical risks largely stemmed from the development history. The system ran on hardware that was outside the mainstream architecture, which had been decided on too late to be included in the system in question. Its somewhat chequered development history added to the technical risk. A number of different technical groups had been involved at different times.

A fairly detailed analysis of the value and risk factors was easily accomplished using the IE approach. The client was then in a position not only to decide whether to invest further in the system, but could see what steps to take to minimize the risks, and thus increase the value of the system.

It is important to stress this separate analysis of value and risk, because it is possible that a number of projects might score the same, or almost the same, overall. For example, one system might be strategically highly valuable, but also very high risk. Another might be a worthy, but comparatively unimportant replacement system, carrying very little risk at all.

Therefore it is important to look at the balance, for any system, of the value and risk scores, rather than the total score, in order to reach a much deeper understanding of its potential.

A look to the future for information economics

There is a further aspect to adaptability which is linked to the question of how relevant the factors are. They appear to be well chosen and cover all the issues. This does not mean that they should be treated as carved in stone. Another strength of the IE approach is that it can be further developed, as well as adapted, to reflect newer thinking or new situations and environments.

Since it has not been used for very long anywhere, certainly not in the UK, it may be thought that it is not yet essential to update it. However, it is essential for IE to take account of new ideas and the changing technology environment. There are stimulating and helpful views coming from research such as the 'Management in the 90s' programme. This programme of research was carried out at the Sloan School of the Massachusetts Institute of Technology. The programme

> was created in 1984 to examine the profound impact that information technology (IT) is having on organizations of all kinds. Its mission was to explore how IT will affect the way organizations will be able to survive and prosper in the competitive environment of the 1990s and beyond. (Scott-Morton, 1991)

Carry on competitive advantage?

The 'Management in the 90s' research leads one to doubt whether an organization can gain competitive advantage from the use of IT, in any simplistic way. Rather it points to the need for management to handle new interdependences, both within themselves and between themselves and other organizations, in order to stay in the race. Such management depends on advanced use of IT. Typically this will involve networks, advanced communications and widespread access to all types of information. Within this overall picture, organizations will put the stress on different strategies. One major emphasis is likely to be on links with suppliers and customers.

There are three areas where one can see that new factors may be developed for inclusion in the IE framework. One concerns what I call 'competitive capability'. This is about using IT as an enabler, giving organizations the opportunity to invest in added innovations in order to stay well ahead in the race.

A second area may be characterized as 'external linkages' or 'customer/supplier services'. Here one may see IT as supporting active and mutually helpful relationships between, say, supplier and customer organizations, in place of the adversarial purchasing approach that is often destructive (Carlisle and Parker, 1989). IT can give organizations the capability to conduct joint problem-solving exercises, with the ultimate aim of maximizing customer satisfaction.

A third area, which may indeed subsume the other two, is the concept of the 'networked organization'. Here the emphasis is perhaps more on internal linkages, or interdependence between various people and groups within the organization. We may also adduce here the idea (Drucker, 1988) of the business enterprise as an orchestra rather than a hierarchy. Information technology is essential to facilitate communication between individuals and groups. These ideas, with their implications for the evaluation of the role of IT, can be incorporated in the IE framework. In a few years' time, we may even see a very changed group of factors. Nevertheless, the essential IE approach will still be there.

Conclusions

Without claiming the IE approach as a panacea, there is evidence that it has been found helpful to organizations grappling with the problems of justifying their investment in information technology and systems. It is certainly practical. It is inexpensive. It demands management interest and the willingness to work cooperatively, rather than money and resources. It is flexible and adaptable, important considerations in times of flux.

British private and public enterprises are increasingly interested in information economics. Those who have tried it – for example the Prudential Assurance experience described in the next chapter – are enthusiastic. It could inexpensively lead to a solution of a key problem for all enterprises seeking to improve their return from investing in information technology.

References

Angell, I. O. and Smithson, S. (1990) Managing information technology: a crisis of confidence? *European Management Journal*, **5** (1), 27–36.

Brunsson, N. (1989) *The Organization of Hypocrisy*, Wiley, Chichester.

Carlisle, J. and Parker, R. (1989) *Beyond Negotiation: Redeeming Customer–Supplier Relationships*, Wiley, Chichester.

Drucker, P. (1988) The coming of the new organization. *Harvard Business Review*, January–February, 45–53.

Freeman, C., Sharp, M. and Walker, W. (1991) *Technology and the Future of Europe: Global Competition and the Environment in the 1990s*, Pinter, London.

Guimaraes, T. and McKeen, J. D. (1988) Organizational bias in the selection of MIS projects. Omega. *International Journal of Management Science*, **16** (4), 297–307.

Hughes, C. and England, J. (1991) Planning and controlling IT budgets, in *Computing Services Association Official Reference Book 1991* (ed. J. Kavanagh), Sterling Publications Ltd, London.

Lederer, A. L. and Sethi, V. (1991) Critical dimensions of information systems planning. *Decision Sciences Journal*, **22** (1), 104–19.

Mintzberg, H. (1987) Crafting strategy. *Harvard Business Review*, July–August, 66–75.

Parker, M., Benson, R. and Trainor, E. H. (1988) *Information Economics: Linking Business Performance to Information Technology*, Prentice-Hall, London.

Price Waterhouse (1991) *Information Technology Review 1991/92* (ed. K. Grindley), Price Waterhouse, London.

Scott-Morton, M. (1991) Introduction, in *The Corporation of the 1990s: Information Technology and Organizational Transformation* (ed. M. Scott-Morton), Oxford University Press, New York.

Sullivan, C. (1985) Systems planning in the information age. *Sloan Management Review*, **26** (2), 3–12.

Thurow, L. C. (1991) Foreword, in *The Corporation of the 1990s: Information Technology and Organizational Transformation* (ed. M. Scott-Morton), Oxford University Press, New York.

10

Beyond return on investment

Tom Coleman and Mark Jamieson

Introduction

This chapter first describes the conclusions from some research carried out jointly by the authors (Coleman and Jamieson, 1991). Over 100 of the Times top 200 companies provided data on how they carried out IT investment appraisal, in particular how they managed, or more usually ignored, the intangible benefits. This adds to the picture on evaluation practice developed in Chapters 2 and 3 of this book.

The results of this research formed one of the foundations for the Prudential project appraisal method (PAM). The chapter also describes the methodology used to develop and implement this system, which at the time of writing is being used to evaluate IT projects within the traditional arm of Prudential Assurance, the Home Service division of the Prudential.[1] Throughout we use the terms information systems and information technology interchangeably.

Evaluating *all* the benefits of information technology

There has always been plenty of depressing news about how information systems (IS) projects fail to deliver the promised benefits. Several studies have claimed that up to 70% of all IS projects fail to deliver the claimed benefits, in many cases

Information Management: The evaluation of information systems investments.
Edited by Leslie Willcocks.
Published in 1994 by Chapman & Hall. ISBN 0 412 41540 2.

providing no measurable gains at all (Hochstrasser and Griffiths, 1991). If people honestly believe that spending money on IT is at best a waste of time, and at worst a damaging waste of money, then there is no logical reason why such expenditure should continue.

Despite this, expenditure on information systems continues to rise and there are no real signs that the growth of IT expenditure is slowing to a halt (Butler Cox Foundation, 1990). Even in the current recession, the Gartner Group recently predicted that IT spending would climb to 9.5% of revenue by 2002 compared to its current level of 5.2% (Gartner Group, 1992).

In spite of the negative reports, we believe that there is widespread acceptance that investment in IT is beneficial. The problem is in understanding what exactly is being produced by the technology. To paraphrase a well-known advertising truism: 'I know that I am wasting 50% of the money I spend on IT, I just don't know which 50%.' The failing is not in the use of technology itself, but in understanding what benefits it brings.

This chapter, therefore, concentrates on techniques for evaluating the benefits of information systems. The emphasis is on evaluating **all** of the benefits. We believe that the investment appraisal techniques in use in most organizations concentrate exclusively on the tangible benefits. Our research found that where an evaluation is carried out, there is overwhelming use of techniques that push decision making on the basis of return on investment (ROI). Our results reinforce those detailed in previous chapters. These techniques ignore the contribution of benefits that cannot be measured in cash terms, even though they can form a crucial part of the deliverables of a project. Among the respondents to our survey, the feeling was that, on average, nearly half the value of IS projects is contained in intangible benefits. If the benefits are not identified in the first place, or if measures of success are not put in place, it is hardly surprising that the feeling remains that nothing of great importance has been achieved.

The title of this chapter expresses the view that in order to understand what information systems produce, techniques have to be used that go beyond the tangible measures used in ROI techniques.

We shall describe the broader aspects of appraisal systems, discussing in detail some of the techniques that have proved successful. In the area of intangible benefits, there are no generally accepted techniques in use, and so we go further to describe a methodology that has been developed for, and is used by, the largest division of the Prudential. Before we do this, however, we shall discuss further the limitations of current techniques in order to establish why a new approach is needed.

Investment appraisal in practice: research conclusions
Beyond ROI

To understand the limitations of ROI measures, it is worth while considering what it is we are trying to do when performing an investment appraisal. We are trying to express the benefits and costs in terms that the decision makers understand, and with ROI measures, we are estimating both of them in cash terms, which is something that everyone understands. However, this approach runs into trouble in three main areas (Levy and Sarnat, 1986):

- When the ROI is zero or even negative
- When the costs or benefits cannot be expressed in cash terms
- When there is no clear, causal relationship between the information system and achievement of business goals.

Zero or negative return on investment

Return on investment methods are based on an 'investment' view of decision making. Managers are seen as having a certain amount of money under their control and they decide to 'invest' in the projects that will bring the largest return. This process sometimes has the sophistication of a 'hurdle' rate, a minimum rate of return from a project before it can be approved. However, some investment decisions do not fit in with this 'investment' view of the business world. For example:

- A building society is trying to make an investment decision as to whether to join a nationwide network of cash-dispensing machines in order to provide a type of service that they believe some of their customers will demand. The return on investment in this situation is almost certainly negative. As well as paying to set up the link, they will have to pay ongoing charges for the service. In addition, their internal costs may increase, as experience indicates that provision of cash dispensers results in a larger number of transactions of smaller value. Although the business case includes positive benefits, such as fewer tellers, more efficient use of their accommodation and potentially more customers, they will be difficult to realize and are outweighed by the hard costs.
- However, the building society decides to go ahead with the investment, because not to do so would almost certainly result in their losing customers to other societies that provide a fuller range of services.

Another example:

- An insurance company sets up a claims handling system to process claims more quickly, in order to improve the level of service it provides. But it does not expect any increase in sales to offset the disadvantage in cash flow, as well as covering the costs of the new system. Why not? Because they are merely reacting to initiatives set up by their competitors and attempting to use improved service and image to maintain their market position.

These two examples highlight situations described as 'competitive response'. The investment decision is not based on how much extra revenue or profit will flow into the company, but on something more powerful, the price of staying in business. In a competitive industry, and particularly in mature markets, there will be few opportunities to produce positive returns on investment. As soon as one company establishes a short-term advantage its competitors will be forced to invest merely to retain their share of the market.

It has been suggested that this 'competitive response' is a major impetus in IT investment decisions (Ward *et al.*, 1990). There is certainly a lot of cross-checking between competitors to ascertain the size of the IT budget and the type of project undertaken, and this can often appear to be the main criteria in setting the IT budget and systems plan.

Despite this, many organizations still have stringent financial criteria to satisfy (Thomas, 1992), including widespread use of hurdle rates, payback periods, internal rates of return, etc. The challenge, then, for the project sponsor is how to satisfy these financial criteria in order to allow projects crucial to the organization's survival to be approved.

We have encountered many devious techniques used to establish a certain ROI, usually by analysing only part of the project. For example, a large financial services company provided a justification for a major systems initiative on the basis of a comparison between doing it with in-house staff or contracting it out to a facilities management company. This hurdle rate was cleared and the project went ahead, but the expected benefits of the project were never seriously analysed.

Equally common is a quasi-deliberate optimism over the total project costs. By the time anyone can prove that there is a serious negative financial variance, the organization is committed to having the project at almost any cost. The result is 'good money thrown after bad', but eventually the system is delivered, albeit at the price of another public cost overrun by IS development.

The other main technique is something known as 'backward justification'. This is where the tangible costs are identified, and then benefits are identified until the hurdle rate is achieved. First the tangible benefits are identified, such as headcount reductions or space savings, then the less tangible benefits, such as efficiency savings or proposed increases in sales, and, finally, if desperate, some values are put on basically intangible benefits, such as improved decision making.

In this case the financial plan is usually carefully filed on a dusty shelf and never referred to again. Such analysis may at least satisfy the project sponsor (and possibly the internal auditors) but it does little to ensure that the benefits are effectively managed on system delivery or that maximum value is obtained from the project.

Intangible costs and benefits

As Hochstrasser suggested in Chapter 8, return on investment relies on ascribing a cash value to a benefit. But there are many benefits of information systems that are difficult or impossible to quantify – the intangibles. In our research we discovered that certain types of projects gave great difficulty in justification. These were:

- Infrastructure projects
- Management information systems and executive information systems
- Office systems
- Replacement systems
- 'Strategic systems'.

In all of these the majority of benefits are intangible in nature. For example, a key benefit of a management information system is to allow improved decision making by the management of a company. It is difficult to determine whether decision making will in fact improve once the system is installed, and very difficult indeed to determine what the cash value will be.

As discussed in other chapters, justifying infrastructure expenditure causes problems for almost all organizations. Information technology is an enabler, i.e. it does not provide direct benefits but enables other areas of the business to achieve them. Infrastructure projects are therefore 'enabling the enabler' and are thus one step further away from the cold realities of profit generation.

However, even with architecture or infrastructure projects there are benefits from consistent appraisal. The Prudential use the benefit profile described later, on technical systems projects initiated by the systems developers rather than by the business, if only to ensure that the architecture planners have fully considered the business advantages that will come from the technologies.

Dos Santos and other contributors to this book point out that strategic systems also cause problems for conventional management accounting appraisal. Considerable investment has been made in recent years in systems which are seen as strategic to the organization's success, but which provide no benefits of a tangible nature. Return on investment measures are little help in evaluating these types of projects. In fact reliance on ROI can cause considerable distortions in the investment appraisal process. As an example, in one organization a large office system was justified on the basis of reduced secretarial headcount because of improved word-processing facilities. The efficiencies in typing fulfilled the requirements of the justification process. However, in the post-implementation review the main benefits of the system were identified as:

- improved effectiveness of professional staff, by improving communication through use of electronic mail
- improved customer service, by providing access to a centralized message facility from remote offices; staff visiting remote offices could still receive messages from their home office whenever they logged into the system.

These benefits were made possible by the widespread provision of workstations to professionals, and of an extensive electronic network to provide messaging facilities. These could not easily be justified on the basis of the tangible secretarial headcount savings originally identified.

Care also needs to be taken when quantifying managerial productivity gains through the use of office systems. The usual justification techniques look at the amount of time spent in administrative tasks as opposed to managerial tasks. The time saved in administrative tasks, described as a percentage of overall time, is multiplied by the salary bill to provide the cash saving. When implementing an office system, however, it is often the case that professionals spend more time in 'administrative' tasks, such as typing, than they did before they were given a word-processing package (Peltu, 1986). It is managerial effectiveness that typically provides the benefits from office systems, not efficiency.

Causal links between IT investment and profitability

Many activities in business do not have a direct link to profitability. The impact from investment in activities such as marketing or human resource initiatives is very difficult to measure. Expenditure on information systems is similarly very difficult to relate to profitability. Paul Strassmann (1990), in his book *The Business Value of Computers*, goes to great lengths to investigate if there is a direct link between IT investment and profitability. He concludes that there is no direct relationship. But

ROI measures assume that such a relationship exists.[2] That is, if I put in x amount of expenditure then I get out y amount of profit.

One reason for this difficulty is because information systems support or enable business initiatives. The benefits are obtained outside of the control of the IS department. The efficacy of information systems should be measured by the extent to which they support business processes and ROI measures cannot assess this relationship. At best they tend to measure the overall impact of the business initiative, not the contribution of IT.

Of course, business initiatives themselves may not have a direct link to profitability (Peters, 1990). Examination of the strategic plan of any large organization reveals many objectives that do not necessarily result in increased profits. If an IS project is supporting such an initiative it is nonsensical to insist on an ROI from it when the business activity cannot support such an analysis.

This does not mean that expenditure on IT is akin to throwing money into a large pit and hoping for the best. In some cases IT expenditure can result in direct savings. Many document image systems, for example, have been justified on direct improvements in clerical speed and efficiency, along with the space savings from converting paper records to optical disk-based ones (Coleman, 1990).

These limitations of ROI have implications for the identification of benefits and the management of projects. If we want to determine the extent to which IT will benefit business processes, the best judges are the managers of the business (Computer Finance, 1992). The onus for benefit identification should be on them, rather than the IT department. Similarly, the responsibility for achieving the benefits should be theirs. The IT department performs its role by providing the system. The achievement of the benefits for the business ultimately depends on the business managers and they therefore need to understand the limitations of ROI in appraising IT projects.

Building the business case

Although there are serious limitations in using ROI for the investment appraisal of IS projects, as Wiseman argues in the previous chapter, measurement of tangible costs and benefits still has its uses. The problems occur when it is the **only** measure used in investment appraisal.

Major users of IT that we interviewed recognized long ago the limitations of ROI as the only measure of value for IS projects. They concentrate on building a more complete picture of the costs, benefits and risks associated with IS projects. In almost every organization this is called the business case. Return on investment is but one of many measures that are used. In the remainder of this chapter we shall examine what the components of the business case should be, and describe how such an approach has been formalized in the Prudential.

The uses of investment appraisal?

We have argued earlier that most business decision makers are dissatisfied with the quality of their IT investment appraisal. They believe that a high proportion of the expenditure is wasted and that they are not achieving the competitive advantage that has been promised over and over again during the past decade.

Their focus on efficient and effective use of resources has been heightened during the recession when costs have become critical for many organizations. Boards and shareholders are looking to IS to share the strain along with all of the other functions and achieve more benefit with less budget. In effect they are demanding optimum value for money and the best possible return from the use of scarce resources. In these circumstances appraisal techniques have two major uses:

- **Project selection**. There are always more potential projects than resources to complete them and every organization must have *some* processes for winnowing and prioritizing them. Companies use a multitude of techniques – for example, project selection may be informal or formal, controlled by the accountants or internal audit, tightly or loosely linked to the business and IT strategies, etc.
- To initiate **benefit management planning**. There is a widespread misconception among IS development staff that if the system meets the specification and is developed within the budget then it is a success. However, success is really only achieved by the business using the system to generate additional profits. Benefit management plans encourage the business users to focus on exactly how they will make the system pay off and contribute to the company objectives. As discussed earlier, intangible benefits are becoming an increasingly important part of this.

Project appraisal is inevitable. You can argue that it is redundant for mandatory projects where a company must go ahead no matter what the cost, but there may well be choices to be made between technical or business options and the delivery of the benefits still needs managing. The evidence suggests that only a very small proportion of projects are truly mandatory, i.e. failing to do them will cause critical damage to the business. Almost all are really discretionary in nature. Providing it accepts the consequences, a company can choose not to go ahead with the project without any calamitous effects on their short-term survival prospects, although the champions of the projects may well argue differently.

Although we believe every company uses project appraisal, most current approaches are far from optimal. They lack reliability, validity and consistency. Even more critically the results of project appraisal are simply not believed by the very people it is aimed at.

This situation is now beginning to change. Tools and techniques are being developed which provide major advantages to both business and IS communities (Parker *et al.*, 1988). As we have found within the Prudential, the gains can amount to a significant percentage of the IS budget. The remainder of this chapter will cover our experiences of developing, and introducing, investment appraisal systems in more detail. It will describe both the methodology and the tools used within it and touch upon some of the pitfalls we have encountered in implementing a full system.

Our development methodology

Implementing a system that will radically alter the way value for money is achieved from IT investments is far from easy. Because most firms have a long history of failure in this area there is often tremendous inertia to overcome as well as a severe lack of credibility in the way business managers regard IT plans. The change process needs managing from a total organizational context, getting all of the various levels of stakeholders to buy in through involvement and feedback. The appraisal system needs to match not only the explicit company goals but also the underlying strategies and individual needs. The business managers need to be convinced that they will get increased quality and higher value systems, and that they will have more control over IS developments. On the other hand, system developers need to be convinced that they will be supplied with clearer user priorities and that they will be protected from the worst extremes of changing requirements.

Properly managed, the change process itself provides beneficial side-effects, with the end-users becoming used to the concepts of benefit management and being more prepared to be involved in a partnership with IS. To satisfy these requirements the Prudential used the IT investment appraisal methodology briefly described below to develop and introduce the process of 'Total Benefit Management', including the appraisal tools which are packaged together internally as the PAM (project appraisal methodology) (Coleman, 1992).

1. **Investment appraisal audit and business objective review**
   Aim – to understand the existing senior management level, business priorities and IT investment strategies
   This phase is basically a review of existing mission statements, goals, objectives, KPIs, CSFs, etc. Identifying where the top level management are trying to move the business, and what are the supporting IT strategies.

2. **Investment analysis tool selection/development**
   Aim – to develop and validate a tool set which matches the organizational culture and the business objectives
   An iterative approach is used, working with senior, line and project managers. See below for further details.

3. **Define change initiation and investment appraisal processes and structures**
   Aim – to establish common terms, processes and measures for managing the value of IT with the business and IS managers
   In our experience this phase should determine what the consensus views are, and then highlight any disagreements, rather than attempt to force a common set of definitions on reluctant business or IS groups.

4. **Integration of investment appraisal into the IS development life-cycle**
   Aim – to make sure the IS development process is focused on achieving the desired benefits
   Physically integrating the tools, although very important, is only part of the task. Obtaining support and acceptance from the stakeholders is vital.

5. **Training and roll-out**
   Aim – to ensure that the approach is universally adopted
   Using awareness seminars, training material, one-to-one walk-throughs, cascade training, etc.

6. **Support and maintenance**
   Aim – to accommodate changing business and user requirements
   The business objectives and priorities inevitably change from day one. The tools also require maintenance and possibly further development, although in our experience thorough initial design will keep this to a minimum.

7. **Programme management**

Aim – to focus both IS and business management on benefit management and value for money

Portfolio management can be defined as the aggregation of all of the planned and current work. We believe that organizations need to move on further to programme management, where you appraise and manage benefits that would not happen unless the projects are considered as an integrated whole.

The phases are not interdependent and will almost certainly overlap. Effective change management, which is the key element of programme management, is essential throughout the whole development of the investment appraisal system. Business users **have** to be convinced that a formal system will benefit them directly; no easy task if the proponents come from IS rather than the business itself.

Prudential experiences to date suggest that, for large organizations, implementing an investment appraisal system will take at least six months. There is always an existing system, albeit ad hoc, and some of the tools recommended are likely to be totally new to the organization and thus require a significant familiarization and learning period. However, if necessary, results can be shown relatively quickly by carrying out a small-scale IT audit, e.g. on one division's current portfolio or on the options for a major project.

The Prudential IT investment appraisal system

This section covers the tools developed for the Home Service division of the Prudential Assurance. Home Service deals with all individual life and general insurance products, employing several hundred application developers, with a total IT budget of over £50 million.

The methodology and appraisal tools were developed over some 12 months between 1991 and 1992. The long development period was partly due to the learning experience. We believe few companies have focused on total benefit management in this fashion and pioneering new areas inevitably leads you down a few blind alleys. However, an equally important factor was the intense organizational and cultural change proceeding at the time, both in the systems development area and Home Service generally.

The tools developed for the Prudential fall into the three areas of:

- financial appraisal
- risk appraisal
- strategic or intangible benefit appraisal.

The tools are used across the whole life-cycle of a project with some aspects, e.g. benefit management, potentially extending years past the implementation date. Figure 10.1 shows how the main tools within the project appraisal methodology (PAM) are used over the various phases of selection, development and implementation.

Our primary reason for using the tools is to maximize the value for money that the Prudential gets from its investment in information technology. This objective remained clear and constant even though our sub-goals changed during the PAM development; e.g. in the emphasis placed on portfolio/programme management as opposed to single project appraisal.

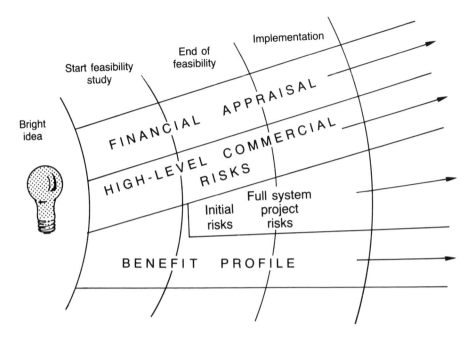

Figure 10.1 The Prudential project appraisal method.

Developing and tuning the appraisal tools required several iterations, testing them out against a meaningful sample of both successful and unsuccessful project proposals. This would have been extremely difficult if the systems groups had been perceived as the sole drivers. However, from the start, business area involvement was high; we collaborated in the tool development and the business decision makers are among the strongest supporters.

Financial appraisal

Almost all companies have standards for financial appraisal. Often ownership lies with the finance department with complex procedures being laid down and audited by the accountants. Although we have argued earlier that hard benefits alone are an inadequate measure for information systems, this does NOT mean that they are unimportant and the quality of the CBAs should be a key concern for the business.

The main objectives for the Prudential were to produce high-quality CBAs more reliably and much more quickly. One of the major reasons behind inadequate CBAs is that few business or systems people have a formal grounding in the principles of project accounting; thus it was vital to raise the financial awareness of all the staff associated with IS projects.

The Corporate Finance Groups provide guidelines on how project cases should be presented to them. These then form the basis for business area regulations covering the production of CBAs. However, all of these documents were intended to be used by trained accountants. We simplified the guidelines to make them appropriate for both business and IT project managers and have run a number of seminars on the subject.

An associated spreadsheet template was constructed to automatically calculate the required measures such as NPV, Paybacks and IRRs. The spreadsheet also included macros to encourage the use of sensitivity analysis. We also took great care to avoid encouraging a 'no brain' attitude to creating a CBA; thinking through the financial case and clearly putting down the assumptions used is as important as the bottom line result. We have found that this is best encouraged through individual training, using a project manager's current appraisal tasks as the basic educational platform.

Of the three areas, the financial tools should have been by far the easiest to standardize and roll out. However, in practice, producing a CBA for a reasonably complex project needs the assistance of an accountant or appraisal specialist, who is fully familiar with the local conventions and modus operandi and can guide the project managers through their complexities.

Risk appraisal

Over the last decade information technology has proved to be revolutionary in both accelerating change and in creating a demand for that change. As a result, IT systems have increased in power and sophistication faster than our ability to manage the risks involved in introducing them. This problem is exacerbated by the volatility of business requirements; companies need to respond quickly to competitors' moves and market opportunities while still delivering high-quality products cost-effectively.

'Right First Time' is not so much desirable as essential; even in the short term significant damage can be caused if IS fails to support the business needs in a timely fashion. A critical factor in delivering systems effectively, and then delivering the business benefits that the systems enable, is competent IT risk analysis and management (European Security Forum, 1990).

Risk analysis can be defined as a systematic process for helping management understand the risks involved in a particular endeavour. What is needed is to clearly identify the organization's exposure to risk, plan those risks which can be controlled, and take account of any residual risks. Additional approaches to risk are discussed in the next chapter, as well as in Chapter 4.

Three risk tools are used within the Prudential PAM:

1. High-level commercial risk appraisal questionnaire
2. Initial system/project risk appraisal questionnaire
3. Full system/project risk appraisal tool.

The first tool examines the high-level business or commercial risks. Designed primarily for the business sponsor, it is a simple one-page tick-list dealing with medium- to long-term risk areas, which could affect both delivery of the projects benefits and the ability of the company to capitalize on them. Forty risk areas are covered in the tool, categorized into the domains shown below:

- Organizational/cultural
- Legal/political
- Business volatility and competition
- Technical
- Social and customer.

The tool is designed to be a prompt for the project sponsor and is carried out in the initiation phase. Disciplined use of the tool in the early stages exposes risks and potential errors, and ensures that they are considered before spending time and resources on systems work.

The second questionnaire is a simplified system risk questionnaire. It is intended to be used in the early stages of a project, i.e. the initiation or early feasibility study phase, to focus attention on the main system development risk areas. The results are used to produce an initial risk management plan as input into the decision-making process before a heavy investment is incurred.

The last tool is a full system risk multiple choice questionnaire, investigating risks in the following categories:

- The system is delivered late, or never
- The system costs too much
- The system does not meet expectations or requirements
- The system fails in production or does not meet the service level agreements
- The system is non-maintainable
- The system goes against the business or IT strategy.

It is used within the Home Service development methodology (based around SSADM) to investigate the risk of the project failing to meet its implementation goals and key deliverables. Both the impact of a risk factor and its probability are estimated, together giving a prediction of the likely hazard. The manageability of the high hazard risks is then considered with the results being fed into the risk management plan.

This tool is first used in the feasibility study phase, being administered by the project managers. A simple PC programme supports the process, encouraging the project manager to frequently re-run the analysis in order to indicate the effectiveness of the risk plan and the residual risks remaining.

Strategic and intangible benefit appraisal

The third part of the Prudential investment appraisal system deals with the softer intangible benefits. The main deliverable is a benefit profile and accompanying textual bullets, which provide a simple representation of the total contribution that a project makes to the company objectives. The profile has to be customized to the individual corporation, company or division using a combined top-down and bottom-up approach.

Working from the top, input from the senior business decision makers is used to clarify the company's mission and the high-level objectives. The desired outcome is a clear, unambiguous set of critical performance indicators and goals that are shared by all of the high-level stakeholders. At the same time the current portfolio of projects is reviewed, asking project managers and line IS and business management what factors of their projects could reflect on the emerging list of intermediate performance indicators or goals. The end deliverable is a set of questions that make sense to the interviewees, i.e. they are comfortable with the scoring mechanisms and can see how they relate to their projects. The questions also are directly related to the strategic objectives via the intermediate goals and weighting techniques described later.

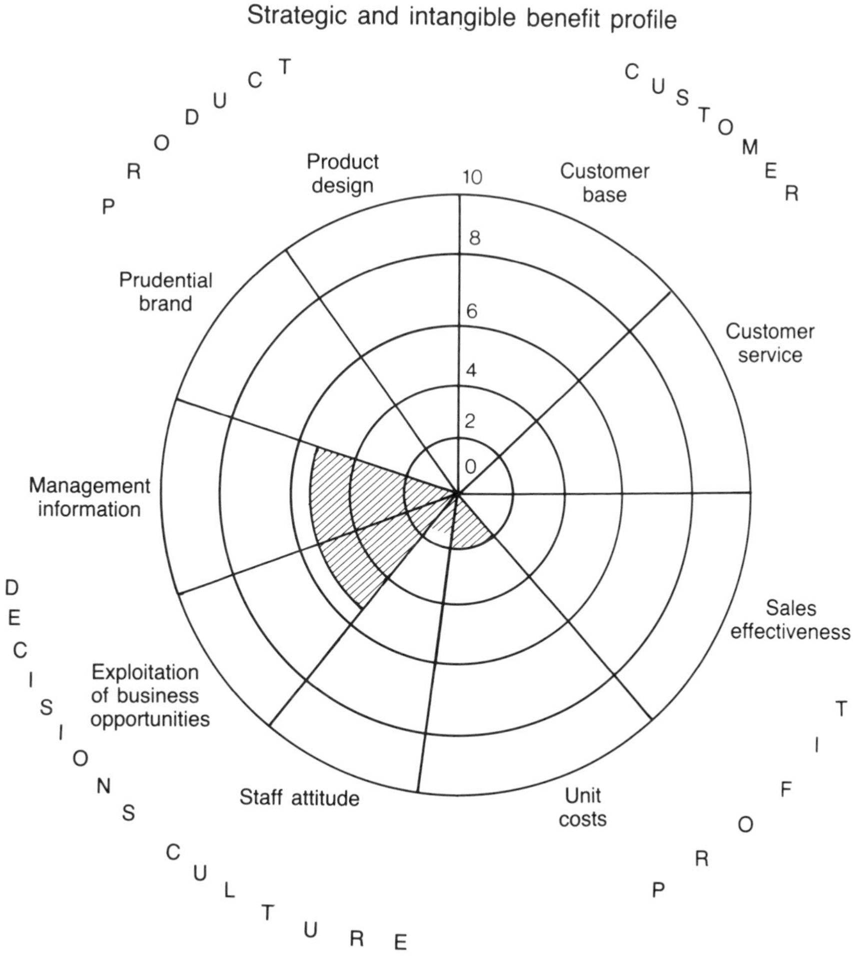

Strategic and intangible benefit profile

Client/server pilot: The pilot is partly a 'proof of concept' project. While there are benefits against the HS objectives (as shown in the profile), a major objective is to gain experience of downsizing via client/server environments and to quantify the effects on mainframe charges, productivity and user control. The pilot will also provide business area feedback on the open system strategic architectures.

Unit costs: The pilot will not reach a payback point within the 3-month trial, approximate cost savings on the existing system are £20k. However, there is potential for either scaling up trial or running system longer than one quarter. Additional possible savings include £90k discount if we decide to purchase a new product in 1993, plus a £6k reduction in maintenance per annum. These sums are for the limited trial only with relatively low savings.

Exploitation of business opportunities: The building block approach to management control information, when combined with the potential for networked information aggregation/transfer, should improve our internal change management capabilities.

Management information: Pilot provides minor benefits because of limited scope. Enabler for providing timely cost information to all (e.g. an extension of the weekly flash), particularly focusing on expense control via current MIS data. Increased accuracy due to avoidance of rekeying.

Figure 10.2 Intangible benefit summary.

Table 10.1 High-level business objectives

Benefit category	Business objective	Example weights
Customer	1. Customer base	60
	2. Customer service	80
Profit	3. Sales effectiveness	80
	4. Unit cost	70
Culture	5. Staff attitude/morale	100
Decisions	6. Exploitation of business opportunities	70
	7. Management information	75
Product	8. Prudential brand	90
	9. Product design	75

The process is an iterative one requiring significant testing and refinement, with the eventual result being a set of tools which produce a profile of the type shown in Figure 10.2.

In the Prudential Home Service system there are nine separate classes of benefit in the profile, divided into five categories (Table 10.1). The weights refer to the relative importance of each category as defined by the senior management decision group. In the profile the weights are represented by the size of each segment. The weighting system provides the tool with a high degree of flexibility. Changes in company or divisional emphasis can easily be introduced without having to revisit or rescore each project.

To create the profile an appraisal specialist fills in a short questionnaire with the business sponsor and/or project manager. In the Prudential system there are 16 questions which are used to give quantitative information about the softer, intangible benefits of projects. These values are then aggregated to produce a score for nine benefit categories. Finally, the benefit profile can be automatically drawn up using PC software.

On average the interview takes approximately 30–40 minutes, with approximately 1 to 2 hours required for the complete process. The duration primarily depends upon the phase of the project and the extent of the information already known to the sponsor/managers.

The use of an investment appraisal specialist to facilitate the answers and scores is crucial if there is to be a reasonable base for comparison across projects and divisions. Within the Prudential we use a small team of business analysts and managers who have a reasonable knowledge of IT. These specialists determine the scores that are entered, which balances both the natural optimism of most systems project managers and the occasional desire of the business champion to see his or her preference thrive above all others.

Most of the questions are scored along two dimensions:

• Impact – Will the project have a major or minor effect upon the benefit category?
• Range – How many policyholders, policies, transactions, staff, etc., will be affected?

To give an example, a project might reduce transaction turnaround by 25%, providing a major impact on customer service. If, however, it only affects a small number of policies the overall score could well be below that of a project which speeds up the

Table 10.2 High-level goals + related metrics

Business objective	Contributing factor	Question definition
Product optimization	1. Prudential brand	Extent to which key brand values are maintained. Quantify effect on values X, Y, Z and give metrics.
	2. Product design	Risk and risk exposure of new or changed product. Compliance with design standards. Potential revenue to expense.
	3. Compliance	Turnaround times for all processes.

processing by a small amount but for a large number of policy types. Table 10.2 shows sample questions for one of the areas plus brief definitions.

This process also provides an analysis of the total benefits of the project, confirming exactly what is expected to be achieved as well as the key issues and assumptions. Our users are enthusiastic about the tool as a means of clarifying their own ideas **before** incurring any system costs.

If the tool is being used at the 'bright idea' phase of project initiation, there is inevitably considerable imprecision in the answers. This does not affect the overall value of the tool which is designed to appraise the project, insofar as it is understood, at any point of its life-cycle.

The verdict on the appraisal tools

At the start the main intention was to develop a system to aid project selection and prioritization, although, for the developers of the investment appraisal system, high-quality benefit management was seen to be at least of equal importance. Both objectives rely upon being able to estimate accurately a project's total contribution to the Prudential's business goals and a key design criterion was to make sure that the results were credible to all levels of business and IS management. The overall opinion is that the tools have succeeded and that they provide benefits to both the business users and the system developers.

The tools are relevant to projects or system enhancements of any size, which includes both new developments and enhancements. Even with very small projects, quickly applying the intangible benefits appraisal and the shortened risk questionnaire increases the understanding of why the change is being made and helps to minimize the risks involved.

A frequent comment from the users is that the very act of applying the techniques is extremely useful in clarifying the project's objectives, and that they appreciate the advantages of using the tools at the earliest stages of a project for a very low cost. A key benefit is that they help business and systems personnel achieve a mutual understanding of the project's purpose and risks, before significant resources have been spent on analysis and design.

The tools are far from being set in stone. A key design objective was to build in flexibility, a goal which has proved particularly pertinent given the rapid changes that have taken place in the various Prudential divisions.

Conclusions

The primary conclusion from our work is that ROI on its own simply does not work as an appraisal mechanism for information systems. This holds true for even the most sophisticated discounted cash flow measures. There are no effective techniques for converting all of the benefits of IT into hard, bottom-line returns. What is needed is an extension to appraisal techniques which predict and measure the total contribution to the business objectives and goals. Specifically the intangible benefits need to be dealt with in a consistent, valid and reliable manner.

The appraisal techniques should accurately deal with all types of IS project. Mandatory projects are relatively few, most IT work can be foregone if the organization is prepared to bear the cost, and in any case the benefits from 'must do' projects should be analysed along with the discretionary work.

Information technology infrastructure and architecture projects are notoriously difficult to judge (CCTA, 1989) and tend to be considered purely in system terms. However, we have found that it is possible to make a case for that type of project in terms of medium/long-term business advantage. The benefits of getting IT practitioners to think in these terms are considerable.

Persuading IT practitioners to consider business value for money is just one aspect of what is arguably the hardest and the most important task for improving benefit management. That is getting the roles, responsibilities and accountabilities clarified and fully accepted by both business users and system developers. Ideally, one person should be accountable in all stages of project development and one user clearly accountable for capitalizing on the business benefits once achieved (Hurford, 1992).

The difficulties arise not only from differences in language and culture between business and IS but also because the business is reluctant to accept responsibility where it feels it has no real authority over development. We have a lot of sympathy with this view and believe that the answer lies in developing a true partnership where the business sponsor is the senior member.

A final point is that all parts of the organization need to focus on quality throughout the system's life. An IT project does not finish with the successful delivery of a working system; it continues as long as benefits are being accrued to the business. Achieving maximum value for money means not only picking the right 'goods' to buy, but also using them productively for as long as makes economic and organizational sense.

Notes

1. We would like to thank all those people within the Prudential who have helped Tom to develop the PAM (project appraisal method) and to roll it out within the Home Service division. In particular we would like to thank Brian Thomas, manager of the Business/Systems Co-ordination Group, who has provided many invaluable ideas and who has remained the PAM champion even when its implementation and acceptance seemed doubtful.

2. There is some doubt in the author's mind about this. There is growing evidence that IT expenditure has a multiplying effect on management effectiveness. Thus, for companies already in the top quartile of effectiveness, increased spend brings

increased advantage, whereas for companies with ineffective management, increased IT expenditure merely exacerbates their problems.

References

Butler Cox Foundation (1990) *Getting Value from Information Technology*. Butler Cox, London.

CCTA (1989) *Appraising Investment in Information Technology*. Information System Guides, Vol. B4, HMSO, London.

Coleman, T. (1990) Matching image systems to business requirements. *Proc. Document Image Processing '90*, Blenheim Pubs, London.

Coleman, T. (1992) *Project Appraisal Method (PAM) – An Overview*. Internal Document, Prudential Assurance plc., London.

Coleman, T. and Jamieson, M. (1991) *Information Systems: Evaluating Intangible Benefits at the Feasibility Stage of Project Appraisal*. MBA thesis, City University Business School, London.

Computer Finance (1992) *Measuring the Intangible*, APT Data Services, London, September, pp. 23–4.

European Security Forum (1990) *Security Status: Consolidated Survey Results*, Coopers & Lybrand, Europe.

Gartner Group (1992) Central IS budgets shrink while IT spending climbs. *Inside Gartner Group This Week*, 5 September 1992, 5–7.

Hochstrasser, B. and Griffiths, C. (1991) *Controlling IT Investment: Strategy and Management*, Chapman & Hall, London.

Hurford, C. (1992) Getting value for money from IT. *Proc. UKCMG 7th Annual Conference*, pp. 291–6.

Levy, H. and Sarnat, M. (1986) *Capital Investment & Financial Decisions*, Wiley, Chichester.

Parker, M. M., Benson, R. J. and Trainor, H. E. (1988) *Information Economics: Linking Business Performance to Information Technology*, Prentice-Hall, New Jersey.

Peltu, M. (1986) New Approaches brings benefits and justifies the investment. *Computing*, 24 April, 38–9.

Peters, G. (1990) Beyond strategy – benefits identification and management of specific IT investments. *Journal of Information Technology*, **5**, 205–14.

Strassmann, P. (1990) *The Business Value of Computers*, The Information Economics Press, New Canaan.

Thomas, L. C. (1992) Financial risk management models, in *Risk Analysis Assessment and Management* (eds J. Ansell, and F. Wharton), Wiley, Chichester.

Ward, J., Griffiths, P. and Whitmore, P. (1990) *Strategic Planning for Information Systems*, Wiley, Chichester.

11

Risk and information systems: developing the analysis

Leslie Willcocks and Helen Margetts

Introduction

Risk and information systems receive a variety of treatments in other chapters. Thus Ward put forward an approach for identifying and spreading risk across the information systems portfolio. Peters in Chapter 5 showed how business risks could be identified and information systems use could be related to minimization of those risks. Wiseman described the usefulness of the information economics approach for risk identification, and elements of both Chapters 8 and 10 have shown how this approach can be tailored to produce usable, practical analytical frameworks. This chapter seeks to build on these contributions in several ways. Additional frameworks for risk classification at the investment appraisal stage are assessed. A further framework, drawn from the organization studies literature, is then applied to several cases illustrating risk in information systems applications in different organizational settings. The chapter argues the merit in interpreting risk operationally as not just inherent in certain structural features of the environment or of a project, but also arising as a result of distinctive human and organizational practices and patterns of belief and action. Building on the argument made by Wiseman about the criticality and neglect of organizational risk (see Chapter 9), this chapter suggests that more comprehensive frameworks for risk assessment are needed to complement the all too

Information Management: The evaluation of information systems investments.
Edited by Leslie Willcocks.
Published in 1994 by Chapman & Hall. ISBN 0 412 41540 2.

frequently encountered truncated forms of assessment developed from the project management, operational research and financial management fields.

Risk in computer-based information systems (IS) projects is surprisingly under-managed in both the private and public sectors (Coleman and Jamieson, 1991; Farbey, Land and Targett, 1992; Keen, 1991; Willcocks, 1992a). The surprise comes when the large size of information technology (IT) expenditure, and the history of disappointed expectations is considered (see Introduction). Moreover, against predictions of continuing rises in IT expenditure generally, surveys regularly report IT introduction and usage in work organizations as a high-risk, hidden-cost process. Let us look at two examples. A 1992 survey based on 56 000 IT budget holders predicted the size of UK overall spend increasing from £15 015 million in 1991 to £15 295 million in 1992 and from £15 897 million in 1993 to nearly £18 000 million in 1994 (KEW Associates/Computer Weekly, 1992). OTR Group (1992), in reviewing IT projects over the previous 10 years in 200 organizations, found that for projects over £660 000, 90% were over budget, 98% had changed specification, 60% were over time, and 20% were inappropriate. Despite this, at the level of managerial practice as well as in academic studies, risk is more often regarded as added to the system when it is in operation, and usually relates to systems security, the need for backup in the event of systems crash, or issues connected with data protection legislation and/or the prevention of fraud. The omissions at investment appraisal stage were indicated in Chapter 3 where little formal risk analysis was identified among respondent organizations, except that embraced by financial calculations, e.g. discount rates. OTR Group (1992) found only 30% of the companies surveyed applying any risk analysis. Some insight into lack of managerial use of risk analysis in capital budgeting decisions generally is given by Pike and Ho (1991). They found that managers lacked the required understanding to apply formal approaches and/or were unable to find an approach that is systematic, easy to apply and cost-effective.

This chapter focuses on the types of risk incurred when designing, developing and introducing computer-based information systems into organizations. How far do organizations face risks in IS projects? What types and levels of risk are experienced? Is there anything to be learned from past projects? How far do larger developments in the contexts of introducing and using IS ameliorate or raise new risk issues and set the risk agenda? We investigate these questions with a view to contributing to a neglected area of study and practice. An additional reason for surprise at this neglect is that there already exists a body of research findings on risks incurred in IS projects; additionally, a number of frameworks for classifying such risks have been developed. The next section reviews this work. This review is used to develop an understanding of risk and a framework that can then be applied to analysing case histories in greater detail. We then supplement existing frameworks by proposing a framework for IS risk analysis derived from the research studies, including our own detailed case study work.

Throughout the paper IT and IS are used as largely interchangeable terms, though a distinction can be made between IT as hardware, software and communications technologies – essentially equipment – and attendant techniques, and IS as a wider concept referring to how designed information flows attempt to meet the defined information requirements of an organization. IS may be more, or less, IT based (Willcocks, 1992a). The systems under review here are highly IT based.

Risk assessment and information systems

Risk is involved in all IS projects. In the risk literature the terms analysis, assessment, estimation and evaluation are frequently differently defined (for example, Charette, 1991; Warner *et al.*, 1992). Here risk analysis and assessment are used interchangeably to mean the study of decisions subject to uncertain consequences. As a subdivision risk estimation includes identifying outcomes, their probability and the magnitude of their associated consequences. Risk evaluation is concerned with establishing the significance of identified risks/hazards to those concerned with or affected by the decision.

According to Loudon and Loudon (1991) and Stringer (1992), risk is taken to be a negative outcome that has a known or estimated probability of occurrence based on experience or some theory. This interpretation owes more to a managerial perspective than to classical decision theory. Risk here refers to exposure to such consequences as: failure to obtain some or all of anticipated benefits due to implementation difficulties; implementation time much longer, and/or costs much higher, than expected; technical systems performance significantly below the estimate; incompatibility of the system with selected hardware and software. This listing is only illustrative. Risk of a negative outcome only becomes a salient problem when the outcome is relevant to stakeholder concerns and interests. Different settings and stakeholders will see different outcomes as salient. For example, in government, the policy impact as well as the administrative efficiency of an IS, and thus the risk of negative outcomes on this further dimension, all may well be deemed significant. Risk is taken on a broad definition in this chapter. We see a range of risk factors that may contribute to negative outcomes of varying degree. Emerging from the research studies reviewed below, in terms of factors there are those that appear inherently risky (for example, risk increases with size and complexity of project); those that are inherent in contextual factors about which organizational members and project managers can do little (for example, time limits set by government or a holding company); and those shading in varying degrees into mistake and/or inadequate action. Our purpose here is to examine all such risk factors as they emerge in the research studies and from our case analyses.

Frameworks

Apart from those already encountered in this book, a number of frameworks have been generated from experience, and from research, to assist risk assessment at the feasibility stage of IT projects. Thus Cash *et al.* (1992) suggest that there are at least three important dimensions that contribute to the riskiness inherent in project implementation risk. These are: project size (staffing levels, elapsed time, cost, number of departments affected), experience with the technology, and project structure (a highly structured project with fixed, certain outputs not subject to change during the lifetime of the project experiences less risk). A version of how these factors relate to one another, and engender different levels of risk, is shown in Figure 11.1. This provides a simple and useful starting point for analysing risk, though it does leave out many factors identified as potentially significant by the research work reported below.

Earl (1989) has proposed a cost–benefit framework for assessing on economic,

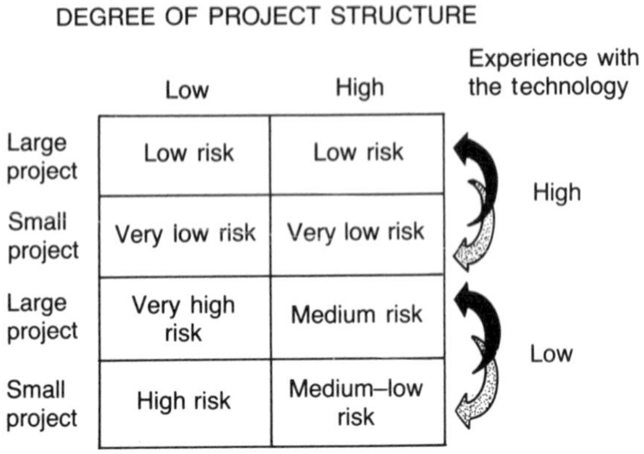

DEGREE OF PROJECT STRUCTURE

Figure 11.1 Risks in project implementation (from Cash *et al.*, 1992).

technical and operational criteria the viability, risks and opportunities represented by the IT investment. This provides a useful heuristic device at the general level. Corder (1989) suggests high-risk factors as project size, project definition, user commitment and stability, project time, and number of systems interfaces. Medium-risk factors include functional complexity, number of user departments, newness of technology/ vendor, user experience of computers, the project team's experience of the user area, newness of technology to the organization, number of vendors/contractors. Low-risk factors include number of geographical sites, functional newness and number of project phases. This again is useful as a starting point, but from which to develop a more organization-specific analytical framework. The process of reviewing such a framework against a particular organization's circumstances could assist in identifying additional risk factors or different weightings for the risk factors, and could lead to developing a scoring system against which projects could be assessed.

Risk versus reward

A fundamental part of risk assessment is to identify the risk in terms of its probability and organizational impact, then evaluate what might be the acceptable trade-offs between risk and reward. It is useful to support the risk assessment process with a number of now widely available financial estimation and statistical techniques (as examples only, see Hull, 1990; Post and Dilz, 1986; Williams, 1990). Typical financial techniques are discussed in other chapters. Statistical techniques include outcome probabilities, simulation, sensitivity analysis, game theory and variance measures. Responding to the need for easy-to-apply tools, Figure 11.2 shows two frameworks that can then be used to model the results of such deliberations. However, as other chapters make clear, if financial and statistical techniques are under-used in risk assessment, they also come in the 'necessary but insufficient' category. There are difficulties in establishing, for different types of IS project, appropriate discount rates or payback periods; the subjectivity of choice and the limited availability of information are often disguised by the seeming certainty when risk is expressed in figures. Most figures in such calculations contain uncertainty; however, they may also be very sensitive in the sense that quite small changes in

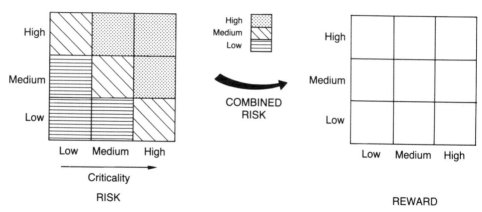

Figure 11.2 The trade-off between risk and reward.

calculations can point the way to quite different decisions being made. Furthermore, it is all too easy for figures to be arrived at without a thorough analysis of the nature of the risk. This suggests that other methods of risk assessment need to be deployed to assist in the understanding of risk and lead on to their management.

A further point is that decisions on the risk–reward trade-off are invariably arrived at in organizations through what Symons in Chapter 12 calls a formal–rational analysis. These assume a high degree of objectivity in the calculations; moreover, the appearance of objectivity can be enhanced by expressing the calculations and results in numerical form (Mintzberg, 1989; Strassmann, 1990; Walsham, 1992). However, the influence of perception, politics, culture and attitude to risk cuts across all such analyses and decision making in quite fundamental ways. Formal–rational analysis in fact frequently has a strong ritualistic element, often acting as a symbolic expression of a belief in rational management rather than a reliable aid to decision making (Currie, 1989; Kumar, 1990; Symons and Walsham, 1988). Different stakeholders will perceive IS issues, and value the attendant risks, in different ways. Thus in an IS project in a major oil company, studied by one of the authors, the project manager saw risk in terms of those factors that would prevent the project being delivered on time and within budget. The commissioning manager was concerned with those factors preventing the delivery of an acceptable and effective system. There are various attitudes to risk in the oil, insurance and health services sectors, for example. Specific organizations develop their own risk cultures. An illuminating example is that of the US Space Agency NASA and the Space Shuttle Program (Collingridge, 1992; Shenhar, 1992). In fact NASA built into its culture the belief that risk was not minimized by quantitative risk analysis but by improving the reliability and quality of design. The proportion of rocket launch failures was driven down between 1958 and 1986, contributing to a culture of increasing success. When a safety board suggested they should be working on figures of failure as 1 in 1000, NASA recommended 1 in 10 000 'due to unique improvements in design and manaufacture of solid rocket fuel boosters (SRBs)' (quoted in Charette, 1991). For political reasons, and partly to maintain government funding, risk was downplayed; as one example the space shuttle was designed as an airliner, suggesting similar reliability. An SRB failed on the twenty-fifth space shuttle launch, in 1986, killing all the crew. NASA now applies quantitative risk analysis together with its quality design approach and uses a 1 in 78 failure rate for its SRB launches. Clearly attitudinal, cultural and political issues can greatly influence risk perception. One conclusion must be that these aspects themselves are neglected risk factors that need inclusion in analyses and evaluation of risks to be managed.

Research studies

More detailed research supports the frameworks and issues discussed above as representing the major risk factors, while also indicating a range of other factors differently significant from project to project. In a comprehensive review of the literature Lyttinen and Hirschheim (1987) found 12 groups of reasons for information systems failure, including: lack of sophisticated technology; lack of fit of the IS to user capabilities or to the organization or organizational operating environment; deficiencies in the IS development process relating to lack of adequate and powerful methods, or lack of sufficient attention to types of decision supported, nature of work, contingency factors, organizational implementation or to the fact of biased or wrong assumptions driving development; and finally insufficient skills and capabilities on the part of IS professionals and/or users. More recent research tends to focus on limited sections of this listing, but also supports generally the finding that the major risks and reasons for failure tend to be through organizational, social and political, rather than technical factors (see, for example, Beath and Ives, 1989; Johnston and Vitale, 1988; AT Kearney, 1990; Scott-Morton, 1991; Willcocks, 1991, 1992b).

Another way of assessing risk is through utilizing innovation theory. Thus Harrow and Willcocks (1992) adopt from Rogers and Kim (1985) five attributes of innovations that affect adoption rates in public sector contexts. In terms of IS projects, innovations with:

- greater relative advantage (over preceding practices)
- more compatibility (with potential adopters' needs and values)
- less complexity
- more trialability (testing possible on a limited basis)
- more observability (results visible to others)

are more readily and rapidly adoptable than others. The research literature supports strongly the first three factors as major determinants of IS success or failure defined typically in terms of IS usage and/or user satisfaction with the system (Cooper and Zmud, 1990; Earl and Runge, 1987; Kwon and Zmud, 1987; Tornatzky and Klein, 1982). However, a range of support factors probably need to be incorporated into innovation theory if robust risk frameworks are to be developed. Thus, in the public sector, Willcocks and Mark (1989) show innovation and support factors coming strikingly together in the rush to implement IT designed to provide management information crucially supporting the general managers appointed following the Griffiths proposals for the UK National Health Service in the mid-1980s. Furthermore, again taking into account the public sector context, a further finding by Willcocks and Margetts (1991) is that even situations diagnosed as low risk – that is, where many of these innovation factors tend to support IT adoption – risk can be reintroduced by financial and time constraints imposed by central government that does not reflect the realities of project managing robust, usable systems into the organization.

Developing the analysis: a framework

So far we have investigated information systems as risk at a general level. It is useful to carry out a complementary but more detailed, processual and longitudinal analysis using case histories. To facilitate the analysis, an analytical framework will be deployed. In studies of a variety of organizations Pettigrew and colleagues (1985, 1991, 1992) rightly strove to avoid the ahistorical, aprocessual and acontextual character of much research on organizational change. In a development from their work six conceptual, interplaying categories can be brought into analysing the development, introduction and use of information systems (see Figure 11.3):

- **Context (external):** Such factors will be the givens that the organization and its members need to respond to and accommodate, e.g. the economy, politics and governmental policy, markets, competition, supplier availability and expertise, and in the public sector, department or local government guidelines, procedures, funding arrangements.
- **Context (internal):** Characteristics of the organization itself are included here such as strategy, structure, rewards system, management, human resources and industrial relations arrangements, IS infrastructure and management. Given the importance often assigned to it in information systems research studies, for analytical purposes the additional aspect of organizational and related **histories** is shown separately in Figure 11.3.
- **Content:** This includes proposed changes, including their substance, e.g. type of technology, size and extensiveness of project, whether radical or incremental in impact, 'risky' or 'safe'.
- **Process:** This covers how things are done and issues perceived; the 'how' of IS development, implementation and usage; the normal patterns of action and behaviour; the types of action that are seen as legitimate. Here it is given more specific reference to include such issues as user training and commitment, project team experience, IS staff retention rates.
- **Outcomes:** These may be planned or unanticipated, desirable or otherwise. Outputs typically assessed in IS projects include cost; time; technical performance; operational efficiency; stakeholder, business and financial impacts; stakeholder acceptance, satisfaction and/or usage.

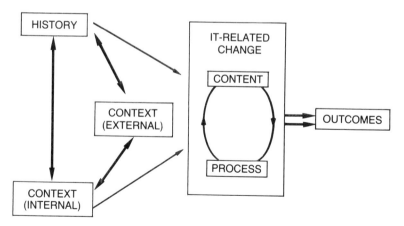

Figure 11.3 Framework for risk analysis.

Issues of risk in information systems are pursued in the next sections through several case studies. A strength of case study analysis is that it can demonstrate the linkages and mutual influence of categories in the framework. The cases do not represent a random sample; nor can statistically significant findings be derived from their analysis. Nor are the cases illustrative of every risk factor discussed in the above sections. Rather the purposes here are to demonstrate how risks arise through the ways in which content, process and context relate in relationship to information systems development, introduction and usage. The findings from this and other studies cited will be used to develop a more process-oriented and organization studies-based framework for risk analysis to complement other frameworks discussed in this book. In most cases the material represents summarized case histories generated in the course of several of the authors' research projects. We have re-analysed these to address the issue of risk in developing and implementing information systems in work organizations. In several cases we have also reviewed, and utilize extensively, secondary material. One case is largely derived, in its factual base, from Walton (1989). In some cases, as a condition of publication, anonymity of the respondent organization is observed.

Case studies

Two cases in IS infrastructure risk

IS infrastructure risk relates to how far the entire IS organization needs, is prepared and is able to support a specific IS project (see Chapter 9). Hodgkinson (1991) has argued that the real challenge in the management of the IT function is to provide centralized direction and coordination simultaneously while also realizing the benefits of decentralized decision making, user department involvement in development, and distributed IT. Between them the following cases illustrate the risks inherent in poor IS professional–user department relationships, historically conditioned IS professional skill sets, and inappropriate organization of the IT function. Two large multi-divisional companies – Concordia Casting Company (CCC) in the USA and WH Smith in the UK – came to a better understanding of this problem set in the 1980s, and the cases illustrate the risks identified through that process.

Concordia Casting Company

In the mid-1980s CCC was a large multi-divisional manufacturing organization. It had four business segments – automative, machine tools, precision parts and fluid controls. Each operated as an independent business unit and profit centre. Additional independent companies were being acquired while price competition in the industry was becoming intense and just-in-time manufacture and delivery becoming increasingly adopted. It was recognized that a fully centralized information systems division, inherited from the 1970s, was no longer appropriate for CCC. By 1984 a 'distributed' organization was in place. Corporate data-processing functions were clearly separated from work done for the operating divisions. Several regional data centres serviced clusters of operating divisions, while corporate IS staff would focus on corporate systems development, decision support, long-range planning, policy setting, database management, corporate DP standards, and business systems consulting throughout the company. A decision was also made to convert to IBM equipment. This meant that IS staff would need to be increased in numbers and upgraded. None had been trained on standard IBM systems. The recruiting process proved successful, but a high labour turnover in technical staff developed, and widespread use of consultants proved expensive and rarely to the satisfaction of user department managers.

A major problem developed in the speed and quality of systems delivery to user departments. The combined IS staff could not handle the conversion of old applications let alone the demand for new ones. This was no more clearly demonstrated than in the CAPS conversion project. CAPS was the production control system at the heart of CCC's business; it consumed the most resources, was highly visible, and running it was the responsibility of the central IS division. It was estimated that the total conversion process would take some 75 programmer years of which half would need to be dedicated to the CAPS system. The problems in CCC illustrate IS infrastructure risk. While the IT function had developed a distributed organization, responsibility was left with technical staff. In practice most of the development and conversion projects were not implementable without much more active involvement by user department and senior corporate managers. This was particularly the case for the major CAPS conversion project. There was a lack of congruence between organizational environment, structure and direction on the one hand, and how IT was organized and controlled on the other. This was exacerbated by the fact that the newer IS professional staff, though technically competent with IBM technology, often had little knowledge of CCC business objectives and systems, and rarely developed good relations with user department managers and staff.

WH Smith

WH Smith in the period 1989–92 illustrates further dimensions of this problem set. WH Smith is a £2 billion business and the leading UK retailer of books, magazines, stationery, recorded music, and video, and the leading UK distributor of newspapers, magazines and office supplies. The group also has large interests in the do-it-yourself market and overseas. The group is made up of some 16 strategic business units (SBUs) which are operationally autonomous to a large degree. The businesses have their own clearly identifiable cultures, and often adopt different approaches to the same business functions. The group spends about £30 million a year (1.5% of revenue) on operational IT. Up to 1989 information technology was provided to all SBUs by a group head office function known as Management Services Division. However, this proved dysfunctional for the provision of IT for business needs within each SBU. The main problems with the centralized IT organization were that it was unresponsive; there was no SBU ownership of systems; there was no SBU control over central overhead costs; and SBU needs were frequently not met. Additionally, in IS projects the group encountered most of the IS infrastructure risks and limiting factors detailed in the CCC case.

The underdeveloped use of IT, together with some less than satisfactory outcomes with a number of IT projects, led to the decision in 1989 to devolve responsibility for IT to each of the SBUs. It was felt that IT investment would then more closely match the needs of the individual businesses. A small number of functions were retained at the centre and continued to be provided by the Information Services Division (ISD).

The ISD retained a number of responsibilities, including approval of all IT capital spend and significant projects within the group; overall management of the group's IT suppliers; monitoring and advice on IT projects within each SBU; establishment of group-wide standards and policies for the use of IT; provision of consultancy services in areas of relevance to the group as a whole. This type of model, often called the federal IT organization, has been found to be applied increasingly in multi-divisional companies in the late 1980s and early 1990s in the UK. Adoption may well serve to reduce IS infrastructure risks in specific IT projects (Hodgkinson, 1991).

Corporate personnel systems in a manufacturing company

This case illustrates a number of typical risks in IS projects. These include risk of systems crash/failure; risks associated with leaving systems development and implementation primarily to technical staff, suppliers and/or consultants; and risk of supplier bankruptcy or failure.

As at the beginning of 1991, XYZ plc was an international organization based in the UK, with annual sales approaching £800 million and 12 000 employees world wide. The organization consisted of a range of operating companies variously manufacturing motor cars, medical equipment, automotive technology, alloys and components for the aerospace industry and military vehicles. As a decentralized organization it had a small group of head office functions based in London. This case focuses on implementation of an IS in the corporate personnel function in the period 1990–92. The major role of corporate personnel was to provide timely and accurate data on the recruitment, training, progress, career development, assessment and severance of the 400 most senior managers within the XYZ group. An attempt to bring in a computerized personnel system had been made in 1984. After three years in place the ICL DRS20 system was still unable to provide even the most basic of data. In particular, it produced dated, incomplete and inaccurate data, was difficult to use, presented data poorly and could not produce summary reports. As a result, periodic corporate personnel reports had to be produced by hand. Given the pressure on staff numbers, a more usable, flexible on-line database system, linked to the computerized salaries and pensions system, seemed appropriate.

One significant risk rested with the lack of in-depth technical appreciation of computerized systems within any of the corporate functions, including personnel. Risk was also increased by the lack of a history of IT projects at head office. The decentralized structure of the organization also contributed to this, with a little sharing of expertise on IS across divisions and between divisions and head office. As one result it was decided that the system could not be developed in-house. The contract for installing the IS was awarded to a software company called Niche Software Ltd (NS). The strongest rationale for this decision was that the company was already employed by XYZ, installing a new system for salaries and pensions, and this presented an opportunity to network the two systems. In practice, after three months the contract was cancelled, and a total refund of fees made. While ex-NS staff continued to work on the salaries and pensions system, NS had ceased trading as a software products company. The in-house project manager later concluded that the risk of supplier bankruptcy had been inadequately analysed. He commented that, as a small company, NS had seemed closer to the customer and more flexible in their response to customer needs, but in retrospect NS had very limited resources and became vulnerable when workloads increased and deadlines approached. He also indicated other insufficiently anticipated risks. 'Definitional uncertainty', that is, lack of clear requirements at the design stage, led to problems at implementation, and together with the change in supplier led to the original implementation time of six months being extended to 18 months. Moreover, in contracting a second supplier – Business Advisors Ltd – its packages had to be accepted, and the facility for networking with the salaries and pensions department was lost.

In XYZ plc a number of historical factors contributed to suboptimal IS outcomes for management. Lack of relevant in-house IS experience in combination with a lack of a history of IS failure led to an under-analysis of the risks inherent in utilizing a small IS supplier. An internal contextual factor – decentralized structure – contributed to this situation by cutting off sharing of IS experience within the company. These factors, in combination with content issues – in particular, 'low degree of project structure' and 'small size of project' – created in terms of the Cash *et al.* (1992) matrix a classic high-risk project. By admission, the smallness of the project and financial outlay also caused management not to investigate closely for comparative purposes alternative sources in the IS supplier/consultant marketplace. It is interesting in this case that a number of 'content' factors considered by many commentators as being inherently high risk – large size, complex project, technical uncertainty, a large number of departments being computerized – were **not** present, but nevertheless there were suboptimal IS outcomes. Feeny *et al.* (1989) have argued that newness of the technology to the organization is a critical factor influencing success. Where technology is new, it needs to be developed in-house with a high degree of user participation, or the relationship with the contracted IS supplier needs to be very close and participative, with a 'user' rather than a 'specialist' focus. In the case of XYZ plc neither process approaches prevailed, and this may provide on this issue some further support for Feeny and co-workers' own evidence.

Kwik-Fit: risks in IS success

This case illustrates how early success with applying IT to organizational objectives, despite lack of IS experience, can engender an under-analysis of risks in future IT-related change projects in an organization. In this respect a history of IS success can lead, first, to undertaking large risks with new technology and new suppliers and consultants, and, secondly, previous success can lead to a belief that success can be repeated on the basis of a similar, cursory analysis of the risks to be undergone. The case also illustrates project/organizational risks in IT-related projects.

Kwik-Fit is a UK car-servicing company focusing on a narrow range of simple services, mainly exhaust and tyre fitting and the replacement of standardized parts. In the early 1980s growth in the number of depots providing these services was constrained by an administrative structure that, in the words of its chief executive, 'was good for 50 outlets but not for 180...the whole structure began to creak' (Gallagher and Scott, 1988). The need to maintain competitiveness, together with the requirement to match structure and information systems with business growth, provided the context in which, despite the lack of IS experience and know-how within the company, computerization seemed to be the way to move.

A US system seemed compatible with the Kwik-Fit operation and by March 1982 some 200 terminals had been installed. The machines performed all essential functions of a centre's administration including quotation and invoice production, recording of customer and banking transactions, confirmation of stock levels and recording of staff working hours for payroll. Depot managers, not programmers, helped to draw up the specification for the computer system. Mainframe computers at central office would process data overnight and produce management information ready for depot managers next morning. The system, with several enhancements over the years, proved highly successful to the extent that it was the subject of a published case study (Gallagher and Scott, 1988).

Our own research reveals a different picture for the 1987–91 period. In the early and mid-1980s Kwik-Fit management had circumvented the risks associated with little IT history and experience, and reliance on outside suppliers, through their insistence on user involvement, an emphasis on the job content implications and the search for system 'compatibility' with the organizational capability, structure and processes. A 1987 system review suggested the need to increase mainframe capacity and change to a system usable in any country. Kwik-Fit employed new suppliers for both the mainframes and to rewrite programs. Off-site consultants were employed for the work. According to the chief executive, Tom Farmer, they offered little commitment and frequent delays were experienced. Systems turned out to be inappropriate, there were delays by suppliers who failed to supply what was wanted and over-promised on what could be delivered. There was also internal mismanagement, including the failure to keep the project under Kwik-Fit control. The new systems incurred enormous time lags and costs running into many millions over budget to get them even adequately working. The chief executive suggested that a major reason for this failure was, ironically, previous success as a first-time IT user in the early 1980s. This had led them to severely underestimate risks associated with lack of in-house IT expertise, and in the selection process and use of external suppliers and programmers.

The Kwik-Fit experience forms an interesting case for risk analysis, because ostensibly it runs counter to the notion that lack of technical expertise together with newness of technology engender high risk in IT projects. In fact Kwik-Fit was successful in its first early 1980s IS implementation because of low technical and definitional uncertainty in the project, the user/organizational focus adopted in the process of change, and close relations between management, users, and the system designers and suppliers. The second system's implementation in the late 1980s shows high risk being created through a combination of historical factors – a lack of relevant IS experience, and, ironically, previous IS success; external contextual factors, in particular under-analysis of risks in the supplier/consultant markets; content factors, particularly relatively high technical uncertainty; and process factors, mainly concerned with how projects were organized and controlled.

Thorn-EMI: human and organizational issues

This case, the facts of which are mainly derived from Walton (1989), is used here to illustrate risks in respect to 'strategic maturity' (the ability of the organization to operate strategically), 'organizational readiness for change' (see Willcocks and Margetts, 1991) and what Parker et al. (1988) call organizational/project risks.

Thorn-EMI Electronics International rented home entertainment equipment in the

UK and 21 other countries. It had 1100 stores in the UK in 1987. Unlike many organizations in both private and public sectors, who thus created many risks in IS implementation (see Willcocks, 1992c), it had also aligned its business, IT and human/organizational strategies. The business emphasis on marketing, service and growth was paralleled by moving IT use, organizational structure and management of human resources from a control, administration and cash accounting emphasis, to one of decentralization, user and employee commitment, and value-added business activity (Walton, 1989). However, such alignment proved an insufficient condition for effective IS implementation at Kendal in 1987.

Three systems – an inventory system, a service management system and hand-held units for service technicians – were installed in the Kendal area. The area consisted of eight showrooms and a new service centre and served 30 000 customers. A year later the systems were working but had fallen short of expectations in managing stock, service commitments and service personnel, and supporting marketing and selling. For Walton (1989) the first-level explanations relate to both management and workforce: too little training and knowledge; failure to provide additional people during start-up resulting in severe overload; rewards that emphasized operational efficiency; heavy use of IT to monitor quantitative aspects of behaviour and performance; over-reliance on the IT for remote communication. At a deeper level management underestimated the requirements for additional resources, management attention and workforce training because they focused almost exclusively on the technical system. Despite a 'commitment' as opposed to a 'control' philosophy for employees, managers went back, in their use of IT, to what they were used to doing, that is emphasizing control and efficiency. Furthermore, they underestimated the magnitude of the human resource task – for example, the implications for job content, social relations, rewards – because of the implicit assumption that technology would drive the necessary change. They had also declined to involve organizational/human resource specialists, who might have focused greater attention on the people aspects of systems implementation. However, Thorn-EMI did take corrective action, thus avoiding another risk – that of not learning from its mistakes in computerization.

Inadequate managerial action in aligning human resource, business and technical strategies can create large risks in IS projects. The Thorn-EMI case shows the risks attendant in not ensuring that organizational, business and IT objectives remain aligned not just at the strategic level but through the development, implementation and imbedding stages of an IT project. Furthermore, organizational history and culture did have considerable bearing on the shaping of the computerization process. Thus the Kendal project serves to indicate the problems consequent on underestimation of organizational/project risks and underestimation of the human and organizational implications of a proposed system.

Three cases: context and timescales

Outer and inner contextual pressures, constraints and characteristics can lead not only to heightening the probability and organizational impact of risk factors, but can also raise new risk issues that must be faced. We have argued and detailed elsewhere how this is particularly the case in respect to introducing and using IS in UK public sector settings, notably in UK central and local government, and in the case of the

Department of Social Security Operational Strategy (Margetts, 1991a,b; Margetts and Willcocks, 1993; Willcocks and Margetts, 1993). Below we examine how risks have arisen in the distinctive context of the National Health Service (NHS), and also show that some comparison can be made with risks engendered in private sector contexts.

The National Health Service

National Health Service reforms proposed by the UK government throughout the 1980s and early 1990s have been heavily dependent for their success on the delivery of effective IT systems. Much of the story has been that of disappointed expectations. NHS computing has confronted major risks in this period, the main risk factors being:

- environmental/government pressures;
- tight deadlines;
- changing organizational direction and needs;
- lack of in-house IT expertise;
- lack of user IT training;
- scale and complexity of projects/tasks.

A significant risk relates to environmental/government pressures. The fast pace and substantial volume of change demanded from NHS management and information initiatives have in themselves created extensive IT implementation difficulties. The lack of in-house IT expertise and lack of user training and know-how have also been pinpointed, along with the underfunding of training (National Audit Office, 1991).

Risks have also been incurred through poor project management. Typical short-comings have included incomplete feasibility studies; loose contractual arrangements; inadequate planning; weak control; and lack of post-implementation reviews. The National Audit Office observes that these failings did not affect all IT projects, but tended to have much greater adverse impacts on larger scale projects. There are also risks attendant on the scale and complexity of the tasks. As one example, a Worcester hospital has 2 million handwritten patient records waiting for transfer to computer. There are some 2500 UK hospitals at various stages in the computerization process. The magnitude of the data entry task may also contribute to the risk of inaccurate data. Indeed, suggestively, on estimates of their own systems by several NHS managers and consultants there are inaccuracies in perhaps one in five entries (Collins, 1992). Willcocks (1989, 1991) shows organizational/project and 'compatibility' risks arising due to insufficient management attention to social, political and organizational implications of IT-based systems. Internal organizational turbulence also makes it difficult to implement a system that will be usable. In this case 'definitional certainty' – that is, a clear specification of user requirements – may actually be a disadvantage as user requirements are likely to change all too quickly. In such an environment there are risks associated with 'definitional certainty' as well as with 'definitional uncertainty'. The latter may, of course, be all too readily encouraged by such an environment. Not surprisingly NHS managers have increasingly relied on external consultants, thus engendering many of the associated risks discussed in earlier cases (see above).

Some feel for risks engendered in public sector settings can be gained from looking at IT implementation in one Regional Health Authority. In 1984 North West Thames hired two consultancy firms to advise on new systems for general ledger and payroll functions. Despite recommendation of two systems it was not until 1989 that both were implemented. A major problem between 1985 and 1989 was a series of changes – not only had the technology changed, but so had management requirements. A further frequent risk in every IT project is that of underestimating systems capacity. In this case the consultants specified inadequate hardware. The Region had to add a second ICL machine to double the power. A further machine had to be added but required too much electricity and was left unused (Collins, 1992). The risk of escalating costs became real as the original estimate of £5 million became over £12 million by 1992, with the users of the system, the Districts, increasingly dropping out of the scheme.

North West Thames was also involved with five other Regions in the 1980s to share costs with the supplier to develop and maintain a common patient administration system (PAS). The system, known as converged product (CP) comprised two major elements: the PAS and District/Regional information systems to meet Kornerstipulated information requirements. High risks were associated with the size and complexity of this project. However, the necessary project management standards to meet these risks were not always forthcoming. This was partly due to the tightness of Korner deadlines (an 'environmental' pressure). This led, for example, to inadequate testing of the full system before going live (National Audit Office, 1991). A common risk in projects is that of falling behind time schedules, frequently due to lack of consideration of social and organizational implications of computerization (Chew *et al.*, 1991; Willcocks, 1991). In this case tight time schedules actually created problems in these areas, including inadequate advice to users, lack of training courses and materials, and an absence of well-defined requirements creating user overexpectation about what the system would deliver.

Private sector comparisons

Several private sector cases illustrate variants of these sorts of risks. The tight deadlines set by the UK government for the computerization of the London Stock Exchange in 1984 led to a considerable rush among related organizations to be ready by the October 1986 deadline. On the opening day the stock exchange systems themselves crashed due to underestimation of the size of user demand (see Willcocks and Mason, 1987b, for a more detailed analysis). A recent study of developments in settlement systems for brokers found many abandoned part-way through development or shortly after the 'live' date. Many brokerage houses installed 'card-board' systems to cope with the 1986 changes in UK securities trading practices, but had to rethink their systems with the stock market crash of 1987. The study estimates that stockbrokers had written off over £100 million on computers between 1986 and 1992 (reported in *Computer Weekly*, 16/7/92). Risks are also incurred in incompatibilities between timescales arising from business decisions made within an organization, and the time and expense required to put in or modify supporting IT-based systems. Thus, in a major international ferry company the IT director commented that a major difficulty was getting to know early enough likely business decisions. Business managers were constantly searching to attract new customers. There was a downside to this entrepreneurialism, which was that too little thought was then given to the IT implications. In one marketing example special deals for customers were advertised in newspapers. However, rates for these deals had not been set up in the reservation system, so that as the system processed the thousands of requests for booking, many were rejected.

While these cases help to illustrate the risks engendered by setting tight deadlines for delivering IS to organizations, the NHS case also helps to illustrate how risk arises through the complex interpenetration of a range of contextual, processual and substantive factors ranging from inherently risky characteristics of the context and IT project, through to varying degrees of mistake and inadequate action on the part of key stakeholders. One ironic learning point from the ferry company experience may be that, as central government increasingly encourages entrepreneurialism among public sector managers, associated IS risks will become increasingly prevalent in public sector organizations.

The DSS Operational Strategy: risks in large projects

The Operational Strategy (OS), the project to fully automate the Department of Social Security (DSS), provides an example of computerization and risk on a much greater scale. As at 1993 the DSS was one of the largest government departments, consuming 30% of public spending and employing around 10% of central government staff. The OS was a plan involving the construction of large-scale computer systems and the installation of 40 000 terminals in 1000 local offices and unemployment offices. It was claimed to be the largest programme of computerization ever undertaken in Europe, on 1992 figures costing in excess of £2 billion, with originally planned £700 million savings on DSS operating costs by 1995 as a result of computerization.

Work carried out on the OS fell into three stages. The planning and design phase lasted from 1982 until June 1985. In 1985 the government announced its plans for the reform of social security in a two-volume Green Paper. This had far-reaching implications for the systems in the strategy and new plans had to be made to account for the subsequent restructuring of benefits. The third stage started in 1987 when it became clear that many of the projects had slipped behind their original target dates. The speed of implementation after 1987 was fast and furious, and subsequent target dates for individual projects were largely met. More detailed descriptions of the history of the OS, and the risks engendered in the project, appear elsewhere (see Margetts, 1991b; Margetts and Willcocks, 1993; Willcocks, 1992b). Therein we question the extent to which the objectives of cost savings, system robustness, increased job satisfaction for staff and improved quality of service will now be achieved. The following represents only a summary of our findings.

Within the overall context of high risk due to the large size, high complexity, large number of divisions being computerized and length of time for project completion (from 1982 to 1999), a number of additional risks can be demonstrated in the DSS case, some of them distinctive to the public sector. The major risks in the DSS Operational Strategy are listed here, and we provide some commentary on these below.

1. Large number of divisions
2. Length of time for completion
3. Separation of IT management from policy making
4. Large size
5. Difficulties in aligning business/IT/organizational strategies

6. Insufficient IT expertise
7. Industrial relations risk
8. High complexity
9. Environmental turbulence/pressures
10. Isolation of IT in development phases
11. Newness of, and changing technologies

The history of a soured industrial relations climate, flowing in part from a seven-month 'pensions' strike at Newcastle computer centre in the mid-1980s, caused difficulties in securing employee commitment to the project, while the strike itself caused significant disruption to project timings (Willcocks and Mason, 1987a).

Overall a major risk was that of costs running out of control. In fact costs rose from the original estimate of £700 million to over £2.6 billion by 1993. It is unlikely that any of the cost savings, estimated in 1989 at £175 million, will now be achieved (Margetts and Willcocks, 1993; National Audit Office, 1989).

The OS also underwent risks associated with the organization not possessing sufficient IT expertise. In fact the OS has struggled with IT staff turnover rates of 45%. In practice, the DSS dealt with the problems of skills shortages almost exclusively via the use of consultants. In 1986–87, the department employed around 150 consultants at a cost of £12.1 million, thus making real the risk of spiralling costs. After 1987 the number of consultants used on the project increased significantly. Half the internal programmers working on the OS project were moved to other areas because they were seen as a strike risk. The number of consultants employed in 1987–88 was 235, at a cost of £22 million, nearly five times the cost of equivalent in-house staff (National Audit Office, 1989).

Further risks were inherent in the separation of IT management from policy making. As contextual factors social security reforms between 1985 and 1988 had far-reaching effects on the project. Little development work had taken place on the main projects at the time the social security reforms were introduced, but the changes meant that project plans had to be altered within a relatively brief period of two years up to April 1988. According to many sources, those involved in planning the OS were not consulted until the Green Paper was published. The speed demanded for modification of supplementary benefit software to income support software in time for the introduction of the new benefit created considerable problems. Many of the smaller projects, largely those designed to improve quality of service, were dropped from the plans. While those in charge of administration appeared unconcerned with policy issues, it also seems that politicians were reluctant to equip themselves with an understanding of information technology (Margetts, 1991b).

There were considerable risks inherent in the isolation of IT in the DSS. All the problems encountered seem to point to this one major feature. While succeeding in bringing the computers themselves to the heart of the organization, all expertise in information technology has been kept largely on the periphery. While much of the design and specification of the system has been carried out by consultants, those with experience of actually using the DSS administrative systems were relatively excluded. The isolation of IT could be increased by the introduction of the agency structure to the UK Civil Service. Further marginalization of computer expertise in the DSS seemed likely after April 1990 when all the DSS's information technology staff were moved to an Information Technology Services Agency (ITSA), deepening the division between IT and clerical staff. In future the worth of ITSA can be measured against its competitiveness of the computer consultancy market; if the newly created Contributions Agency or the Benefits Agency are dissatisfied with the service they get they can go elsewhere. However, it is far easier for users of computer services to define what they want when they possess an understanding of what is possible. If most technological expertise has been moved to the periphery of the organization, it seems unlikely that the DSS will know whether they are dissatisfied or not.

Using the framework in Figure 11.3, a range of risk factors come strikingly together in the history of the DSS Operational Strategy. In terms of outer context, government pressure, imposed deadlines and the many legislative changes in the 1980–92 period all created a riskier climate for the delivery of robust IS. Additionally, historically, the organization lacked relevant IS experience and skills. Reward systems in the organization created labour market problems and exacerbated IS skills shortages; in a soured industrial relations climate against tight deadlines, the policy became to cut off staff participation in systems development and pull in external consultants. This put pressure on cost targets, left systems design largely to IS professionals, and put at risk stated objectives on job satisfaction and systems quality. At the same time a number of inherently risky factors feature in the OS, in particular the large size, high complexity, large number of units being computerized, a high degree of technical and definitional uncertainty, and the 17-year time span for project completion. Furthermore, the processes of change saw little user commitment and training to 1990, mainly through tightening deadlines, management decision and the perceived high cost of further delay. Much of the case evidence indicates that the major risks and reasons for suboptimization are as much through organizational, social and political factors as through inherently risky or merely technical factors. The complex nature of risks in large IS projects are well exemplified in the DSS case, with the public sector setting also bringing distinctive outer and inner contextual factors to bear.

Towards a usable framework

From a review of the frameworks, research studies and cases detailed in this chapter a more comprehensive, directive framework for risk analysis can be tentatively put forward. It is suggested that this can be used to complement, rather than replace, other methods for risk analysis, but that a major advantage of carrying out this additional, deeper analysis is to enrich the degree to which risk analysis informs and enables subsequent risk management.

Major factors that seem to bear critical study during IS development, implementation and usage are shown in Figures 11.4 and 11.5. For clarificatory purposes we discuss illustrative examples of these factors; however, these examples receive considerable support from the other evidence presented in this chapter.

A **history** of information systems' success or failure seems to have a bearing on subsequent risks experienced. In the DSS case the Operational Strategy followed on a previously failed, high-profile project in the department; in the Kwik-Fit case, previous IS success led management to underestimate risk in future IS development and introduction. In the NHS a history of disappointed expectations creates sceptical user communities at many organizational sites. A lack of relevant IS experience at CCC, XYZ plc, the DSS, the NHS, in the City and to some degree at Kwik-Fit contributed to subsequent risk development in each case. Organizational history of

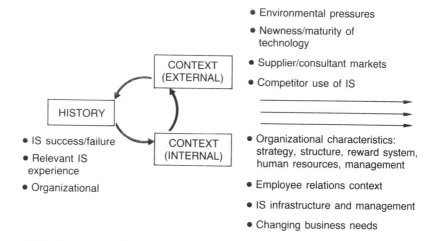

Figure 11.4 Diagnosing risk (1): history and context.

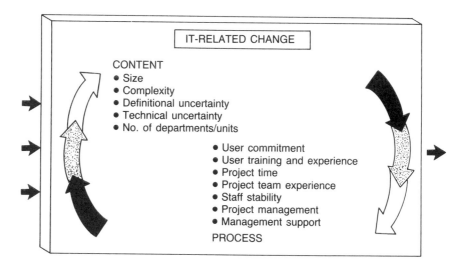

Figure 11.5 Diagnosing risk (2): content and process.

industrial relations problems directly impinged upon computerization in the DSS case.

The way in which **external contextual** factors contribute to the 'riskiness' of computerization is demonstrated in the public sector cases (government deadlines and the speed of new legislation), and in the case of the stock exchange (externally imposed deadlines) and the ferry company (turbulent, competitive markets). The 'newness of technology' factor was discussed in detail in the case of XYZ plc, but also applies to the DSS, NHS and City/stock exchange cases. This factor often led organizations to expose themselves to the vagaries of the consultancy/supplier markets, as discussed above in each of these cases. We take 'competitor use of IT' from the information economics framework (see Chapter 9) because it is also endorsed by the ferry company, CCC, Thorn-EMI and Kwik-Fit cases. Vitale (1986) has also added to our understanding here, pointing to the growing competitive risks associated, ironically, with IS success. In a competitive arena the development of a successful IS may prove a disadvantage in certain circumstances – for example, where the IS changes the basis of competition to a company's disadvantage, lowers entry barriers to the industry sector or increases customers' or suppliers' power to the detriment of the innovating firm.

Internal contextual factors also have a critical bearing on levels and types of risk engendered. As examples: misfits between organizational and IS structure/infrastructure can cause problems (CCC, XYZ plc). The degree to which the organization possesses relevant IS experience can influence the risks subsequently undergone (CCC, XYZ plc, Kwik-Fit). Managerial, cultural, human resource and evaluation and reward systems issues can feed into the degree of risk experienced in computerization (Thorn-EMI, DSS). The DSS case also illustrates the impact of the industrial relations climate on project risk. Changing business needs can also greatly affect the riskiness inherent in IS development and introduction, as seen in the ferry company, NHS and CCC cases.

The **content** issues in IT-related change listed in Figure 11.5 emerge strongly from all studies, but particularly clearly from XYZ plc and the DSS cases, each at the extreme in terms of size and complexity and number of units being computerized, but both illustrating the risks inherent in 'definitional' and 'technical uncertainty' (see Parker *et al.*, 1988). The organizational/project risks associated with **process** issues also flow through all the cases but are particularly clear in the Thorn-EMI and DSS cases.

A further point relates to the study of desirable **outcomes** in computerization. Typical outcomes pursued in the cases we have detailed are summarized in Figure 11.6. This listing does not exhaust the possibilities, of course.

What becomes important in analysing preferred IS outcomes is discovering whose perceptions and vested interests these represent. If defined outcomes are not representative of the desired objectives of salient stakeholders who can affect the course of computerization, then this may decrease the achievability of those outcomes. Clearly a detailed stakeholder analysis can assist in defining the type, size of impact and probability of risks becoming real here (Willcocks, 1991; Willcocks and Mason, 1987b). However, the dominant point that must emerge from our analyses and this discussion must be that it is the relationships between all the risks listed in the DSS case and the factors detailed in Figures 11.4 to 11.6, and the way in which

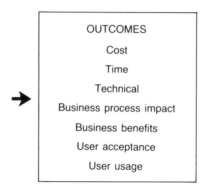

Figure 11.6 Diagnosing risk (3): outcomes.

they interconnect to engender risk, that deserve analysis. The study of such inter-relationships receives too little attention in other risk analysis approaches, and the present framework can provide a useful, complementary, heuristic tool.

Conclusions

This chapter has sought to consider and demonstrate the many types of risks that arise in a variety of ways in IS projects in both private and public sector contexts. Computerization remains a high-risk process but the degree and type of risk is in-fluenced considerably by environmental and organizational contexts and pressures.

From a practitioner perspective there would seem to be some merit in interpreting risk operationally as not just inherent in certain structural features of the environ-ment or of a project, but also arising as a result of distinctive human and organiza-tional practices and patterns of belief and action. It is clear that certain features are inherently more risky than others. However, we have also sought to develop the notion of risk to take into account factors which shade into mistakes and inadequate action by stakeholders and participants in IT-related change processes. This has been done deliberately to see if there are any other typical mistakes and inadequate actions that can be identified in such processes. In this chapter we have tried to be suggestive rather than conclusive on this area, but it would seem to be a productive subject on which to pursue further research. A further development here has been the attempt to introduce into the study of risk – and to demonstrate the usefulness of – a more comprehensive framework for exploring the interrelationships between history, outer and inner contexts, processes, content and outcomes of IT-related change. This is to begin to suggest coherent alternatives to the all-too-frequently encountered truncated forms of risk assessment used in work organizations, or to the situations where little formal assessment of risk is carried out at all. One direction for future development, not attempted here in any detail, would be to extend the assessment of risk by focusing on broader, possibly more desirable outcomes than those most often encountered – that is, limited assessments of risk against 'in time, within budget, to acceptable standard' type criteria (see also Introduction to the book and Chapter 12). A further development, not detailed here, would be to put in place an organizational process for monitoring risk across systems life-time (see Willcocks and Lester, 1993). Much of this argues that those who wish to study and/or influence risk levels in IT-related change processes need to apply as much learning from organization studies as from the more traditionally utilized project manage-ment, operational research and financial management fields.

References

Beath, C. and Ives, B. (1989) *The Information Technology Champion: Aiding and Abetting, Care and Feeding*. Oxford Institute of Information Management Research and Discussion Papers RDP 89/2, Templeton College, Oxford.

Cash, J., McFarlan, W. and McKenney, J. (1992) *Corporate Information Systems Management*, Irwin, Boston.

Charette, R. (1991) *Application Strategies for Risk Analysis*, McGraw-Hill, New York.

Chew, B., Leonard-Barton, D. and Bohn, R. (1991) Beating Murphy's Law. *Sloan Management Review*, **5**, 5–16.

Coleman, T. and Jamieson, M. (1991) *Information Systems: Evaluating Intangible Benefits at the Feasibility Stage of Project Appraisal*. Unpublished MBA thesis, City University Business School, London.

Collingridge, D. (1992) *The Management of Scale*, Routledge, London.

Collins, T. (1992) Health computing: the wasted millions. *Computer Weekly*, 7 May, 32–4.

Cooper, R. and Zmud, R. (1990) Information technology implementation research: a technological diffusion approach. *Management Science*, **36** (2), 123–39.

Corder, C. (1989) *Taming Your Company Computer*, McGraw-Hill, London.

Currie, W. (1989) The art of justifying new technology to top management. *Omega*, **17** (5), 409–18.

Earl, M. (1989). *Management Strategies for Information Technology*, Prentice-Hall, London.

Earl, M. and Runge, D. (1987) *Using Telecommunications-based Information Systems for Competitive Advantage*. Oxford Institute of Information Management Research and Discussion Papers RDP 87/1, Templeton College, Oxford.

Farbey, B., Land F. and Targett, D. (1992) Evaluating investments in IT. *Journal of Information Technology*, **7** (2), 100–12.

Feeny, D., Earl, M. and Edwards, B. (1989) *IS Arrangements to Suit Complex Organizations: 2. Integrating the Efforts of Users and Specialists*. Research Paper RDP89/5, Templeton College, Oxford.

Gallagher, J. and Scott, R. (1988) *Kwik-Fit Holdings*. Case 388-007-1, Case Clearing House, Cranfield.

Harrow, J. and Willcocks, L. (1992) Management, innovation and organizational learning. In *Rediscovering Public Services Management* (eds L. Willcocks and J. Harrow), McGraw-Hill, London.

Hodgkinson, S. (1991) *The Role of the Corporate Information Technology Function in the Large Multi-business Company*. Oxford Institute of Information Management Research and Discussion Papers, RDP 1/2, Templeton College, Oxford.

Hull, J. (1990) Application of risk analysis techniques in proposal assessment. *Project Management*, **8** (3), 152–7.

Johnston, H. and Vitale, M. (1988) Creating competitive advantage with interorganizational systems. *MIS Quarterly*, June, 153–65.

Kearney, AT (1990) *Breaking the Barriers: IT Effectiveness in Great Britain and Ireland*, AT Kearney/CIMA, London.

Keen, P. (1991) *Shaping the Future*, Harvard Business Press, Boston.

KEW Associates/Computer Weekly (1992) *UK IT Market Analysis*, Autumn 1992 edition, Computer Weekly, London.

Kumar, K. (1990) Post-implementation evaluation of computer-based IS: current practices. *Communications of the ACM*, **33** (2), 203–12.

Kwon, T. and Zmud, R. (1987) Unifying the fragmented models of information systems implementation, In *Critical Issues in Information Systems Research* (eds J. Boland and R. Hirschheim), Wiley, Chichester.

Loudon, K. and Loudon, J. (1991) *Management Information Systems: A Contemporary Perspective*, Macmillan, New York.

Lyttinen, K. and Hirschheim, R. (1987) Information systems failures – a survey and classification of the empirical literature. In *Oxford Surveys of Information Technology*, Vol. 4 (ed. P. Zorkoczy), Oxford University Press, Oxford, pp. 257–309.

Margetts, H. (1991a) Information technology in the public sector: new risks, new dangers. Paper at the *ESRC/LSE Seminar Series on Hazard Management, 'IT Developments and Hazard Analysis'*, London School of Economics, London, November.

Margetts, H. (1991b) The computerization of Social Security: the way forward or a step backwards? *Public Administration*, **69** (3), Autumn.

Margetts, H. and Willcocks, L. (1993) Information technology in public sector settings: disaster faster? *Public Money and Management*, **13** (2), 49–56.

Mintzberg, H. (1989) *Mintzberg on Management*, Free Press, New York.

National Audit Office (1989) *Department of Social Security, Operational Strategy*. Report by the Comptroller and Auditor General, HMSO, London.

National Audit Office (1991). *Managing Computer Projects in the National Health Service*, HMSO, London.

OTR Group (1992) Report detailed in *Computer Weekly*, 12 December, p. 12.

Parker, M., Benson, R. and Trainor, E. (1988) *Information Economics: Linking Business Performance to Information Technology*, Prentice-Hall, Englewood Cliffs, New Jersey.

Pettigrew, A. (1985) *The Awakening Giant: Continuity and Change in ICI*, Blackwell, Oxford.

Pettigrew, A. and Whipp, R. (1991) *Managing Change for Competitive Success*, Blackwell, Oxford.

Pettigrew, A., Ferlie, E. and McKee, L. (1992) *Shaping Strategic Change*, Sage, London.

Pike, R. and Ho, S. (1991) Risk analysis in capital budgeting: barriers and benefits. *Omega*, **19** (4) 235–45.

Post, G. and Dilz, D. (1986) A stochastic dominance approach to risk analysis of computer systems. *MIS Quarterly*, December, 362–75.

Rogers, E. and Kim, J. (1985) Diffusion of innovations in public organizations, in Innovation in the Public Sector (eds R. Merritt and A. Merritt), Sage, Beverly Hills.

Scott-Morton, M. (ed.) (1991) *The Corporation of the 1990s*, Oxford University Press, Oxford.

Shenhar, A. (1992) Project management style and the space shuttle program (part 2): A retrospective look. *Project Management Journal*, **23** (1), 32–7.

Strassmann, P. (1990) *The Business Value of Computers*, The Information Economics Press, New Canaan.

Stringer, J. (1992) Risk in large projects, In *Operational Research Tutorial Papers* (ed. M. Mortimer), Operational Research Society, London.

Symons, V. and Walsham, G. (1988) The evaluation of information systems: a critique. *Journal of Applied Systems Analysis*, **15**, 119–32.

Tornatzky, L. and Klein, K. (1982) Innovation characteristics and innovation adoption implementation: a meta-analysis of Findings. *IEEE Transactions on Engineering Management*, February, 28–45.

Vitale, M. (1986) The growing risks of information systems success. *MIS Quarterly*, December, 327–34.

Walsham, G. (1992) *Interpreting Information Systems in Organizations*, Wiley, Chichester.

Walton, R. (1989) *Up and Running: Integrating Information Technology and the Organization*, Harvard Business Press, Boston.

Warner, F. *et al.* (1992) *Risk: Analysis, Perception and Management*, The Royal Society, London.

Willcocks, L. (1989) Information technology in public sector settings: towards effective systems. *International Journal of Public Sector Management*, **2** (3), 15–29.

Willcocks, L. (1991) Information technology and human resource issues in the 1990s: integration through culture. Paper presented at the *Fifth Annual Conference of the British Academy of Management, 'Business: Advancing the Horizons'*, University of Bath, 22–24 September.

Willcocks, L. (1992a) Evaluating information technology investments: research findings and reappraisal. *Journal of Information Systems*, **2** (3), 1–26.

Willcocks, L. (1992b) The manager as technologist, In Rediscovering Public Services Management (eds L. Willcocks and J. Harrow), McGraw-Hill, London.

Willcocks, L. (1992c) Strategy development and delivery: dealing with the IT evaluation question, In *Creating a Business-based IT Strategy* (ed. A. Brown), Chapman & Hall, London.

Willcocks, L. and Lester, S. (1993) How organizations evaluate and control information systems investments: recent UK survey evidence. Paper for the *IFIP WG8.2 Working Conference – Information Systems Development: Human, Social and Organizational Aspects*, Noordwijkerhout, The Netherlands, 17–19 May.

Willcocks, L. and Margetts, H. (1991) Informatization in UK public services: from implementation, through strategy, to management. Paper at the *EGPA Conference – Informatization in Public Administration*, The Hague, The Netherlands, August.

Willcocks, L. and Margetts, H. (1993) Informatization in public and private sector settings: distinctive or common risks? *Informatization and the Public Sector* (forthcoming).

Willcocks, L. and Mark, A. (1989) IT systems implementation: research findings from the public sector. *Journal of Information Technology*, **4** (2), 92–103.

Willcocks, L. and Mason, D. (1987a) The DHSS Operational Strategy, 1975–1986. *Business Case File in Information Technology*, Van Nostrand Reinhold, London.

Willcocks, L. and Mason, D. (1987b) *Computerising Work*, Paradigm, London.

Williams, T. (1990) Risk analysis using an embedded CPA package. *Project Management*, **8** (2), 84–8.

Part Four

Process and Perspectives

12

Responsibility for IT: a grey area of management

Catherine Griffiths

Introduction

The question of where responsibility for IT should reside in an organization is one which is causing increasing concern. Senior managers are coming to realize, often through bitter experience, that treating IT project proposals as one-off investment decisions is not the way to achieve solid business benefits for their companies and positive financial returns for their shareholders (Hochstrasser and Griffiths, 1990). For IT to provide benefits to a company it has to be managed and directed and this cannot be left as a part-time activity, linked exclusively to financial planning and short-term crisis decision making (Strassmann, 1985). The management of IT investments therefore needs to progress from a nursery stage of management practice to a full-time process of management, over time.

In many organizations there is an unstructured approach to the management of IT and, as a result, it is left to some individuals to assume IT responsibility while others simply have it thrust upon them. The pressure to ensure that there is some clear focus of responsibility is coming from the fact that many companies are poised to make major decisions driven by the urgent need to cut costs and ensure a better return on their investment (Atkins and Galliers, 1992). The European Community has measured the turnover of the IT industry in Europe as being 700 bn ECUs

Information Management: The evaluation of information systems investments.
Edited by Leslie Willcocks.
Published in 1994 by Chapman & Hall. ISBN 0 412 41540 2.

(£490 bn) which is nearly 5% of the Community's gross domestic product. This fact alone illustrates the scale of the potential problems for companies. With IT being a major part of the infrastructure for many companies, requiring as much as 22% of non-taxed revenue in some cases, the indiscriminate slashing of IT budgets cannot occur without the threat of inflicting terminal damage on some of the core business areas.

Business and technical personnel are realizing that responsibility for IT cannot continue as the grey area of management. There is, however, no current consensus of how IT investments can be coordinated and better directed. The result is that a number of different approaches to handling IT responsibility, this new management phenomenon, are evident. In some companies it is traditional to link IT responsibility to another main corporate function, most commonly finance, while in other companies it has led to the creation of completely different job roles and new reporting structures. What is certain is that the whole domain of IT responsibility is now under the microscope. In the following sections this chapter will outline the current management dilemmas surrounding the issues of IT responsibility. It will introduce the need to link responsibility to the key areas of authority for IT and accountability within the company. Some new ways of structuring management processes to incorporate these IT management issues will be discussed.

IT responsibility

In a recent study, the Kobler Unit contacted 34 companies to discover where they placed IT responsibility. In total, 60 senior managers participated in the investigation. The organizations involved varied in size from small partnerships with a turnover of under £1 million to multi-national corporations with more than a £500 million turnover. The companies were drawn from a wide range of business sectors including financial, manufacturing and retailing. Whereas for all large traditional business functions such as personnel, finance and marketing it is common practice to have a

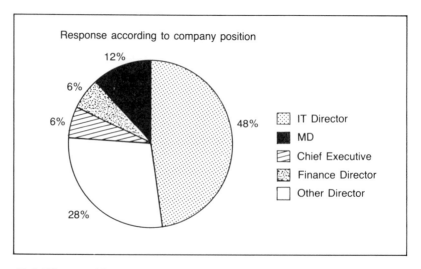

Figure 12.1 Whose problem is it anyway?

board level director as the head of the function linked to a well-defined reporting structure, this is not necessarily the case for IT. Often there is no obvious, well-qualified, person to whom matters of IT importance or funding can be addressed (Figure 12.1). According to the particular type of company this might mean that IT itself falls within the scope of some other key functional responsibility.

Does this lack of a directional focus for IT really matter? The indications are that it does because it shows that the underlying management problem is more complex than has first been assumed. The real issue is concerned with three areas of:

- authority for IT
- responsibility for IT
- accountability.

These three areas are relevant to all companies regardless of size, industry or specialization.

1. **Authority** for IT might rest with a single person, or with a group, as well as ultimately with the board. Having authority means having the power to make decisions, in particular about resource allocation, personnel, project priorities and delegation. It means being ultimately answerable for the outcome of decisions made. Responsibility is implicit in authority but is not identical.
2. **Responsibility** for IT can lie with a wide range of people and be at many different levels in an organization. The definition of responsibility needs to be integral to each person's job role and function, whether technical or non-technical. The degree of importance attached to any responsibility will be reflected in the seniority of the role and will vary across the organization. Roles that carry responsibility do not necessarily carry authority.
3. **Accountability** means providing direct feedback and communication of the decisions made. Formalized procedures are necessary, as accountability does not occur automatically; it must be made explicit. A strong emphasis on accountability reinforces the importance of both authority and responsibility. It ensures there is a link between them and it minimizes the arbitrary nature of some decision making.

Perhaps the problem that many organizations face is already becoming clear: that is, **these three areas have not been addressed with sufficient thought**. Many companies are therefore finding it difficult to make decisions which include consideration of IT. They try to provide a coherent policy towards IT without first setting in place the necessary management processes (Earl, 1989; Lincoln, 1990). When IT investments are made without clear definitions of authority and responsibility, these can be assumed by whichever power base within the organization is strongest. Usually this means it is assumed by one of two groups: either a user group or by the technologists themselves.

If the users take charge it can be found that the resulting systems are inconsistent, incomplete, expensive and only used to a fraction of their full potential (Hochstrasser and Griffiths, 1991). When this happens dual practices can develop, leading to information being kept in separate systems. The result is that some information is updated on an IT system which may function erratically while some information is maintained and updated on paper-based systems. In many companies serious problems have developed when it becomes uncertain which systems are current and the most relevant. The question is then raised of what to do when particular information is no longer consistently available through either system.

If the technologists take charge of IT the resulting systems can be user-unfriendly, over-engineered, unduly complex and isolated from securing the business aims (Strassmann, 1990). When this happens technology tends to take over. The IT department may, as a result, seem to be justifying its existence by providing technical solutions which are looking for problems to solve. The outcome of this can be that the users suffer from either information overload, where too much information is hiding salient facts, or from information starvation, where not enough information is available to the right people at the times required. The outcome can be that business personnel resort to blaming the IT section for poor support. In many cases this may lead to a lowering of morale in those sections of the company most affected. Accountability, in this type of anarchic situation, can become entirely lost along the way. Regaining control then becomes a painful and expensive process. While most companies may not be totally run by only the technologists or only the users, there is ample evidence to indicate that the issues of authority, responsibility and account-ability are not being effectively addressed (Atkins and Galliers, 1992; Kaplan and Norton, 1992). It is suggested here that this lack of clear corporate delineation is a major contributing factor to the underlying cultural and communication gap existing between technologists and users, particularly at senior levels. This problem has been highlighted in a recent Kobler Unit study (Hochstrasser and Griffiths, 1990).

When managers were asked to indicate the main constraints to optimizing their IT involvement, three out of four pointed to the problems of communication gaps between IT and the users:

- 38% stated poor understanding of the potential of IT by senior management
- 35% considered themselves constrained by poor understanding of business plans by IT professionals.

As pointed out in the Introduction and in Chapter 5, many companies have intro-duced IT without planning how it will integrate with the business. In other words, there has been an expectation that IT and business will align naturally, without the need to make specific decisions about who is responsible for which tasks. At the most senior levels, this reflects an abdication of decision making by those with the authority to initiate the required changes and new role definitions.

Further evidence of this problem has come from a recent survey undertaken by the computer systems house Sequent (1991) of a sample of 56 companies from The Times Top 500. It was found that 57% of DP managers felt their board lacked knowledge of IT issues while only 5% of directors believed their DP managers knew the business 'very well'. A suggested solution of appointing IT directors to the board was turned down by 83% of the companies, who indicated they were not con-sidering the creation of such a post. If technologists are questioned they perceive that the business users need to become more involved and indeed business users state the same of technologists. This situation is not likely to resolve itself without manage-ment intervention and leadership.

Unfortunately this does not appear, in many cases, to be forthcoming. The NCC/ Impact programme investigations, CE Perspectives on IT Performance? (1991), show a current willingness on the part of senior management to push the IT issue away from their own level of decision making. The study found that 'the consensus was that the IT director should strive to make IT as well integrated with the business, and business procedures as possible'. Once again responsibility for the integration of IT with the business is seen to be passed down, with expectations that it will somehow be resolved independently of senior management involvement. IT is not seen to be a broad management responsibility. Case studies show that when managers are prepared to abrogate their responsibility despite 'recognizing the pervasiveness of information systems which affect everyone' they are likely to experience a poor return from their IT investments (Hochstrasser and Griffiths, 1990; Scott-Morton, 1991; Strassmann, 1990). Moreover, experience points to the fact that IT will not become an integral part of the business unless a broader approach to IT management responsibility is adopted and a more precise definition is made of authority linked to accountability.

Where should responsibility for IT lie?

What is evident, with only a few exceptions, is that responsibility for IT is being slotted into the traditional hierarchy of organizational structures without any recognition of the broader impact that IT has on existing processes, communication practices and organizational structures (Ciborra, 1991). Very few companies are reorganizing their human resources and the tiers of management to reflect the pervasiveness of information systems or to reflect the importance of information as a valuable resource (Willcocks, 1991). The result is that large unofficial and unrepresentative power structures can develop which, if left undirected, can undermine the very business objectives that are being aimed for by the existing management.

How can managers overcome this latent threat to long-term management effectiveness and business survival? There are two prerequisites. First, it is clear that the personal skill set of the individual responsible for IT is the most critical single factor contributing to effective IT management. The relevant skill set is developed through a broadly based process of education which includes understanding of the issues that surround IT. Effective management of IT is always a function of individual talent and ability. Secondly, the personal skill set can only be exploited to maximum corporate advantage if the particular individuals are then placed at the most appropriate level within the organization. For many companies this might mean that it is necessary to make some changes: to define new roles and to delineate new areas of authority and responsibility. Obviously, introducing new positions alone will not automatically improve management effectiveness but if individuals who have appropriate skill sets are given new remits then the changes can become effective. The current problem for many companies may well be that the skilled people in the organization are not being placed at the most effective level to provide the sought-after corporate benefits.

Most companies, regardless of size, culture or market sector, have handled the whole issue of responsibility for IT in a similar way (Atkins and Galliers, 1992; Hochstrasser and Griffiths, 1991; Rockart, 1988). IT responsibility usually remains focused on one of the following four functional groups:

- IT director
- finance director
- business units
- the board.

It is found that when responsibility is focused exclusively on one of these functional areas there can be drawbacks as well as benefits for companies:

What happens when IT directors are in charge of IT?

If responsibility for IT is left exclusively to the IT function it is found that major alignment problems tend to develop. Without direction and feedback from the business units on a regular basis, IT personnel are left to plan and implement the technology without reference to the strategic business requirements. When no strong links exist with the business it becomes difficult to achieve the benefits that were intended when the IT investments were first made. Furthermore, the preoccupation with technical matters means that little time is directed towards the serious consideration of human and organizational issues. The result is that many systems, once operational, are not fully exploited because the users do not have sufficient training and organizational support to facilitate their work. When the IT director is not on the company board and there is no direct link to the board, these problems continue to undermine the value of investments and ensure that IT continues to be regarded essentially as a cost. In this situation, the IT managers in most companies do not have the authority to force business managers to make the decisions necessary for effective IT investments, aligned to corporate needs.

When IT responsibility remains within the IT department, companies can directly benefit from systems that are planned on an extensive and technically accurate basis. Centralizing IT control means that systems are usually technically efficient, speedy and reliable. It becomes easier to enforce standards of coding and documentation, as well as provide security of sensitive data. There is also a strong awareness of potential compatibility problems so subsequent integration can be achieved more smoothly. Furthermore, it is found that personnel in the IT function often have a broad knowledge and understanding of the types of technology that are being developed for future commercial use (Rockart, 1988). This means they are well placed to exploit innovative technology as it becomes available (Figure 12.2).

What happens when finance directors are in charge of IT?

Cost–benefit analysis techniques already have strong control over the corporate psyche. If finance directors are left with exclusive responsibility for IT there is sometimes a counter-productive emphasis on the use of this approach for the evaluation of all IT investments. Obviously financial evaluation procedures are useful and necessary but they are limited in their application (Kaplan and Norton, 1992). If

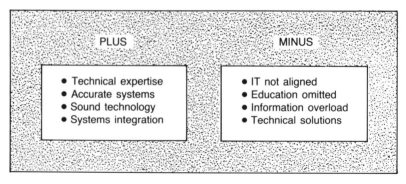

PLUS	MINUS
• Technical expertise	• IT not aligned
• Accurate systems	• Education omitted
• Sound technology	• Information overload
• Systems integration	• Technical solutions

Figure 12.2 IT responsibility: IT directors.

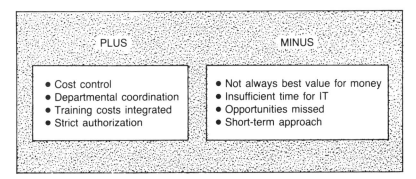

Figure 12.3 IT responsibility: finance directors.

used as the only measure of the effectiveness of IT it is frequently found that valid broader business benefits, which are not so easily quantifiable, are not included. The annual budgetary cycle, the whole process of submissions for budget requirements, and the demand for benefits within short timescales dominate the corporate thinking. This means that often larger investments which may be of group or company significance are not adequately addressed by a director who has other responsibilities. Opportunities can be lost when short-term benefits are exploited at the cost of the longer term benefits. In the final analysis it cannot make solid business sense to link two such important functions as finance and IT under one umbrella post, when both require full-time management to be effective. The argument for leaving responsibility for IT investments with the finance director is indeed a powerful one. The finance director is a key member of any board. Placing IT with finance does ensure that a company is strongly aware of the obvious costs. Strict financial authorization procedures are comprehensively enforced. The processes under which investments are made are widely understood and business-aligned proposals can result which are financially justified. Some of the additional requirements are also financed at the outset – for instance, training and some form of backup support. Clear standards and procedures are generally applied when obtaining funding for existing and future projects. The combined effect of this is that strong central control exists and that there is a broad level of coordination across the whole company. Undoubtedly, many companies have operated with this approach: financial control becomes a synonym for good management (Figure 12.3).

What happens when business units are in charge of IT?

When business units are left exclusively with responsibility for IT implementation and management, there is a risk that some decisions are taken for the benefit of the business unit at the expense of the company as a whole. No individual business unit wants to incur costs that are for the benefit of other units when they are faced with consistent pressures to ensure cost minimization. Resources can be wasted as a result of the unnecessary duplication of efforts and lack of coordinated support for new initiatives. It is found that internal competition for limited resources can lead to artificial barriers being created which can undermine company-wide benefits. As a result, cross-divisional learning may become a problem and incompatibility issues

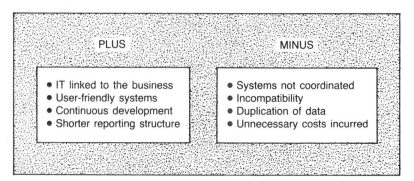

Figure 12.4 IT responsibility: business units.

may start to feature more strongly as a point of concern. The combined effect of these factors is that individual business units can continue to repeat past mistakes which have been expensively learned elsewhere in the company. Usually companies with this type of structure do not create appropriate management processes to ensure that these gaps in communication are filled.

Nevertheless, there are advantages if business units retain responsibility for IT investments. This approach does provide opportunities for closer cooperation between the business and technology communities. Joint developments can lead to more user-friendly systems which can be better directed to individual user needs. Adjustments to systems become easier as flexibility is built into systems at the outset. Delegation of decision making to business units, when accompanied by strong board level direction, clear delineation of responsibility and authority as well as formalized processes of accountability, can indeed make good business sense (Figure 12.4).

What happens when the board is in charge of IT?

Clearly the board always has ultimate responsibility for a company and all its operations: the board is where responsibility and authority come together. In a later section of this chapter it is shown how the board can strengthen the management processes for making decisions about IT investments. The focus here is on what happens when direct IT responsibility is assumed by the board without the necessary organizational infrastructure in place to provide support.

If IT responsibility is left to the board in general, without any clear role definitions, IT issues are often addressed only superficially. IT tends to feature on the agenda only when further resources are required or when some crisis precipitates the need for action. Lack of board level interest in IT is now widely experienced as a problem. When this exists together with a lack of any personal experience or knowledge of the broader IT implications, major organizational problems can occur. Additionally, lack of concern for the logistical details can lead to companies installing expensive systems that are only used to a fraction of their full potential.

The board is, however, in a unique position. It is able to appreciate the strategic implications and wider impact of departmental policy decisions. This perspective is not possible at lower levels in the organization. Providing a corporate overview can ensure that there is a strong link with the business and that investments in IT are

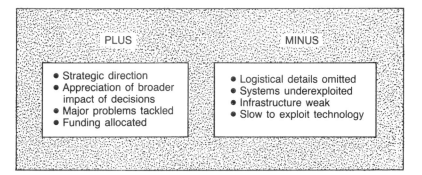

Figure 12.5 IT responsibility: the board.

only made when there is a strong drive from the business itself. Major problems can be handled at the strategic level, leading to the allocation of the necessary resources, and removal of the inevitable red tape. The convergence of authority and responsibility means that the board can make things happen. Ensuring that these 'things' are right is, of course, the measure of management judgement (Figure 12.5).

Whose responsibility is IT anyway?

As this section has shown, the answer to this question is neither simple nor straightforward. It seems, though, that traditional approaches to allocating and devolving responsibility have usually attempted to solve this problem by forcing IT responsibility into an existing framework of management; one which is no longer appropriate to the issues involved. No blueprint solution exists of how responsibility should be structured and how it should be related to authority and accountability. These complex issues require that every company must address them for itself, taking into account size, structure, culture, resources and business emphasis (Ciborra, 1991). The issue cannot be avoided in the long term, because it is found that effective IT management will not flow automatically from decision making structured around traditional corporate hierarchies. Authority, responsibility and accountability need to be redefined in order to provide the seamless linking of IT with business in all organizations.

The solution for all companies is to examine their existing processes; to analyse those that work but have evolved outside the traditional corporate hierarchy, and then determine how they can be incorporated into a newly defined management structure. The changes necessary to be effective, have to be more fundamental than the introduction of new titles or positions to an organization; they have to be representative of the actual business processes (Kaplan and Norton, 1992). Some successful companies are already meeting these challenges by adapting their traditional hierarchies to reflect the emphasis on facilitating a directional role rather than a control role, linked to static job descriptions. This, it is found, is the key to managing IT investments more effectively, both in the long and short term. When companies recognize this, then the range of IT management processes will be handled more competently, rather than as an erratic series of disjointed decisions, often fraught with political overtones.

The hybrid manager

One approach to overcoming the shortcomings that have been outlined as existing in traditional methods of managing IT is to break down functional barriers by introducing 'hybrid managers'. The term hybrid managers was first coined by Michael Earl and David Skyrme (1990) in their investigations for OXIIM, Templeton College, Oxford. Earl, acting as the David Attenborough of the management jungle, selected a number of companies that were classified as managing their IT investments effectively. He then defined the types of characteristics and competences of those individuals who were key to this successful management process. He found that these individuals were neither specialists in technology nor specialists in business. They had a degree of knowledge about each field, hence they were hybrids (Figure 12.6).

The term hybrid manager has since become familiar terminology to describe anyone who is knowledgeable in two or more management areas. In fact, the success of this term has often meant that it has become divorced from the context in which it was originally developed. While the concept of the hybrid manager itself has integrity, a great deal of hype has since attached to it which is distracting from what can realistically be achieved by organizations in practice, within short time-

AREA	COMPETENCES
Business knowledge	General business knowledge Knowledge about firm's specific business knowledge–markets, products, competitors
Organization-specific knowledge	Culture Structure Processes Key people and their motivation
IT knowledge/experience	Experience of managing projects IT applications in firm's business Awareness of existing potential Knowledge of who can provide expertise on specific technologies
Management competences	Change management skills Interpersonal skills Conceptual skills Motivational skills Team/peer group skills Communication skills

Figure 12.6 Competences for hybrid managers (adapted from Earl and Skyrme, 1990).

scales. Many companies, anxious to achieve success, now see the development of hybrids within their companies as a necessary first step to successful management of IT and integration with their business. Two distinct approaches to developing hybrids have become evident. The first is the approach taken by some individual companies to develop 'home grown' hybrids. These companies select key personnel and provide them with an accelerated career path through their organization. The hybrid candidates are placed for short periods of time in all the main business and technology divisions of the company. Given that these candidates will be exposed to a diversity of experience, and given access to considerable opportunities, it is likely that many of them will become good-quality senior managers in the longer term – not necessarily hybrids in the original sense of the term.

The second approach has been the growth of new hybrid courses at business schools and the endorsement, by the British Computer Society, of initiatives which include a focus on the training of hybrids. Given the time constraints of most of these courses, they cannot include sufficient opportunities to gain extensive practical experience. As a result, one vital component inherent in Earl's definition of hybrid managers – the need to have solid business experience and knowledge of how a particular firm operates both overtly and covertly – is missing. A well-planned course will provide many potential managers with exposure to new ideas, but so far it has not proved to be a solution to the communication and cultural gap existing in many companies.

While it is too early to establish whether existing managers can be converted successfully into effective hybrids, experience has shown that good managers are not made simply by moving people around organizations. Hybrids refer to good-quality key personnel who have broad management skills and who will facilitate effective communication across divisions. Those organizations that are attempting to 'grow' hybrids through having a policy of moving people through their organization have yet to be seen to succeed, because the relevant hybrid knowledge will only be acquired over time.

Hybrid managers are not themselves, however, the whole answer to the question of IT responsibility within organizations. Returning to the original work by Earl and Skyrme, a fact that is often omitted from the current arena of discussion is that hybrid managers cannot effectively work in isolation. Hybrids will only be effective if they are able to work with a number of other key managers. Earl defines three additional roles in particular: the visionary, the leader with the idea of what IT might do for the business; the impresario, who is usually the IS director with authority to allocate the necessary resources; and the technical expert, who can design and develop the technology.

The creation of this type of structure and level of communication is difficult in any organization. The idea that most companies may have to wait until the new hybrids and their colleagues have been trained makes this solution impractical for most companies in the short term. They certainly may form part of the answer longer term, but principally what this identification has forcefully defined is the need for wider concepts of learning to be introduced and adopted within companies. The requirement for hybrid managers has effectively highlighted the need to focus on the definition of individual job roles that can add value to organizations. When a company starts to redefine job roles the traditional organizational structure itself is put under pressure to change. New definitions for authority, responsibility, and the introduction of mechanisms to ensure accountability are an integral part of this process.

Federal structures

A few companies have recognized the pressures that have grown, partly as a result of IT, on their traditional organizational structures. They are making far-reaching corporate changes to reflect different job roles and processes: they focus on improving information flow and wider communication. Some helpful research defining the structure of an information handling organization is defined in Hodgkinson (1991) and the Butler Cox Foundation report *Managing the Devolution of Systems Responsibilities* (1991). The latter report argues for a strongly directed realignment of IT responsibilities to reflect the devolved nature of most business decision making. It suggests that managers change the structure of their organizations from bureaucratic hierarchies to federal organizations. Centralization and devolution of IT decision making can then coexist to the benefit of the whole business.

Undoubtedly, this makes sound sense in theory, but, as many companies have already found to their detriment, there is a danger in changing to a devolved structure simply because it is fashionable. The problem, as Christopher Lorenz has summarized in the *Financial Times*, is that following a trend has 'all the attendant risks of half-baked decisions, inadequate execution, frustrated expectations and ignominious climb-downs – a vicious cycle from which some companies are already beginning to suffer'. The laudable objectives of cutting back on corporate bureaucracy and costs are frequently pursued without the necessary planning, control and support structures needed to be effective. As a result, the way in which many companies have attempted to introduce organizational changes has increased rather than decreased their corporate costs and not brought about the required business gains. What tends to happen in practice is that decisions affecting devolution are made in a vacuum, without sufficient planning or understanding of the complex organizational implications. Great disruption to the business then results, when attempting to change from a centralized to a devolved control structure in one traumatic switchover.

Introducing organizational change will always present a whole range of management problems. The main one is the resistance that can be encountered from a company's employees. This is particularly severe when those managers at the centre of a company are threatened with the loss of authority and responsibility as control passes to the divisions or business units. To facilitate a change in the organizational structure any redefinition of job roles needs to be accompanied by a broad programme of education linked to good corporate communication aimed at minimizing company disruption. Clear guidelines need to be set in place to address exactly what central control is to be enforced and what local control is to be allowed. Forward planning needs to be undertaken to establish the links between them so that communication is maintained and the move to a federal structure delivers the company advantages sought. In the final analysis the main reason for establishing a federal structure for IT investments must be to enhance the effectiveness of the organization through its ability to handle and use information. Introducing organizational changes in order to obtain cost reductions has, for too many, proved to be a false objective.

A federal structure will only provide a better management solution for IT: if the correct balance is struck between the degree of central control and the degree of devolved systems' responsibilities; if decisions are made to ensure that key areas are not left undefined; if reviews are regularly undertaken and adjustments are made where necessary. The critical issues of authority, responsibility and accountability still need to be defined and planned within the new organizational structure. Realisti-

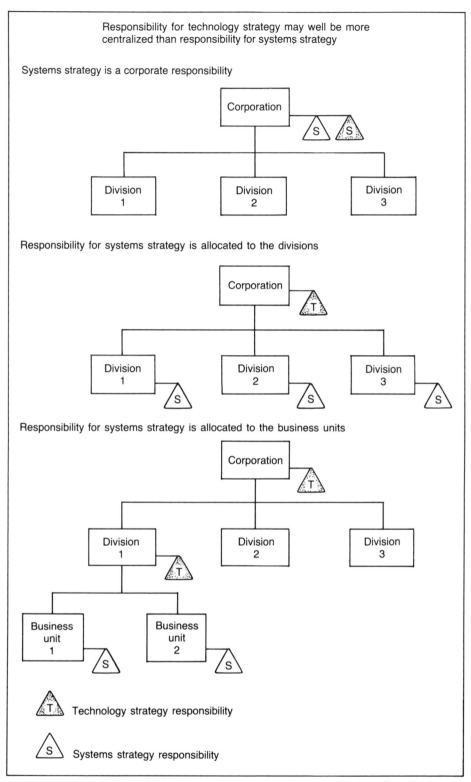

Figure 12.7 The federal model for technology strategy organization (adapted from Butler Cox Foundation, 1991).

cally, some systems such as infrastructure support need to be managed centrally, while others can be devolved effectively to the business units, in ways which enhance business alignment, allow user flexibility and enable more effective IT management. As a result, it becomes possible to match more closely the sometimes very different needs of individual business units in the same company, without introducing total isolation and potential chaos. In the Butler Cox model their suggested mechanism for addressing the management of the balance between central control and local autonomy is the establishment of a central coordinating committee reporting to the board. This committee has responsibility for service definition, service supply, for agreeing and mandating group-wide IT policies and for resolving conflicts of priority between corporate and business unit strategies.

Figure 12.7 illustrates how a federal model would work. It shows how the control of IT, in a multi-national company with different business units, would be split. Many of the principles outlined in the hybrid manager concept and the federal organizational structure illustrate ways of achieving a new balance of responsibilities. They are not, however, an instant solution for every company as they do not address all the practical problems. For too long now many organizations have oversimplified the IT responsibility issue – they have swung from one extreme, that of total centralization which signifies cost control, to the other extreme, that of devolved anarchy which signifies profligacy.

Information

It is suggested here that one way of assessing what could realistically work for any individual company is to make information itself the main subject. This then provides further scope for some additional new thinking about the way to handle IT and its impact on the issues of role, responsibility and communication. The Kobler Unit recognizes that all businesses are fundamentally about information, in some guise. Therefore, to understand a company and its problems it is necessary to return to the essential elements of information and information flow. Based on an understanding of the business from this perspective it becomes possible to define how IT can be introduced to achieve solid benefits. For most companies, as IT is neither the main product nor the topic to which company managers wish to be side-tracked to address unnecessarily, this might seem to offer an attractive approach. However, many companies are still unnecessarily technically focused (Strassmann, 1990). As a result, they fail to address the whole function of IT management from the information perspective; there is a need to concentrate more on the 'I' for information rather than on the 'T' for technology.

When information is the main focus there are three issues to be addressed and clarified:

- the content of the information that is required, i.e. the information that will add value
- the form in which the information is presented
- the procedures for accessing information, including security standards.

Taking this approach presents a new way to assess the value of existing information and to gauge the suitability of the processes that have evolved to handle it. For many companies this raises the question of who should be responsible for undertaking this task: it is not a one-off exercise that can be executed in a short timescale. It has to be part of a process that is integral to the very core of the business and will include the necessity of planning for the management and coordination of information over time. The answer is to take a radical step and create new roles in companies to ensure that information is treated as the important resource it is so often argued to be. The role definitions need to break away from the traditional boundary areas of finance and marketing to focus on maximizing the reliability, accessibility, security and relevance of information for use throughout the company. Emphasis needs to be put on what information is currently available, what information is exploitable from elsewhere in the organization, and what can be obtained additionally that is of beneficial use. In summary, for many companies this may require a cultural change in attitude towards the way they handle their information. It would no longer be handled on the basis of personal or functional ownership but on the basis of being a valuable corporate resource.

In the United States, the idea of having an information officer was first proposed by Synnott in his work *The Information Weapon* (1987). He envisaged that a single person fulfilling this new role could be effective if he or she was at a board level position. CIOs are now common appointments in USA. This is not what is proposed here. These information coordinators are not at board level but are a function, in large corporations, of several people effectively fulfilling this role. In some companies this might mean that these positions are outside the traditional divisional hierarchy, but the personnel would report to board level directors. The organizational chart would not necessarily map exactly the authority chart on a one-for-one basis. The line of authority would need to be clear and the terms of reference for the work would require new definition (Ciborra, 1991; Gupta, 1991).

In order for information coordinators to be effective across the whole organization, three further levels of responsibility need to be explicitly defined and understood on a company-wide basis. These are:

- Who owns the information?
- Who has responsibility for updating the information regularly?
- Who has access to the information?

This approach does not imply that all information should be accessible to everyone but rather it shows the responsibility levels for information that need to be defined if information and IT are to be used effectively.

The information coordinators are not the owners of the information. The owners of the information need to be defined and need to work closely with the information coordinators to ensure that business people can extract what is critical as well as ensure that salient information is available in a form required. Other individuals need to be appointed to be responsible for updating and verifying this information on a regular basis. Further access (viewing only) for other individuals in the organization needs to be planned. Links can then be made to allow other configurations of information if necessary, without endangering the integrity of the original information. The information coordinators will facilitate the necessary hierarchy of security coding to assist with this process.

In total the information coordinators will be aiming to improve communications across and between functions; to assess the business from the information angle; and to identify new opportunities for improving information use.

A change of management emphasis

In an earlier section, the drawbacks of leaving board level responsibility for IT as only vaguely defined were outlined. Generally this approach is found to lead to erratic and inconsistent IT management which does not ensure alignment to business needs. Collective board level direction is crucial, however, when making fundamental changes to the structure of any company. Making the strategic choice to introduce information coordinators requires an entire change of management emphasis within most companies. This cannot be achieved without the involvement of the board, both to initiate and then to support new processes over the longer term. It requires that companies give a greater emphasis to the general strategic importance of information as a means to gaining business advantages, rather than automatically meaning tightening central control. This change of emphasis is increasingly found to be necessary for every company, regardless of size or sector (Gupta, 1991). The process by which it is achieved will vary according to company type and complexity of structure.

The first requirement for the majority of companies, particularly those with a heavy dependency on IT, is for the position of the IT director to be at board level. This has been shown by Coulson-Thomas (1991a,b) to be critically important for companies aiming to integrate their IT with their business. It facilitates communication within the organization and provides a mechanism, at the right level, for accessing knowledge of the potential of IT. This will also mean that the IT director becomes an integral part of the investment decision-making process although not automatically part of all business decision making. Only in this way can the effective coordination of information, and subsequently the management of IT, begin to become a full-time process.

Secondly, clear lines of authority and responsibility will need to be defined, ensuring that information coordinators report to specific board directors. This reporting link requires early definition. It is unlikely that the information coordinators will report to the IT director as they are essentially facilitators for the user community and are sometimes working under the supervision of several functional directors.

Taking an information led approach to the management of IT means that a much wider range of non-technical issues will be part of the realm of decision making. As a result, other responsibilities will need to be defined. These have been outlined in detail in the publication *Controlling IT Investment* (Hochstrasser and Griffiths, 1991). They are:

- evaluation issues
- cost issues
- organizational issues
- policy issues
- people issues
- control issues.

Full technical guideline plans will need to be enforced for:

- technical issues
- systems issues
- implementation issues.

If board level decision making focuses on these issues then, in effect, management will be dealing with the very core of their business: IT will then realistically start to become integrated with the business.

Management think tank

Changing the emphasis in management from technology to information might seem a neat theoretical answer to the current problems of managing IT. It does, nevertheless, provide a more relevant way of taking the topic of IT to the board. It overcomes the problems of limited technical knowledge which have handicapped many board members and caused them defensively to marginalize their IT function.

Ensuring the management of IT on a continuous basis does however require some further radical approaches (Ciborra, 1991; Willcocks, 1991). In some organizations it may be appropriate to introduce a small 'think tank' which reports directly to the board. The composition of this think tank (not a committee) determines the value the organization extracts from it. Each significant business and support unit, including IT, should be represented. The think tank's role is to feed in ideas, as well as respond to and help refine ideas, that might originate in other sections.

The way the think tank operates is that there would be a limit of one year at a time for each participant. In fact, it is also recommended that internal promotion beyond a certain seniority level is dependent on a person having spent at least one period with the think tank. The existence of this think tank would allow:

- the opportunity for serious study of alternative scenarios for company (and divisional) development by individuals highly qualified and highly motivated but temporarily without operational responsibilities;
- the opportunity for those who may eventually help lead the company to get a strategic perspective of the business and a better understanding of the constraints and opportunities provided by information technology and other support activities;
- the opportunity to view how competitors are developing and to search for new opportunities, possibly outside the current company activities;
- the opportunity to better monitor and, if necessary, draw attention to potential conflicts arising from bottom-up initiatives and to apply planning standards across the whole company;
- the opportunity to study more objectively and quantitatively board suggestions for development diversification or divestment.

As with any group or committee, there is a danger that it may become ineffective and irrelevant unless there is strong, effective management. The aim of the think tank is to provide an underlying and reliable core of strategic thinking to the company. As Porter (1987) has observed: 'Criticism of strategic planning was well deserved. Strategic planning in most companies has not contributed to strategic thinking. The answer, however, is not to abandon planning. The need for strategic thinking has never been greater . . . few have transferred strategic planning into the vital management discipline it needs to be.' The role of this type of think tank is to contribute to the corporate thinking not to become 'just another planning group'. Its value is directly linked to the calibre of its personnel and the degree of direction and management it receives from the board. At the end of a secondment the members of the think tank return to their original business areas. They take back with them a broader understanding of the strategic issues involved relating to their company, a greater understanding of the work of other divisions, an important strategic overview and the experience of interacting with the board at the centre.

Currently in most organizations decisions are based on incomplete information. This can often be attributed to the fact that no single division or individual has the time or resources to collect and structure information in ways relevant to the company. The introduction of a think tank enables this gap to be filled and provides a mechanism for a continuous cycle of thinking and learning to develop on a company-wide basis. As with other initiatives, its contribution will be totally dependent on the calibre of the management which directs and supports it.

Conclusions

The expectation that a single function can be responsible for IT and all its implications has proved to be false. This chapter has shown the need to develop corporate responsibility for IT and to change existing company command structures to reflect this. It is found that the existing misalignment of authority, responsibility and accountability within many organizations has created communication gaps which are constraining overall company effectiveness. A number of new approaches have been suggested. First, devolving IT responsibility to business units or establishing federal structures can facilitate communication, provided this is accompanied by appropriate corporate-wide standards. Secondly, hybrid managers may contribute to a longer term programme of management education but do not provide an immediate solution to the issue of IT responsibility. A more practical approach to handling IT responsibility is for management concern to move away from a focus on the technology to a focus on the importance of information as a valuable resource. This means introducing new job roles for the coordination and use of this resource. Link to this the establishment at board level of a special think tank and it becomes possible for relevant, broader corporate thinking and learning to occur.

Addressing the problem of IT responsibility presents the management challenge of the 1990s. A process of active corporate participation is required. IT responsibility as the grey area of management will only gain real definition if the core issue of authority is addressed and linked to accountability. Those companies that are focusing on this issue are laying the foundations for future competitive successes; those that are not may soon cease to matter.

References

Atkins, M. H. and Galliers, R. D. (1992) *Human Resource Development for IS Executives.* Warwick Business School Research Papers, No. 36, January.

Butler Cox Foundation (1991) *Managing the Devolution of Systems Responsibilities*, Butler Cox, London.

Ciborra, C. U. (1991) From thinking to tinkering: the grassroots of strategic information systems, in *Proceedings of the International Conference on Information Systems*, New York.

Coulson-Thomas, C. (1991a) Directors and IT and IT directors. *European Journal of Information Systems*, **1**, 45–53.

Coulson-Thomas, C. (1991b) IT Directors and IT strategy. *Journal of Information Technology*, **6** (3/4), 193–203.

Earl, M. J. and Skyrme, D. J. (1990) *Hybrid Managers: What Do We Know About Them?* RDP90/6, Templeton College, Oxford.

Earl, M. J. (1989) *Management Strategies for Information Technology*, Prentice-Hall, London.

Gupta, Y. P. (1991) The chief executive officer and the chief information officer – the strategic partnership. *Journal of Information Technology*, **6** (3/4), 126–39.

Hochstrasser, B. and Griffiths, C. (1990) *Regaining Control of IT Investments*, Kobler Unit, Imperial College, London.

Hochstrasser, B. and Griffiths, C. (1991) *Controlling IT Investment: Strategy and Management*, Chapman & Hall, London.

Hodgkinson, S. (1991) *The Role of the Corporate Information Technology function in the Large Multi-Business Company*. Oxford Institute of Information Management Research and Discussion papers, RDP91/2, Templeton College, Oxford.

Kaplan, R. S. and Norton, D. P. (1992) The balanced scorecard – measures that drive performance. *Harvard Business Review*, January–February, 71–9.

Lincoln, T. (1990) *Managing Information Systems for Profit*, Wiley, Chichester.

Lorenz, C. (1991) Sharing power around the world. *Financial Times*, 29 November.

NCC/Impact Programme (1991) *Executive Briefings: CE Perspectives on IT Performance?*, NCC, London.

Porter, M. (1980) *Competitive Strategy*, Free Press, New York.

Porter, M. (1987) The state of strategic thinking. *The Economist*, 23 May.

Rockart, J. F. (1988) The line takes the leadership – IS management in a wired society. *Sloan Management Review*, Summer, 57–64.

Scott-Morton, M. S. (1991) *The Corporation of the 1990s: Information Technology an Organisational Transformation*, Oxford University Press, Oxford.

Sequent (1991) *The Great Divide*, Benchmark Research, London.

Strassmann, P. A. (1985) *Information Payoff*, Macmillan, New York.

Strassmann, P. A. (1990) *The Business Value of Computers*, The Information Economics Press, New Canaan.

Synnott, William R. (1987) *The Information Weapon*, Wiley, Canada.

Willcocks, L. (1991) Human resource and organisational issues. *Journal of Information Technology*, **6** (3/4), 121–7.

13

Evaluation of information systems investments: towards multiple perspectives

Veronica Symons

Introduction

Computer-based information systems are difficult to evaluate. Information technology (IT) is pervasive in the manufacturing and service sectors: most organizations depend on computers for their routine data-processing operations, and systems designed to give a 'competitive edge' are increasingly common. But successful utilization is by no means automatic. Appraisal of costs and benefits is necessary if value for money is to be obtained from existing information systems and plans made for future applications. Improvements in business performance due to information systems can be extremely difficult to measure, however. Benefits are often qualitative and uncertain, costs diffuse. That this is a hot topic is demonstrated by the fact that there is now software on the market to help in assessment of computing facilities. Yet as other contributors to this book demonstrate, there is no commonly accepted framework or methodology for information systems (IS) evaluation.

According to the Price Waterhouse *Information Technology Review*, 1988/89, a survey of 750 UK computer-using firms showed the amount spent on information

Information Management: The evaluation of information systems investments.
Edited by Leslie Willcocks.
Published in 1994 by Chapman & Hall. ISBN 0 412 41540 2.

technology averaging just under 2% of turnover (around £3 million per company in 1989), but Peat Marwick McLintock found that 44% of top UK companies and public sector organizations made no attempt to quantify the benefits of IT invest-ment (*Financial Times*, 8 June 1989). These figures support the trends discussed in earlier chapters. IT capital spend and penetration is greatest in the financial services sector (Yap and Walsham, 1986), but these companies also find it difficult to measure the contribution made by IT to their business performance. Asked how IT investment was justified, one building society manager was quoted as saying: 'In larger projects, we mostly go by gut feel. If the project is small, we try for a return-on-investment analysis' (*Financial Times*, 13 June 1989). Another summed up the overall attitude with: 'If it is strategic, we just do it. If it is efficiency related, we have to do a cost justification' (*Financial Times*, 13 June 1989). It seems to be the case that the greater the expense and strategic importance of an information system, the less likely it is to be evaluated using a formal methodology. This apparent paradox re-flects the fact that IS evaluation is problematic both conceptually and operationally. The next section sets out some of the issues in the evaluation of information systems.

Issues in information systems evaluation

Certain operational difficulties arise in the evaluation of information systems. Willcocks and Lester have shown in Chapter 3, that the traditional investment appraisal methods, which worked reasonably well when IT was used mainly to reduce costs, are no longer adequate, but remain the ones most commonly used. Western financial management techniques lay heavy emphasis on cost audit and return on investment, the result of which is to discourage innovation by favouring a short payback period. In 1987 Pergamon Infotech reported that managers took a myopic view of investment returns, most refusing to look more than two years ahead, and were more concerned with getting their existing computer systems under cost and quality control than with investing in new and strategic uses of technology. (*The Guardian*, 25 June 1987). The situation is little different today. Developments in evaluation methods have not kept pace with shifts in the use of information systems which have over time widened the scope of their effects.

Evaluation is generally aimed at the identification and quantification of costs and benefits. But the current use of IS in support of business strategy has consequences which are both complex and difficult to measure. The implications of a new system often extend outside the context for which it was initially introduced (Hopwood, 1983). Increasingly, as discussed elsewhere in this book, it is the case that the benefits of IT are strategic or qualitative – improved level of customer service for instance, or 'high-tech' company image. Costs spread over a long timescale for project development are often difficult to determine. Some, such as expenses for training and recruitment of skilled staff, are reasonably clear but it is less obvious how to allocate them fairly. There may also be insidious effects such as a decline in job satisfaction. Quantification of benefits is thus uncertain and subjective, and quantification of costs is subject to the detail of accounting procedures.

Clearly the concept of IS evaluation requires extension. The operational difficulties mentioned above necessitate consideration of two separate but related areas: the linkage of IS strategy to business goals; and the contribution of IS to organizational effectiveness. Since the implementation process is one of the best predictors of operational success or failure, the second area can be conceptualized in terms of implementation issues. The first area, strategy, requires formulation in terms of constraints and opportunities, not just costs and benefits. Evaluation of IS can thus be thought of as comprising the two strands of strategic value and implementation issues.

This leads on to the next point, which is problematic at the conceptual as well as the operational level. What appears as a benefit or opportunity in one part of the organization may be viewed very differently in another. For instance, increased access to information at headquarters may be seen by divisional managers as an erosion of their power base. Individuals, groups and functions may well have divergent (sometimes conflicting) perspectives on the same IS, according to their views and their role within the organization. A failure to understand alternative viewpoints can lead to unanticipated resistance and, hence, operational problems. In conceptual terms, evaluation is never value-free. It is carried out by certain people at a particular time, using criteria based on specific assumptions. Evaluation is therefore properly regarded as the embodiment not of a formal, objective procedure (in the sense of established method), but of a social process involving multiple perspectives. 'Process' is here used to denote a series of actions moving forward in time.

A further point to notice is that evaluation plays a crucial role at many stages of IS development. Before introduction, the ability to evaluate technological innovations satisfactorily is an important factor in the decision to purchase. Such prior justifications commonly take the form of a feasibility study. Evaluation during implementation performs an important learning and control function; it is usually done informally. Post-implementation evaluation, while theoretically valuable, is rarely carried out (Blackler and Brown, 1988). The reason for this is the feeling that a working system is sufficient reward in itself, and that the work involved in post-audit is not really 'productive', coupled with the risk that evaluation might show a non-cost-effective result. Although the basis of evaluation is likely to be different in each phase of IS development, in practice they are not necessarily distinct. As IS development progresses, successive stages of evaluation gradually merge to form a continuous process. Specific evaluative acts and criteria can be 'snapshot' at particular points in time, but cannot be understood independently of the whole process.

Evaluation of information systems is crucially involved in the process of organizational change accompanying introduction of a new system. From his extensive work on continuity and change in ICI, Pettigrew argues that analysis of organizational change should properly explore the relationship and interplay between the content of change, the context of change, and the process of managing change. 'Formulating the content of a strategic change crucially entails managing its context and process' (Pettigrew, 1985). Broadly speaking, the 'what' of change is encapsulated under the label content, much of the 'why' of change is derived from investigation of inner and outer context, and the 'how' of change can be understood from an analysis of process.

Information systems themselves are complex social objects inseparable from the organizational context within which they are situated and the infrastructure supporting them, and are products of history and human agency. Work on IS therefore necessitates an interactionist approach, taking the effects of information technology to be a product of neither the technical nor the social aspects alone, but of their interaction. Evaluation of information systems is in many respects no different from evaluation of any other social organization or change programme, although accompanied by specific types of impact and regarded as more important in today's so-called 'information society'.

The final conceptual issue relates again to the nature of the evaluation process. Evaluation may appear formal or informal, rational or irrational, according to the perspectives of the participants. For example, a formal business case prepared by a junior manager might be used as political rhetoric by the board member who commissioned it. The opinions and judgements by which employees make sense of and understand their work situations in respect of IS are themselves informal assessments. And these have a conditioning role in the evolution of the evaluation process. Politics are generally ignored by researchers, but often play a key part in IS development. Where there are conflicts in hidden goals, IS evaluation becomes an arena for organizational politics.

Although financial and technical evaluation procedures are often dysfunctional, the 'formal–rational' exemplar of which they are instances is commonly regarded as the only acceptable approach to IS evaluation. Currie's research on investment appraisal for IS in manufacturing found engineering management critical of formal budgetary control systems which they regarded as essentially spurious, a ritualistic use of quasi-accounting techniques. But their preferred approach, which was more qualitative and holistic, lacked the historical legitimacy of the formal cost–benefit procedures and was unacceptable to top management (Currie, 1989). Such anecdotes suggest that justifying information systems may be more of an art than a science. Research on evaluation of information systems therefore requires the study not only of formal procedures but of their function and nature as influenced by informal evaluations.

Evaluation of information systems is poorly developed, not because it lacks importance or relevance but because it is sensitive as well as difficult. Progress in this area, we argue, requires that IS be conceptualized as **embedded in organizations** and evaluation as itself a **social process**. The next section illustrates this view by means of a case study of IS development in a manufacturing organization, focusing in particular on the distinct stages of evaluation running through the process. The research methodology used to carry out the study is detailed in Symons (1990). We commence with a narrative description of the main events of the case.

IS development in the Processing Company

The Processing Company was a wholly-owned subsidiary of a large international manufacturing organization. In the early 1980s it had 450 employees and a sales turnover of £25 million. Its original area of business was the manufacture of a product for which the market has shrunk gradually since the 1970s with the entry of newer, technically superior products manufactured by multi-national firms (including the holding company). Increasing competition therefore forced the Processing Company to switch from making to buying in base material, and to diversify into the expanding market for derivative, 'converted', products. By 1986 these accounted for 50% of total sales.

Traditionally the Processing Company had had a small range of products with few customers and a limited number of large orders. Lead times were long and no stocks were held without an order. The business was controlled by means of manual card systems, together with a documentation system running on two IBM PC/XTs, and a Data General CS200 minicomputer and software for stocks of manufactured base material. In addition, an accounts and statistics package was run as a bureau system on the IBM mainframe at divisional headquarters. These programs had been developed over the years by the computer services manager.

The situation in the 1980s was radically different: by 1989 there were some 2000 converted products, of which approximately half were manufactured for stock and half to customer-specified orders. The number of customers increased and orders became smaller and more numerous, with shorter lead times. As early as 1982 it had become clear that the existing systems for converted products were no longer adequate: unacceptably large book/physical stock differences showed that the business was not in effective control of finished product stocks and work-in-progress in this area. The same applied to stocks of packaging materials, and there was no effective system of work measurement. Management determined that computer-based techniques were needed to increase their control over the business, and began to look within the holding company for a suitable system. When the search proved unsuccessful they decided to employ outside consultants, and in mid-1984 the management consultancy branch of their auditors was brought in.

The consultants drew up an invitation to tender (ITT) in conjunction with the project leader seconded from business control. It was proposed to introduce systems in the areas of sales order processing, production planning, shop-floor production control, finished goods stock control, packaging stock control, purchasing, and production statistics. The supplier was to 'provide reliable hardware and software at reasonable cost which could clearly satisfy the requirements of the company; demonstrate experience of successfully implementing systems similar to those required; and provide excellent customer support in maintaining both equipment and software'.

In December 1984 the ITT was sent to five systems houses including, at the insistence of the Processing Company, IBM. This was because IBM and DEC were the preferred suppliers of the holding company, so that to get agreement from the divisional board for the required level of funding (initially around £250 000) the Processing Company would have either to choose IBM equipment or to demonstrate a good reason for not doing so. After receiving the ITT and visiting the Processing Company, IBM in fact concluded that their own package software was not appropriate to the company's requirements; they were then urged to nominate an IBM systems house, and the ITT was passed on to this firm.

In January 1985 four proposals were received; they were evaluated according to equipment, applications programs, and costs, together with the supplier's experience and support available. One of the proposals was rejected on the grounds of excessively high cost, and one because it did not demonstrate a sufficiently deep understanding of the requirements detailed in the ITT. The remaining two were a proposal from Systems House for ProSys software and Data General hardware, and a slightly cheaper proposal for a package which would require significant bespoke development, to run on a relatively small IBM configuration with limited expansion capability. The former was felt to be a less risky option, having a standard package already developed and a wider user base. The consultants thus recommended the Systems House proposal, subject to software modifications which were to be agreed.

By March 1985 the contract was awaiting clearance for funding. When the divisional board realized that the chosen system did not use IBM hardware they expressed concern. The Processing Company was directed to demonstrate the feasibility of data transmission between Data General and the IBM mainframe at divisional headquarters, and this was done satisfactorily. In addition, they were required to send the ITT to a different IBM systems house which had implemented a similar package at another of the subsidiary companies. The project leader and one of the consultants then compared ProSys with the alternative package, point by point against the ITT; the ProSys software was again felt to be superior. Two divisional managers acted as referees, and at a meeting in August 1985 it was reluctantly agreed that the contract be awarded to Systems House.

The contract was signed in September 1985, and installation of the Data General hardware and transfer of existing systems was completed two months later. Work had already started on drawing up specification documents for modifications to the standard ProSys modules. The departments involved were identified, and a 'key user' was appointed in each to represent the users in discussions on modifications, train users, and assist with implementation. The sales order-processing module was to be implemented first, followed by purchasing and manufacturing, with the aim of completing the project by the end of 1986. The specification work for sales order processing and purchasing continued over several months, as it was quickly realized that many more modifications were required than had originally been envisaged. Software began to come in from Systems House in May 1986, and over the summer the project team was simultaneously testing software, setting up the database and revising procedures. They found this period 'horrendous'. The replacement of the old 4-digit part numbering system with a precise 13-digit one was a major change, attempts to explain the necessity of which met with enormous resistance.

Pressure from management to implement the system was building up, and in October 1986 after a stock check the sales order-processing department started dual running. This proved extremely difficult: the workload involved in using old and new procedures in parallel was enormous, and sales clerks were introducing errors because they did not understand how to use the part number codes. In addition, the project team had not finished testing the software and was not satisfied that the system was robust enough. Management decided, however, that cutover could not be delayed any longer; the switch was made in December 1986 for home orders, and in January 1987 for exports. These traumatic months saw 'total chaos' in order processing and despatch: by Christmas hundreds of orders were late, and a lot of business and several customers were lost.

Repetitive training in the importance of the system and continual stock takes to improve the accuracy of the records gradually increased staff familiarity and confidence, until by April 1987 the error rate was down to a manageable level and use of the system had settled into a routine. Not without lingering negative feelings on the part of users, however, and a sandwich student was employed full-time to amend the database whenever a stockout occurred. At this stage work was resumed on specification documents for the manufacturing modules, and the project team and senior management attended a three-day workshop run by Systems House personnel, on the whole area of materials requirements planning (MRP). It was then that they began to understand the system as not simply a piece of software, but 'a whole new philosophy of working'.

The implementation schedule had been extended by 12 months and a steering committee appointed, but management was now concerned that the company did not have the experience, skills and resources required to undertake all the system implementation and organization tasks even within the revised timescale. The consultants were brought in again to address these issues. In October 1987 they produced a review of ProSys implementation and operation, followed in early 1988 by three more detailed reports suggesting a revised organizational structure, implementation plan, and education and training programme.

Soon after this it was announced that the Processing Company was to be merged with another subsidiary recently established, to form ProcessCo, a new business carrying the name of the holding company. ProcessCo, formally set up in April 1988 in order to capitalize on 'major opportunities in rapidly expanding global markets', was to launch a new series of products and would constitute a key site within the division. The old managing director retired in June 1988, and the board members of the Processing Company were replaced by a business director and a four-strong business management team, all much more senior. The new management structure that was superimposed on the Processing Company comprised seven times as many senior managers. The sudden infusion of investment was accompanied by a complete re-evaluation of the information systems required by the new business, for finance as well as manufacturing (including the new production facilities).

Stages of evaluation

The case history of IS development in the Processing Company was a complex one characterized by multiple informal assessments, but punctuated by six stages of 'formal' evaluation. These were, in chronological order:

1. Invitation to tender
2. Selection of computer systems
3. Evaluation of Data General versus IBM
4. Specification of software modifications
5. Organizational review
6. Re-evaluation of information systems for ProcessCo.

We discuss these in turn, drawing out the assumptions underlying each stage of evaluation.

Invitation to tender

The main emphasis in drawing up the ITT lay on the functionality of the system. 'Requirements' were defined in terms of the procedures and functions over which management wished to tighten control. The ITT was drawn up not by employees of the Processing Company but by the consultants, and no attempt was made to understand how staff regarded their 'lines of work'. The board members, having little understanding of the potential of IT and being unclear as to what they wished to achieve, stated relatively low-level objectives and originally focused only on order processing. The consultants convinced them that they should computerize the production side also.

The objective was to automate planning and work-in-progress, when probably more important was information on factors such as product costings which would have enabled a higher level debate about the aims of the business. The formal ITT thus focused almost exclusively on the functionality of procedures. The perspective on information systems implicit in the approach was that of a relatively well-defined machine, best described by objectives, procedures and administrative arrangements over which there was assumed to be consensus. Yet this was not the case in the Processing Company, as was evidenced by strong differences of opinion and a degree of antagonism between the production and marketing departments.

Another objective, that of eliminating the 'informal procedures' by which the old manual systems were frequently overridden, displayed a similarly excessive regard for formal job specification at the expense of the processes by means of which tasks are actually carried out. The increased regulation turned out to be anti-functional, because when the system was implemented its multitudinous small problems and inflexibilities actually necessitated unofficial manual fixes. At the root of this issue lay a conflict of perspective between management and workers over the benefits of computerization. For example, while management viewed the information system as a tool by which to increase their overall control of the business, to the warehouse-staff it appeared as an institution which removed much of their discretion over their work. They no longer had responsibility for home transport arrangements and for making optimal use of the scarce warehousing space, but because they could see where improvements in these would save money for the company they found ways of working around the system. In so doing the warehouse staff were introducing new varieties of precisely the informal procedures the computer system was supposedly designed to prevent. They were reproved by management for their 'bad attitude', and yet it was their commitment to the company as a major employer in their local community which led to their frustration with what they regarded as unnecessarily wasteful rules and procedures.

In summary, then, this first stage of evaluation was viewed largely as an issue of functional specification. The objective of the computer project was not to change business operations in order to bring about improved performance, but simply to automate previous manual procedures. The next stage of evaluation, the selection of computer systems, was similarly technically oriented.

Selection of computer systems

Selection of computer systems in the Processing Company concentrated on technical aspects of the systems and the credentials of suppliers, but gave little consideration to the implementation process. Consultants and managers neglected the definition of user procedures and instruction of personnel affected by ProSys: these factors, according to the later organizational review, 'undoubtedly contributed to the problems experienced'. Some of the older clerical staff, not used to computers, were so lacking in confidence that they continued to maintain their manual records after implementation. The part number and recording system introduced a degree of complexity on the shop floor that the operators had not been used to hitherto, and required much greater discipline and accuracy. Thus, during the 'traumatic' first few months after implementation, the users became highly frustrated because inaccuracies in the records prevented them from carrying out their jobs properly. There was a great deal of scepticism about the benefits of the system, which they viewed rather as an inconvenience and hindrance.

With hindsight it was clear to the board that the implementation was 'under-managed, under-financed, and under-resourced'. In the words of the chief accountant:

> I'm still uncertain whether it was the quality of staff and/or the training that was the problem, but we had a lot of difficulties. . . . It was a big change because the environment here before its introduction was such that people would use their own initiative to move things forward in a random sort of way. With a computer you have to be highly disciplined, and that was a problem.

What was involved was a shift to tighter discipline and interdependence which amounted to an attitudinal and, indeed, cultural change among Processing Company employees. This applied equally to management and workers. The works manager commented: 'I don't think our Managing Director fully understood the concept and what it involved – as a result none of us really threw our weight behind it.'

The formal selection of computer systems was thus based on systems and vendor criteria, to the exclusion of the infrastructure supporting implementation. The essential infrastructural resources supporting an information system include not just physical aspects such as peripherals and a suitable working environment, which were present in the Processing Company, but experience, skills and commitment to organizational change, which were in rather shorter supply. In terms of managerial commitment, the board members were keen to have the system up and running but were not themselves experienced with computers and did not understand the technical and organizational problems involved. They viewed the project as just one among a number of initiatives going on in the company at the time, and did not appreciate the scale of resource it required.

In respect of computing skills and experience, the project leader had significant experience of computers but the team – comprising his deputy (a key user seconded in 1986 from business control), an ex-machine operator who had been injured in a works accident, a temporary employee from purchasing and two sandwich students – did not. There was a serious shortage of effort to undertake data collation: the Processing Company appointed whoever was available, rather than the users or staff with skills and experience. Not appreciating the extent of organizational change involved, senior management did not support the project team in its attempts to gain user participation, and the project leader was not sufficiently senior to enforce this. He was also somewhat lacking in communication and leadership skills.

It was this neglect of infrastructure, leading to under-resourcing and a lack of management commitment in implementing ProSys, which ultimately resulted in the project's failure. While this stage of formal evaluation excluded implementation issues, the next – the comparison of ProSys with a second IBM package – placed more importance on strategic factors.

Evaluation of data general versus IBM

The fact that this evaluation took place at all illustrates the difference between the Processing Company's systems-led approach and the more strategic perspective of the holding company. The divisional board embodied an aspect of organizational context which forced open the otherwise formal–rational evaluation procedure by which the hardware and software were selected. The preference of the holding company for IBM equipment determined the inclusion, among the list of suppliers invited to tender, of first IBM and then an IBM-recommended systems house. Not satisfied that IBM had been given a fair chance, the divisional board then insisted that Processing Company management compare the ProSys proposal with another IBM package. This evaluation was thus not a purely technical exercise, but a social process powerfully constrained by funding arrangements. The objective of the project, as far as Processing Company management was concerned, was to improve control and management information within the business. To the more senior divisional managers, however, data communications between companies within the division and elsewhere in the holding company represented a strategic issue.

This evaluation, then, again originated from a formal–rational perspective. That the choice of hardware was a strategic decision with respect to the division did not alter the outcome at this stage, but was a factor which later resurfaced. Meanwhile, the Processing Company embarked on the task of specifying modifications to the standard ProSys modules. This entailed formal evaluation of the functionality of the system.

Specification of software modifications

Although the Systems House proposal had detailed necessary changes to the standard programs and agreed to meet the functional requirements set out in the ITT at a fixed price, in the event many additional modifications were required and there was some haggling over cost. To make all the changes requested by users would have cost £30 000 over the original price; a compromise was eventually agreed, at a cost of £15 000.

During the last quarter of 1985 the sales order-processing specification went through several iterations (the first issue was published in January 1986) but the amendment schedule was not formally signed until June 1986. The specification documents were written by the Systems House consultant with input from the project team. They were sent to the user managers for comment, but with virtually no response. So, according to the project leader, 'it was really the project team approving and management nodding'.

The purchasing department had early on identified a need for computer assistance to provide better and more accessible data and to reduce clerical effort, and had produced documents setting out their requirements. Work on the purchasing specification document began in February 1986, and after 'a bit of a struggle' the first issue was brought out in April 1986. It was never signed off, however. In view of (a) the purchasing department's apparent difficulty in defining system requirements, and (b) the fact that a second version of the ProSys purchasing module was to be released within the next year, and would probably include as standard some of the required enhancements, it was decided to implement Release 1 of the ProSys purchasing module with minimal modifications. The three or four modifications which were regarded as absolutely essential were agreed in November 1986 and included in the software early in 1987. The purchasing department then commenced implementation of the system, which continued through 1987.

Work on the manufacturing specification, which had commenced in mid-1986, during implementation of the sales order-processing modules was put to one side until April 1987. At this stage the importance of user involvement was recognized and the review of infrastructure supporting ProSys implementation commissioned. Specification of modifications to the manufacturing software continued while the organizational evaluation was being carried out, this time with effective managerial contribution. By October 1987 the document had arrived at issue number 4, which was virtually the final statement, but was never completely signed off because the Processing Company was then completely restructured to become ProcessCo.

The consultants regarded it as very important that the specification study reports be agreed not only by the computer project team but also by the user departments who would eventually have to 'own' and run the system. But since the users were unused to computers and unwilling to change procedures, the outcome of their involvement was not the desired ownership but merely delay in software specification. Management's view that implementation of the system should not be a major change encouraged this unwillingness to change procedures in Processing Company employees. For example, the addendum to the ITT gave a long list of programs to be converted which was in the end dysfunctional: 'the modification spend on ProSys is now well over the original cost, and the sales order processing module has had so many mods we can't take advantage of Systems House upgrades'.

Apart from the long-term problems of so much bespoke modification, the excessive emphasis on functionality of the software was dysfunctional in terms of implementation itself. A pilot system based on a few home orders which ran through the summer of 1986 provides an illustration of this.

Orders were raised by Customer Services but not picked up in the warehouse, so the system was never fully tested. The project leader pointed out to management that the users were not relying on the system, but nothing was done about it. At cutover when the old systems were removed it was immediately discovered that the lot-number control of the system was incompatible with the method of product storage (one lot of material split between several pallets). A major modification to the software was required, which took several months of programming and cost £6000.

The lack of managerial and user commitment to the project thus resulted in a systems-led specification, so that evaluation was overly technical and excluded any consideration of the way staff actually carried out their tasks. The specification documents were supposedly to facilitate use of the new system without significant change in procedures; but effective user involvement was prohibited by a lack of interest and understanding, while the project team emphasized formal task specification at the expense of understanding users' 'lines of work'.

The deficiency of mutual understanding between system designers and system users eventually subverted the enormous cost and effort put into software modification. Finally, Processing Company management realized that they could not develop the procedures necessary to run the information system until they had addressed the organizational issues. They then commissioned the consultants to evaluate ProSys implementation and operation, together with the Processing Company's organizational structure, implementation plan, and education and training programme.

Organizational review

In the light of the dreadful period post-implementation of the sales order-processing module, the provisions for organizational change, implementation plans and training were seen to be inadequate. Processing Company management re-engaged the consultants to evaluate arrangements relating to the whole infrastructure in support of the proposed manufacturing, purchasing and stock systems: system preparation, implementation and operation; training; organization and recruitment; and business issues.

The consultants' investigation of ProSys implementation and operation concentrated on identification of ambiguities in managerial and operational responsibilities. The area of materials planning and control, split between the commercial and works departments, was stated in their report as being the main potential organizational weakness. It was noted that the computer project leader and his assistant reported to the commercial manager while actually working full-time on the computer project, and it was not clear to whom they were responsible. The organizational review recommended that a senior management steering committee be established; also a production project team comprising senior manufacturing managers, and work teams formed to undertake specific tasks. Other actions recommended included the identification of leaders with the necessary implementation skills; definition and communication of quantifiable project goals so that objectives were clear; organization of a formal education and training programme; and establishment of a user-run system with users responsible for the system data.

After two months of deliberation Processing Company management agreed the organizational changes proposed in the October 1987 review of ProSys implementation and operation, and the consultants went on to produce three more detailed reports. The board accepted these findings too but took no immediate action to implement the recommendations, one of which was the appointment of an operations manager. It was agreed that while the restarting of the implementation project was not dependent on this appointment, it should not go ahead without adequate senior management resource, and that, in particular, the chairman of the revised production project team would need to spend at least one day per week on it. Since the works manager – who, in the absence of the new operations manager, would fulfil this role – was unable to spare the time required, it was decided to postpone the start of the project until a new operations manager could be appointed.

The recommendations made in this formal organizational evaluation were concerned with helping to correct the weaknesses identified and reflect the change in focus of the computer project from sales order processing and finished goods control to manufacture and materials management. These latter systems were more difficult to implement because they involved multiple departments and a larger number of users. In addition, the recommendations were designed to help prevent the Processing Company from suffering the three main problems associated with manufacturing computer systems, which are lack of top management support, inadequate education and training, and inaccurate inventory and bill of materials reports (White et al., 1982).

What the formal evaluation was unable to address – although the consultant carrying out the reviews was well aware of it – was the lack of commitment on the part of Processing Company management to the radical and painful organizational change which was essential to improving business performance. He later described this as analogous to the difference in attitude between the chicken and the pig in the preparation of an English breakfast: 'the chicken was involved, but the pig was really committed!'

The consultants attempted to promote an awareness and understanding of the whole business process in the employees (whose perspective was rather limited), but were thwarted in their efforts by the lack of true managerial commitment to restructuring the organization. For example, the consultants were very strongly in favour of devolvement of database control so that users owned their own data and were responsible for its maintenance. They felt that this would result in a greater degree of familiarity with the system and a higher motivation to maintain data integrity. The project leader was indecisive on this point but in the end opted for centralization, feeling that there would otherwise be chaos because users were unwilling to accept the responsibility. Also, the consultants' recommendations on new organizational structure and reporting arrangements were not implemented. The computer project leader commented as follows in respect of this: 'The impression I get is that management are afraid to take on the personalities involved – fearing it would cause too much upset.'

Thus, although Processing Company management were by this time sufficiently cognisant of the importance of organizational infrastructure to commission the review (the cost of which was of the order of £20 000 in itself) and to accept its recommendations at least in theory, their continuing antipathy to organizational change prevented any further definitive outcome. Where previously the ProSys project had been systems-led, aimed at computerization of procedures, this stage of formal evaluation was directed at total control of IS implementation – definition of organizational structure, responsibilities and accountabilities, implementation plan, and education and training programme. These areas were assessed as major features of the organization in which the IS was to be embedded. And yet the evaluation was still subverted by managerial resistance to change.

Soon afterwards, however, the entire organization was subject to radical revision with the formation of ProcessCo, and the new management team embarked on an evaluation of strategy, and information systems in support of the new business.

Re-evaluation of information systems for ProcessCo

The Processing Company at the time of its takeover was described by one of the new business managers as being in 'a pretty fair state of chaos', and therefore it was decided not to proceed with ProSys until they had had a chance to review the situation. With the complete re-evaluation of IS required by ProcessCo the computerization project was in one sense back to square one. Now, however, management commitment, communication processes, user involvement and training were being prioritized, and continuation of the project was delayed until those resources were adequately in place. This relied on prior definition of the new business strategy, a process which took place over the course of the first year of ProcessCo's operation.

Having described the various stages of IS evaluation in the Processing Company/ ProcessCo, the next section analyses the process in terms of its underlying assumptions. The approach is shown to be overwhelmingly formal–rational.

The formal–rational perspective

The IS implementation project in the Processing Company was systems-led, based on a view of systems development as instrumental reasoning (Hirschheim and Klein, 1986). This perspective suggests that IS are all designed to contribute to particular ends, objectively articulated and shared. The role of management is to specify those ends, which are then translated into systems goals. The primary role of systems developers is to be expert in project management, technology, tools and methods of system design. Systems development is primarily technical, with little reliance on human intuition, judgement and politics; it is held to be a formal–rational process.

The assumptions associated with the instrumental reasoning view of IS development have consequences which are likely to prove dysfunctional, as we have seen in the case of the Processing Company. In reality, ends are not agreed: they are controversial and the subject of considerable disagreement and debate. Pre-specified ends benefit certain system stakeholders at the expense of others. As a result the development process meets with resistance.

This case study abounded with multiple perspectives. Yet all those involved with IS development in the Processing Company took a formal–rational approach to it, viewing the information system as a technical system separable from its organizational context, history and infrastructure. Top management, with little understanding and no experience of computers, expected that computerization would automatically benefit the performance of the business. Making no attempt to look at business processes, they effectively took the view that the purpose of the computer was to do their job for them. As the finance and planning manager later commented: 'Management seemed to expect that confidence and enthusiasm for the system would exude from the VDUs when they were turned on.'

Management's conception of ProSys as a technical system resulted in a lack of commitment to implementation which then led to the continuous maintenance of this conception. They initially paid lip service to the project and did not support the project team in its 'uphill struggle' for user involvement. The project leader's lack of experience and leadership skills combined with an under-resourced project team and severe technical problems to make his perspective on the system overwhelmingly formal–rational. As a result he failed to get user managers and key users on board, and there was no active involvement by line management. The project leader commented as follows on the early stages of software specification: 'All this time unbeknown to ourselves we were building up problems by not worrying about the lack of management commitment. At the time we thought we had enough problems with the system itself.' The formal–rational attitude proved disastrous when it came to implementation: for example, the key user in the Customer Services department did not understand the system well enough to be able to motivate her staff to use it.

In consequence of the project team's struggle with systems problems the management and organizational aspects of implementation were neglected, and the users also perceived ProSys as purely technical. Line management tended to view the system as a tool which the computer project leader would use on their behalf. They did not take on board the idea that each manager was responsible for accurate collection, recording and transmission of data, and proper implementation, running and maintenance of the new computer system in his or her area. Lower-level users, too, by refusing involvement with ProSys as an unwelcome change being imposed on them by the project team, made the IS into a technical system which they then resisted because it made no allowance for the social and organizational aspects of their work.

This formal–rational perspective underlay the first four stages of formal evaluation documented above; up until the organizational review the project was systems-led. The final two stages concentrated not just on the IS but on the organization into which it was to be embedded. The organizational review focused on organizational infrastructure and the clarification of managerial responsibilities, taking into account the history and social context of IS development in the Processing Company. The formal selection of IS for ProcessCo was grounded in evaluation of strategic and implementation issues and the management of change. These stages moved away from formal–rationalism to evaluate information systems in the wider sense advocated earlier: as computer systems embedded in organizations. With this altered perspective, ProcessCo management embarked on the difficult task of introducing the cultural change required for successful implementation of IS in the new organization.

Conclusions

We have traced the history of IS development in the Processing Company through six distinct stages of evaluation, seeing the dysfunctionality of the formal–rational perspective eventually give way to an emphasis on organizational infrastructure. This concluding section summarizes this broader approach to IS evaluation.

Information systems are not purely technical systems, but are also social systems. Work on IS therefore requires an interactionist approach, taking the effects of IT to be a product of neither the technical nor the organizational aspects alone, but of their interaction. Information systems cannot be evaluated in isolation from the organization in which they are embedded; history, social context and infrastructure are important elements of analysis; informal as well as formal information flows are pertinent.

More than a one-off 'snapshot', evaluation is a multi-stage activity running through project development and operation; it is a socially embedded process in which formal techniques and procedures are linked with informal assessments. It is inextricably bound up with the content, context and process of organizational change accompanying project development; evaluation can itself be usefully conceptualized in this way.

In terms of content, evaluation should include both the strategic value of the IS and its contribution to organizational effectiveness. These comprise: (a) linkage of the IS to business goals; and (b) a consideration of the implementation process. Successful IS strategy requires the clear definition of business strategy, an understanding of how to use IT in support of business strategy, and the ability to coordinate the two. Implementation issues include specification of requirements, assessment of financial costs and benefits, processes of change, organizational support, and conflict management.

An exclusive focus on the content of change ('what we want to do') fails to take into account the context of that change (the forces for continuity in the situation) and thereby precipitates its own failure. The context of IS evaluation includes the historical and infrastructural elements of information systems discussed above, together with the distribution of knowledge, authority and control within the organization. IS evaluation should also encompass the process of organizational change, i.e. the actions, reactions and interactions of participants.

The formal–rational perspective which commonly underlies IS evaluation is dysfunctional because it places excessive emphasis on the technology at the expense of the organizational aspects of information systems. In so doing it neglects the organizational context and process of IS development, elements which are critical to the successful application of IT in support of business strategy.

References

Blackler, F. and Brown, C. (1988) Theory and practice in evaluation: the case of the new information technologies, in *Information Systems Assessment: Issues and Challenges* (eds N. Bjorn-Andersen and G. B. Davis), North-Holland, Amsterdam.

Currie, W. L. (1989) The art of justifying new technology to top management. *Omega*, **17** (5), 409–18.

Hirschheim, R. and Klein, H. (1986) *The Emergence of Pluralism in Information Systems Development: Stories, Consequences and Implications for the Legitimation of Systems Objectives*, RDP 86/15: Oxford Institute of Information Management, Templeton College.

Hopwood, A. G. (1983) Evaluating the real benefits, in *New Office Technology: Human and Organisational Aspects* (eds H. J. Otway and M. Peltu), Pinter, London.

Pettigrew, A. M. (1985) *The Awakening Giant: Continuity and Change in ICI*, Blackwell, Oxford.

Symons, V. J. (1990) *Evaluation of Information Systems: Multiple Perspectives*. Unpublished PhD dissertation, University of Cambridge, UK.

White, E. M., Anderson, J. C., Schroeder, R. G. and Tupy, S. E. (1982) A study of the MRP implementation process, *Journal of Operations Management*, **2** (3), 145–53.

Yap, C. S. and Walsham, G. (1986) A survey of information technology in the UK service sector, *Information and Management*, **10** (5), 267–74.

Index